Beethoven and the *Grosse Fuge*

Music, Meaning, and Beethoven's Most Difficult Work

Robert S. Kahn

The Scarecrow Press, Inc.
Lanham, Maryland • Toronto • Plymouth, UK
2010

SCARECROW PRESS, INC.

Published in the United States of America
by Scarecrow Press, Inc.
A wholly owned subsidiary of
The Rowman & Littlefield Publishing Group, Inc.
4501 Forbes Boulevard, Suite 200, Lanham, Maryland 20706
www.scarecrowpress.com

Estover Road
Plymouth PL6 7PY
United Kingdom

British Library Cataloguing in Publication Information Available

Library of Congress Cataloging-in-Publication Data
Kahn, Robert S.
Beethoven and the Grosse Fuge : music, meaning, and Beethoven's most difficult work / Robert S. Kahn.
p. cm.
Includes bibliographical references and index.
ISBN 978-0-8108-7418-3 (pbk. : alk. paper)
1. Beethoven, Ludwig van, 1770–1827. Grosse Fuge, string quartet. 2. Beethoven, Ludwig van, 1770–1827—Criticism and interpretation. 3. Beethoven, Ludwig van, 1770–1827. I. Title.
ML410.B42K34 2010
785'.7194–dc22 2010008032

Manufactured in the United States of America.

For
Jane Krochmalny

Contents

Preface

Since Beethoven's day the gap between the general lover of concert music and the contemporary composer has widened into a gulf, and in the twentieth century the gulf became a chasm. The same gulf has opened between the general reader about music and the works of music historians and music theorists, who often write in a language nearly incomprehensible to the general reader.

A writer who tries to bridge this gulf is likely to be derided as a "popularizer," while standing little chance of truly becoming popular.

This is an unfortunate situation: for composers, for music lovers, for historians of music, and for people with a love of culture and reading.

Beethoven and the Grosse Fuge*: Music, Meaning, and Beethoven's Most Difficult Work* is written for people on both sides of that gap, and for those in the middle. It is for people who love music, and think about it, and believe that great music bears with it something important, though what that thing may be is elusive, perhaps unsayable.

I first heard Beethoven's *Grosse Fuge* thirty-five years ago as a graduate student at the Manhattan School of Music. I have not been able to stop thinking about it since then. I have been contemplating and planning this book since then. It is a reaction to the *Grosse Fuge*, an attempt to answer the question which the piece must raise in the mind of anyone who listens to it. That question is: What in God's name is going on here?

I fell in love with the *Grosse Fuge* at once. But my brain asked a second question. Granted that the piece works; granted that it is the most powerful music Beethoven ever wrote—and that means, in effect, the most powerful music anyone ever wrote—still: Why would anyone write something like this?

This book is the shortest answer I could come up with.

Beethoven has been subjected to more than two centuries of intense scrutiny. Yet some aspects of Beethoven's life, and some aspects of the *Grosse Fuge*, have not been revealed with sufficient clarity, possibly because they are in plain sight. This book offers three propositions about Beethoven's life, and three about his music.

First, that the *Grosse Fuge*—not the substitute finale that Beethoven wrote at the insistence of his publisher—belongs as the finale to his Opus 130 String Quartet in B-Flat, and that *there is no evidence that Beethoven ever intended anything else.*

Second, that the creative dry period that Beethoven suffered in his mid- to late forties—roughly from 1814 through 1819—was caused by depression.

Third, that though Beethoven clearly was an eccentric man, many of his quirks, including his furies and resentments, were rational reactions to a social and economic system that was stacked against the independent composer.

These aspects of Beethoven's life are treated in the first three chapters.

As for the music itself, the *Grosse Fuge*, and its companion pieces among the Late Quartets—Opus 132 in A Minor and Opus 131 in C-Sharp Minor—raise the question of whether absolute music can have meaning, and they raise the question more acutely than any other musical compositions have done. Chapter 4 therefore addresses the question of what it means to ask whether absolute music—music without words—can have meaning.

I take the position that absolute music can have meaning, but it usually does not. Only in exceptional cases does music rise to that level, and even when it does, as in Beethoven's Late Quartets, the meaning may be untranslatable.

Second, I propose that in some cases "normal" musical perception can be a form of synesthesia. By normal musical perception I mean the manner in which an average human being listens to music and responds to it. By synesthesia I mean one mode of perception—hearing—being perceived as directed motion through volumes of space. This synesthetic mode of listening seems to occur most often with polyphonic works and in some compositions of the Vienna Classic period.

By hearing interpreted as motion through space I do not mean the motion of a violinist's arm, or the direction a sound comes from, or the space of a concert hall. Nor do I mean that Beethoven was synesthetic, or that musicians or listeners need be synesthetic to understand music. I mean that the manner in which people appreciate some forms of music, particularly some pieces of Western Classic and Baroque music, involves the creation of a synesthetic space: a three- or four-dimensional volume through which sound moves. The synesthetic creation, or mode of perception, is the intuited sense of space—sometimes tremendous space—through which sound appears to move, with direction. That this has not previously been called a form of synesthesia I attribute to the fact that humans have come to take this form of perception for granted, and have not observed what a remarkable thing it is.

The book concludes by observing that the theme of the *Grosse Fuge*, its structure and the transformations through which Beethoven develops it, resemble the structure and transformations of DNA.

I would like to thank Jane Krochmalny, for everything; my sister, Debbie Price; composer-arranger-virtuoso Kenny Goldberg, for his encouragement during the many years it took to write the book; Fred Rivera, for moral courage; Victoria Graham, for help with the word processing; musicologist Mary Ann Morrow, for kindly responding to emails from a stranger inquiring about rehearsal practices in Classical Vienna; Dr. Oliver Sacks, for taking time from his busy schedule to read and comment on the book; and Renée Camus, Jayme Bartles Reed, Sally Craley, and all the editorial and production workers at Scarecrow Press.

Chapter 1

Beethoven and the *Grosse Fuge*

If Beethoven did not exist, and someone found it necessary to invent him, no one would believe it. That the central figure in Western music would write his greatest works after becoming deaf is unlikely. Also unlikely is that his greatest work would receive just three public performances in the seventy-five years after it was written, and that nearly two centuries after the composer's death, few people, even among his admirers, would know his greatest composition, and even fewer would like it upon first hearing. But that also seems to be the case.

Glenn Gould called the *Grosse Fuge* "not only the greatest work Beethoven ever wrote but just about the most astonishing piece in musical literature."[1] But in the 155 years before Gould straightened us out, execration of the *Grosse Fuge* was relentless and vitriolic. The first critical review, in the *Allgemeine Musikalische Zeitung* of 1826, called it "incomprehensible." After the fugue's first public performance in London, in 1887, a critic called it "the biggest, most abstruse, bizarre, and unharmonious piece of musical extravagance ever written." In his 1906 book on Beethoven, Dr. Ernest Walker, director of music at Balliol College, Oxford, called the piece "uncouthly inconsequential." Donald F. Tovey wrote for the 1911 edition of the *Encyclopedia Britannica* that the *Grosse Fuge* was unplayable, that it "surpasses the bounds of musical performance." In 1928 Joseph de Marliave called it a "tiresome waste of sound." Marliave added: "This fugue is one of the two works by Beethoven—the other being the fugue from the piano sonata, Op. 106—which should be excluded from performance." Sidney Grew reported in 1931 that these terms had been used to describe the *Grosse Fuge* in articles published since the 1927 centenary of Beethoven's death: "dour, uncouth, inconsequential, labored, extravagant, cerebral, obscure, impracticable, foolish, mad, illogical, formless, meaningless, and experimental." And in 1947, Daniel G. Mason, composer, critic, and associate professor at Columbia University, wrote: "This long, complicated, and through many hearings repellent if not unintelligible work . . . [of] impenetrable profundity . . . seems to be fostering Beethoven's lifelong capriciousness until it begins to verge on pathological eccentricity. The sequence of moods is irresponsible . . . the most disappointing episode in the entire series of the quartets."[2] Rehabilitation of the *Grosse Fuge* began thanks to the efforts of a few brave string quartets in the 1920s, and took hold in the universities, not surprisingly, after composers and theorists of the serial school came to power in the 1950s and thereafter.

Even those who disagree with the judgment that the *Grosse Fuge* is Beethoven's greatest work will surely concede it's his most difficult—to listen to, as well as to perform. The Great Fugue, Opus 133, was written as the finale to the Opus 130 Quartet in B-Flat, but broken off from it at the publisher's insistence and published separately. It was performed in public just once while Beethoven was alive, then not at all for two generations. The sheer difficulty of performance was not the only reason. The *Grosse Fuge* is a bewildering composition: intellectually demanding, rhythmically disjointed, complex and unprecedented in form, harsh in sonority, with a virtually unsingable "melody," and none of the lush, caressing sound that we have come to call Romanticism.

In 1931, more than one hundred years after its first performance, musicologist Sydney Grew wrote:

> In the whole of music there is no other piece with quite so strange a history as the *"Grosse Fuge"* of Beethoven. Its name has been known for a hundred years to every student or music-lover acquainted with the body of Beethoven's compositions, but on the evidence of what has been said about the composer and his works, in books, periodicals, and newspapers, perhaps not more than half a dozen people in any decade have ever got more knowledge of it than the name and the bare facts of its original production.[3]

In his article, "The '*Grosse Fuge*'—The Hundred Years of Its History," written for "Music and Letters," Grew asked that we "invest the subject with a little more seriousness and reasonableness."

> We have no cause to be proud of what we have thought of the work for the last hundred years—rather the reverse. But we need not be ashamed that it has taken all that time to learn how to understand and play it, for its spirit is so exceedingly fine and lofty that a century was required in the process of education. Nor ought we to blame Beethoven for making the music so very hard: what he had to express could not have been managed in any simpler way.[4]

Beethoven's Opus 133 is a difficult work to play, to understand, and to listen to. An unsuspecting listener who walked in today on a performance of the opening 132-bar fugue might think the piece was written last week in New York. As the longest and most powerful single movement in what are universally regarded as Beethoven's most profound works—the five Late Quartets—the fugue deserves more serious study than it has received in the pages from the forests felled for books about Beethoven—671 books about him in the Library of Congress, and thousands more in which he plays a central part. Books have been written about his "Immortal Beloved," a woman whose identity is not certain, to whom Beethoven wrote a letter he may never have sent and whom he may never even have kissed. In 2000, Russell Martin wrote a very good book about a lock of Beethoven's hair. When a librarian rummaging through shelves at the Palmer Theological Seminary outside Philadelphia in 2005 found a copy of a four-hand piano arrangement of the *Grosse Fuge*, in Beethoven's handwriting, the discovery made news around the world and the manuscript was sold for $1.95 million at Sotheby's auction house. Yet when it comes to the music that is the *Grosse Fuge*, biographers and critics, even the idolators whom Beethoven more than any other composer seems to attract, simply shake their head and pass on. Many find it incomprehensible—though it is the most intellectually rigorous piece Beethoven ever wrote—or they dismiss it as a sad, unhinged result of Beethoven's deafness and his long estrangement from the world. Or they prefer not to mention it. Grew wrote:

> [T]he voluminous literature inspired by the Centenary [of Beethoven's death in 1927] contained—so far as I have observed—practically nothing on the fugue or on what it stood for in the composer's art. Even the great Beethoven numbers of "Music and Letters," for instance, contain only one reference to it, and that no more than a passing one. Such an omission is as curious as would be the omission of the "Hamlet" group of plays from a discussion of Shakespeare, because this fugue is as significant in respect of Beethoven as those plays of tragic failure are in respect of Shakespeare.[5]

Yet it would take another generation after Grew's lament until professional string quartets would begin to restore the fugue in performance, as often as not, to its proper place as the finale of the Opus 130 quartet. The world was unable to accept the *Grosse Fuge* until it had been presented with the music of Bartók, Stravinsky, and Schoenberg.

Even Beethoven's recent biographers often do not seem to know what to make of the fugue. William Kinderman's 1997 biography devotes six pages to "Beethoven's most controversial single work . . . the largest and most difficult of all Beethoven's quartet movements, dubbed '*das Monstrum aller Quartett-Musik*,' in Schindler's derogatory formulation." Kinderman relates the circumstances in which Beethoven decided, or allowed, the fugue to be separated from Opus 130, but as for the question of where the fugue rightly belongs, he says, "a proper assessment of the issue must rest primarily on aesthetic grounds, on our analysis of the music." But Kinderman does not provide the analysis, or offer us an aesthetic judgment, though he states that "Beethoven's composition of the substitute rondo finale cannot be equated with a renunciation of the quartet in its original, 'Galitzin' version, with the *Grosse Fuge* as finale."[6] (The "Galitzin" version refers to Prince Nikolas Boris Galitzin, who commissioned three quartets from Beethoven in 1822, an offer Beethoven accepted in 1823. Galitzin, however, did not pay the debt until 1852, to Beethoven's nephew, and even then, without admitting that he owed the money, "but as a voluntary tribute to the dead composer"[7]—a typical example of the problems composers had in dealing with noble patrons.) Perhaps we can read Kinderman's judgment in the sentence, "As with some of Beethoven's comic pieces, the integrity of this quartet resides in a tension between eccentricity and normality."[8] Kinderman hedges.

His comment that Beethoven's agreeing to write a substitute finale did not constitute a "renunciation" of the fugue, and his remark on the "integrity" of the quartet leads one to believe that Kinderman thinks the fugue is the proper ending for the quartet. But that "tension between eccentricity and normality" indicates uneasiness. And the comparison to comic music is surprising. There is nothing comic about the *Grosse Fuge*, nor the manner in which it presents a titanic struggle overcome. It may have provoked laughter in 1827 because its motivating aesthetic was so far from that of any music previously written—unconcerned with beauty and prettiness, wholly concerned with the inexorable working out of a musical idea.

Barry Cooper's 2000 biography devotes a scant two pages to the *Grosse Fuge.* As is customary with Beethoven biographers, Cooper describes the situation in which the fugue was written and separated from the five movements that precede it, but spends little time on the music itself. Cooper clearly prefers the alternate finale, and states—I believe without evidence—that Beethoven preferred it too, that Beethoven "felt uneasy about it [the *Grosse Fuge*]: however well it absorbed and resolved ideas from earlier in the quartet, it must have seemed somewhat inappropriate. . . ."

> Naturally he expected to be paid extra for the new movement, but the decision to write it must have been made on aesthetic grounds: he would never have compromised his artistic integrity for the sake of a few ducats; nor would he have composed a simpler movement merely because of perceived technical difficulties, or to placate a few friends. Although the *Grosse Fuge* is widely preferred as the finale today, Beethoven clearly intended the new finale to replace it, and the *Grosse Fuge* to be performed as a separate work.[9]

In a previous book, *Beethoven and the Creative Process*, Cooper went so far as to call the fugue "an intrusion into the quartet, rather than the germ from which it sprang."[10] I disagree, and believe not only that Cooper's conclusions are incorrect, but that there is no evidence for them, in Beethoven's life or in the documents that survive from the people who knew Beethoven.

In his 1966 book, *The Beethoven Quartets*, Joseph Kerman devoted 27 pages to the music of the *Grosse Fuge*, which he calls "eminently problematic." Kerman withholds judgment on the fugue, yet seems tremendously relieved when he finishes his pages on it and moves on to the fugue that opens the Opus 131 Quartet in C-Sharp Minor. Perhaps he reveals his attitude to the *Grosse Fuge* in this pithy summation of its 30-bar overture: "This section hurls all the thematic versions at the listener's head like a handful of rocks."[11]

Beethoven specialist Lewis Lockwood, in his 2003 biography, devotes 11 pages to the fugue. Here is how Lockwood sums up the opposing arguments:

> The two sides of the "finale" controversy regarding Opus 130/133 have hardened over the years. Some argue that since Beethoven authorized the separation of the fugue from the rest of the work, published it separately, and wrote the "little" finale in its place, this final decision to separate it should prevail. An-

> other view, championed by Arnold Schoenberg and his associates in the Kolisch Quartet, is that Beethoven's conception of the work entailed the great fugue as its finale from the outset, that his agreement to separate it was not an artistic one but was more or less forced on him by his publisher and close associates—in short, that he let himself be persuaded to publish it with its own opus number and write the new finale, but not as a matter of deep artistic conviction. On this view the "right" version of the quartet has the *Grand Fugue* as finale.[12]

After presenting this fair summary of the argument, Lockwood declines to take a side. "There is justice on both sides, but except in performance we do not have to make an absolute choice," he says, which is true, but unhelpful, if one is seeking assistance in making the choice. A close reading indicates that Lockwood prefers the original version, with the *Grosse Fuge* as finale. He cites a 1957 study by another Beethoven expert, Erwin Ratz:

> Beethoven's agreement to write a new finale was an act of resignation. . . . [D]espite all its geniality, which cannot be denied to the new finale, we must absolutely declare that this movement has no inner relationship to the rest of the work. To any sensitive musician, the beginning of the light rondo finale after the dying away of the unearthly Cavatina must always come as a dreadful shock.[13]

Lockwood points out that this is not the only occasion on which Beethoven separated a movement from its original place and used it in another composition, or as a stand-alone piece. He cites the finale of the Opus 47 "Kreutzer" Violin Sonata, which originally was the final movement of the A Major Violin Sonata, Opus 31, No. 1; and the "*Andante Favori*," which Beethoven removed from the original version of the Opus 53 "Waldstein" Piano Sonata and published separately, without an opus number. The critics and historians, however, never have claimed that Beethoven's separation of these movements from their original places in his compositions indicates that Beethoven "renounced" them.

Lockwood comes about as close as any of the experts do to endorsing the fugue as the proper finale, and it is interesting that rather than say so himself, the world-renowned Beethoven scholar cites another expert's opinion without stating his own. Such reticence is unnecessary. The Opus 130 Quartet in B-Flat—with its companion pieces, the Opus 132 Quartet in A Minor and the Opus 131 Quartet in C-Sharp Minor—are the culminating creations of Beethoven's series of quartets, cornerstones of his work. The outer movements of all three quartets are based upon ingenious variations of the *Grosse Fuge*'s four-note theme. These three Late Quartets address the same problems, musically, intellectually, and philosophically. The first and last movements of all three quartets are thematically related, within each quartet, and across the quartets. But the Opus 130 does not reach this culmination without the *Grosse Fuge* as finale.

To argue that the *Grosse Fuge* could be heard in the light of these other two works without belonging to the Opus 130 is to diminish the Opus 130 Quartet by killing the motivic relationships of its outer movements. The first theme of the Opus 130's first movement is an ingenious derivation and variation of the *Grosse Fuge* theme, with the initial chromatic step in descent rather than ascent, and the upward leap of a sixth delayed. The modulation to G-flat, in measures 55 to 90 of the first movement, anticipates the *Grosse Fuge*'s sudden modulation to that key at the fugue's measure 159. The chromatic accompaniment figure that dominates measures 101 to 130 in the first movement of Opus 130 are merely transpositions of the first two notes of the fugue theme. And the thematic reminiscences in the first movement at measures 94 to 100, and again at 214 to 220, anticipate the reminiscence that will occur at measures 493 to 510 in the *Grosse Fuge*. The stunning breadth and depth of Beethoven's intellectual and musical creations are shortchanged, and damaged, if the *Grosse Fuge* is separated from the first movement of the Opus 130 Quartet.

The *Grosse Fuge* is the most extreme composition of an artist given to extremes. It is the most radical composition Beethoven ever wrote, during a lifetime in which he changed nearly everything about Western music: the range and structural uses of harmony, the nature of melody, the power of rhythm and repetition, the nature, intensity and length of musical development, the limits of form, the violence of contrasts, the demands upon listeners and performers, the social position of the musician, the power of music itself. Enough time has passed that we can say now, with certainty, that the aesthetic ideals and impulses behind the *Grosse Fuge* were almost precisely a century ahead of their time. We live in an age that has learned to value the quartets of Béla Bartók, Arnold Schoenberg, and Elliott Carter, and that accepts the creations of far lesser composers. It is absurd to claim today that the *Grosse Fuge* does not belong as the finale of Beethoven's B-flat quartet, despite the many organic connections tying the fugue to the quartet's first movement, because the fugue is difficult to play and to understand.

Beethoven not only changed music—expanding the range of what is technically and aesthetically possible, and what is acceptable—he changed the way the Western world looks at the artist. Artists in every genre today affect a pose of being misunderstood, disheveled, hostile to polite society, of having a disordered personal life, and of being consumed with greater issues than making a living. Though artists may have felt, and lived, that way for centuries, Beethoven created an image of the artist in the public mind by refusing to cover it up. This may have sprung from Beethoven's odd simplicity and honesty, or, as we shall see in chapter 3, from Beethoven's inability to cover it up. Whichever it was—both elements probably had a hand in it—the attitude that many modern Western artists strike toward society even today springs, to a great extent, from Beethoven.

Wolfgang Amadeus Mozart and Johann Sebastian Bach may not have liked being servants—they certainly did not like it—but that was their place, and they learned how to deal with it. So did Franz Joseph Haydn, and so did the visual artists, all of whom had to cater to an elite clientele of royalty, aristocrats, or priests to wrest a living from art. Beethoven, on the other hand, tried to brain a prince with a chair because the prince asked him more than once to please play the piano.[14] He spoke openly in the taverns, in his loud, deaf man's voice, of the worthlessness of the political regime, during a time of political repression and ubiquitous police spying—even suggesting that the emperor should be hanged from the nearest tree—and he got away with it.[15] That was no pose—that was Beethoven. He provided the model by which most artists—certainly young artists—lived throughout the later nineteenth and the entire twentieth century. He changed the way we think about all the arts. He demanded that the world acknowledge art's importance, and he let even the great and powerful know that if they did not appreciate his music, if they did not consider art as important as Beethoven did, then they were inferior to him. That's an incipient social revolution as well as a musical one.

Along with major political and religious figures, Beethoven is one of the most written-about men of history. The level of scholarship brought to bear upon studying every aspect of his work and life is astonishing. Scholars have correlated the chronological order of his sketchbooks by studying the watermarks of paper manufacturers in early nineteenth-century Vienna, and the pattern of water stains and ink blots that seeped through one leaf of paper to another. Maynard Solomon appears to have identified the "Immortal Beloved" by meticulously searching 160-year-old hotel and police records and stagecoach and postal schedules.[16] Yet these six generations of scholars appear to have missed a few things that always have been in plain sight, including why Beethoven allowed the *Grosse Fuge* to be broken off from the Opus 130 Quartet and published separately. And the answer to that question provides insight into another problem: why the composer's creative output declined so precipitously during the last thirteen years of his life—until his final years, when he wrote the Ninth Symphony and the Late Quartets.

The *Grosse Fuge* and Opus 130

There is no evidence that Beethoven was disappointed with the *Grosse Fuge*. There is no evidence that he agreed to break off the fugue from the B-flat quartet, write a new finale, and publish the fugue separately as Opus 133 because he thought it might have been a mistake to write the *Grosse Fuge* as the finale to Opus 130. Beethoven did agree to publish the fugue separately, and to arrange it as a stand-alone piano piece for four hands. In exchange for these two pieces—the new finale and the piano arrangement—he got 27 gold ducats, or 121½ florins, enough money to live for more than a month.[17]

Let us not forget that Beethoven was a freelance musician. He had been ill throughout his life, and in the summer of 1826, when he sold the *Grosse Fuge* to the publisher Matthias Artaria, he was ill again, from the liver disease that would kill him within a year. He was worried about earning enough to live, and was preoccupied with assuring the financial future of his nephew, Karl. Beethoven had every reason to accept extra money for the fugue, and every inclination to do it. But there is no evidence—none—that he was unhappy with the *Grosse Fuge* or with the quartet in its original form.

It is two centuries of critical hostility, not anything in the historical record, that has created the myth that Beethoven was unhappy with the fugue. At the end of his life, when he wrote the *Grosse Fuge*, Beethoven was one of the most famous men in Europe, certainly its most famous musician. An enormous amount of memoirs, letters, and eyewitness recollections of him survives—including two of his scribbled orders to fishmongers. Nowhere does anyone record Beethoven saying he was unhappy with the *Grosse Fuge*. There is evidence to the contrary that he loved the piece. Kinderman writes: "Beethoven's fondness for the Bb Quartet in its original form is documented in the conversation books of early 1826, where it is referred to as his '*Leibquartett*' ('favorite quartet')."[18]

Karl Holz, a young violinist and Beethoven's great friend at the end of his life, whom the composer asked to write his biography, was present at the only performance of the fugue in Beethoven's lifetime—Beethoven was not. Holz, who did not write a biography, told Wilhelm von Lenz, who did, that the audience that heard the premiere of the Opus 130 demanded that the second and fourth movements—the Scherzo and the *Alla Danza Tedesca*—be repeated immediately. "The fugue passed by uncomprehended. Beethoven was waiting for me after the performance in a nearby tavern. I told him that the two movements had been encored. 'What, those trifles?' he said in exasperation. 'Why not the fugue?'" Some versions of this story have Beethoven calling the undiscerning audience "Cattle! Asses!"[19]

A trustworthy eyewitness was Gerhard von Breuning, the son of Beethoven's childhood friend Stephan van Breuning, who attended the composer so faithfully at the end of his life that Beethoven called the 13-year-old boy his "trouser button." Breuning wrote that he visited Beethoven on his deathbed, found him sleeping, and so sat down and browsed through the latest conversation book, "to see who had been there in the meantime and what they had talked about."

> One thing I found there was: "The quartet of yours that Schuppanzigh played yesterday didn't go over very well." When he woke up a little later, I held that bit up in front of him, asking what he had to say about that. "It will please them some day" was the laconic answer he gave me; and to that he added fully and firmly aware that he wrote as thought fit, and was not led astray by the judgments of his contemporaries: "I know; I am an artist."[20]

Certainly the critics, and many of Beethoven's friends, did not like the *Grosse Fuge*, but there are no records in any contemporary sources that indicate that Beethoven had doubts about it. There is evidence, however, that Beethoven had doubts about the finale of his Ninth Symphony. Alexander W. Thayer, the most trustworthy of Beethoven's biographers, and the closest to the sources (aside from memoirists such as von Breuning and Ferdinand Ries), wrote that Beethoven's pupil Carl Czerny told Otto Jahn in 1852 that Beethoven thought of writing a new finale for the Ninth Symphony, without voices, and held onto the score of the symphony for six months before sending it to be published.

> Sonnleithner, in a letter to the editor of the *Allgemeine Musikalische Zeitung* in 1864, confirmed Jahn's statement by saying that Czerny had repeatedly related as an unimpeachable fact that some time after the first performance of the Symphony Beethoven, in a circle of his most intimate friends, had expressed himself positively to the effect that he perceived that he had made a mistake (*Misgriff*) in the last movement and intended to reject it and write an instrumental piece in its stead, for which he already had an idea in his head.[21]

After evaluating the sources, Thayer concludes, "it is not likely that he gave long thought to the project of writing a new finale."

There are no reports of Beethoven ever saying that the *Grosse Fuge* was inappropriate or a mistake. But reports from first and second hand indicate that Beethoven did question the appropriateness of the chorale finale of the Ninth Symphony. This is seldom mentioned in biographies or critical works because the Ninth Symphony has become a universally beloved work. It was the inevitable choice for two Christmas concerts, on December 23 and 25, 1989, at which residents of the former West and East Berlin celebrated the destruction of the Berlin Wall and the reunification of Germany. The many, often vicious, criticisms of the *Grosse Fuge* come not from anything Beethoven said or wrote about it, but because the fugue's critics simply don't like it.

Beethoven agreed to let Artaria publish the fugue separately as Opus 133. He asked for and received an extra 15 ducats for the new finale, and got another 12 ducats for the four-hands piano version of the *Grosse Fuge*, which was published as Opus 134. In fact, Beethoven insisted on rewriting the piano version, as he was unsatisfied with the arrangement Anton Halm had done for him, for which Halm already had been paid. So Beethoven demanded that the publisher pay twice for the piano arrangement—hardly a sign that he had questions about the work.[22]

That Beethoven agreed to remove the fugue from the Opus 130 is the only evidence there is that he may have had doubts about it. Several biographers and critics insist this is proof Beethoven was unhappy with the fugue—that he never would have consented to alter one of his compositions for mere money, or allow to be published a piece that did not meet his high standards—though every one of these biographers describes numerous instances throughout his life when Beethoven did just that. Beethoven dredged up plenty of songs and chamber pieces that he wrote as a young man and sold them years later, sometimes directing that they be published without opus numbers because he did not want them included among his major works, but sometimes publishing them with opus numbers. Thayer cites the Variations in E-Flat for Piano Trio, written in 1792 and published in 1804 as Opus 44; "Two Preludes Through the Twelve Major Keys for

Pianoforte or Organ," written in 1789, when Beethoven was eighteen, and published in 1803 as Opus 39, though they were "obviously exercises written for Neefe while he was Beethoven's teacher in composition"; and a Trio in C for Two Oboes and English Horn, written in 1794 and published in 1806 as Opus 87.[23]

Lockwood cites the "Dressler" Variations, WoO 63, which Beethoven wrote in 1782, when he was eleven years old, and sold again "more than twenty years later, in 1803, when he was in the flush of maturity and starting full-scale work on the *Eroica* Symphony . . . with only some light improvements made by him or someone else. This initiative is an early indication of his lifelong inability to pass up publication of older and sometimes trifling works in order to pocket a publisher's fee."[24] Then there was the song "*Der Kuss*," published as Opus 128 in 1825, though Beethoven had written it more than a quarter of a century earlier, in 1798. Lockwood calls it an "exhumation." Lockwood also cites Opus 42 and 43—"hack arrangements by others of two of his earlier trios"—and Opus 63 and 64, "unauthorized arrangements of string chamber works."[25] And Beethoven set more than 120 folk songs for the Scottish publisher George Thomson, though he complained that to do the job correctly, as an artist, he needed to know the words of the songs and have them translated. When Thomson did not provide the words or translations, Beethoven set the pieces anyway—forty-three of them for his first commission, in 1809. And he continued setting the songs, for money, for more than a decade. Nor are these the only examples.

To rebut Cooper's statement that Beethoven "would never have compromised his artistic integrity for the sake of a few ducats; nor would he have composed a simpler movement merely because of perceived technical difficulties, or to placate a few friends," we need only quote from one of the most frequently cited letters Beethoven ever wrote, to his student Ferdinand Ries in London, in March 1819. It concerns Beethoven's most difficult work up to that time, the great Opus 106 Piano Sonata in B-Flat, known as the *Hammerklavier*. Along with a long list of corrections, Beethoven wrote:

> Should the sonata not be suitable for London, I could send another one; or you could also omit the Largo and begin straight away with the Fugue [musical example], which is the last movement; or you could use the first movement and then the Adagio, and then for the third movement the Scherzo—and omit entirely No. 4 with the Largo and Allegro Risoluto. Or you could just take the first movement and the Scherzo and let them form the whole sonata. I leave it to you to do as you think best. . . . The sonata was written in distressful circumstances, for it is hard to compose almost entirely for the sake of earning one's daily bread; and that is *all* I have been able *to achieve*.[26]

The *Hammerklavier* Sonata is Beethoven's greatest, most difficult, and ambitious composition for unaccompanied piano. That he was willing to have the piece dismembered, rearranged, and published in pieces does not necessarily indicate that Beethoven was unhappy with it, and critics and biographers never have suggested that he was. What the letter does indicate is that Beethoven was a working musician, without a sufficient source of regular income, who wanted his composition published, and that he knew the piece would be difficult to perform and difficult to listen to. But he wanted it performed, and he wanted people to hear it, and he wanted to be paid for it.

"Beethoven's letter to Ries for the English edition suggesting cuts and rearrangements of the movements if Ries felt the work was too difficult for English taste has no value as evidence of his artistic intentions," Charles Rosen wrote.[27] The same statement can be made about Beethoven's acquiescence to the separate publication of the *Grosse Fuge*.

To sum up: Most commentators are wrong about Beethoven's *Grosse Fuge*. They seem to dislike it, which is their right. They seem to think there is something wrong with it, which may or may not be the case. And they claim, with no evidence, that Beethoven was dissatisfied with it. They claim that the longest and most powerful of the twenty-five movements of the Late Quartets is a failure, and that it is the lone failure among the two dozen other movements in the Late Quartets, all of which are masterpieces. That is not true, and no case can be made for it. A case can be made that the *Grosse Fuge* is the most unusual movement, the most dissonant, the one farthest from the classical ideal of beauty, perhaps the one written with the least concern for beauty, that it is the most difficult to listen to of any music Beethoven wrote, or that anyone had written up until that time. All those statements probably are true. But there is simply no evidence that Beethoven was unhappy with the *Grosse Fuge*.

Why, then, did he consent so quickly to break the fugue off from the quartet and have it published separately? The *Grosse Fuge* presents tremendous difficulties in performance, and quartets in those days were usually played by amateurs, who surely would have struggled with the Great Fugue—as professional quartets still struggle with it today. So Beethoven might have had an eye on the market, as well as on the 15 ducats Artaria offered him for the new finale. But Beethoven's quick surrender to his publisher's demand, and to the suggestions of his friends, almost surely had another source. Beethoven suffered from depression intermittently throughout his life. From his mid- to late forties, he suffered a prolonged depression so severe it prevented him from working for most of six years. He recovered sufficiently to write his profound late works, but he still struggled with the malady until he died. Beethoven had very good reasons to be depressed. And sometimes a depressed man just doesn't feel like fighting anymore.

Beethoven's Depression

Beethoven was depressed for a long time, and that is why his creative output declined precipitously from 1813 to 1819. Beethoven had been through a great personal crisis around 1800 when he realized he was losing his hearing. That crisis, and its results, lasted for the rest of his life. Beethoven was not a talented writer of words, but his anguish is evident in the few letters he wrote to his closest friends about losing his hearing. In his so-called Heiligenstadt Testament of 1802, Beethoven states clearly that he was ashamed of being deaf:

> Though endowed with a passionate and lively temperament and even fond of the distractions offered by society I was soon obliged to seclude myself and live in solitude. If at times I decided just to ignore my infirmity, alas! how cruelly was I then driven back by the intensified sad experience of my poor hearing. Yet I could not bring myself to say to people: "Speak up, shout, for I am deaf." Alas! How could I possibly refer to the impairing *of a sense* which in me should be more perfectly developed than in other people, a sense which at one time I possessed in the greatest perfection, even to a degree of perfection such as assuredly few in my profession possess or have ever possessed—Oh, I cannot do it; so forgive me, if you ever see me withdrawing from your company which I used to enjoy. Moreover my misfortune pains me doubly, inasmuch as it leads to my being misjudged. For me there can be no relaxation in human society, no refined conversations, no mutual confidences. I must live quite alone and may creep into society only as often as sheer necessity demands; I must live like an outcast.

The realization that he was becoming deaf nearly drove him to suicide. The Heiligenstadt Testament continues:

> But how humiliated I have felt if somebody standing beside me heard the sound of a flute and *I heard nothing*, or if somebody heard *a shepherd sing* and again I heard nothing—Such experiences almost made me despair, and I was on the point of putting an end to my life—The only thing that held me back was my *art*. For indeed it seemed to me impossible to leave this world before I had produced all the works that I felt the urge to compose; and thus I have dragged on this miserable existence—a truly miserable existence, seeing that I have such a sensitive body that any fairly sudden change can plunge me from the best of spirits into the worst of humors—[28]

Beethoven had to abandon his career as a piano virtuoso, losing not only a career but his primary source of income. He suffered another crisis in 1812 when he realized that he and his Immortal Beloved would never be together, that he would never have domestic happiness or a family of his own. In the next year, 1813, Beethoven showed obvious signs of depression. He wrote very little that year, after more than a decade of tremendous creativity. He was brought out of his depression—briefly—by being made the musical star of the Congress of Vienna in 1814 and 1815. Beethoven earned more money from public concerts in these twelve months than he did from all the public concerts he gave in the rest of his life.[29] But this period of lionization before the crowned heads of Europe and Russia was achieved by writing the weakest music of his life—*"Wellingtons Sieg"* ("Wellington's Victory") and *"Der glorreiche Augenblick"* ("The Glorious Moment")—the only music Beethoven ever wrote that one might dare call trashy or potboilers—and surely Beethoven knew it. He relapsed into depression when the Congress was over, and this time the depression lasted for years, until his final, great period of creativity in the last years of his life.

There is no need to subject Beethoven to psychologizing at a distance to see that he was depressed. Even if one did want to analyze him, one would surely be cured of it by reading *Beethoven and His Nephew: A Psychoanalytical Study of Their Relationship*, a 1954 book by the Viennese-trained Freudian psychoanalysts Editha and Richard Sterba. Among the insights the Sterbas offer are that Beethoven could not leave Vienna because the city symbolized his mother, and that during his long, tortured relationship with his nephew, Beethoven often signed letters to the boy, "Your father," but he wanted to sign them "Your mother."[30] This takes Freudian psychology to the verge of parody. But the Sterbas' book is valuable for the lengthy legal documents it contains from Beethoven's legal dispute for custody of his nephew. The desperate and bitter tone of these documents provides evidence of the state of Beethoven's mind at this time—a subject, however, which can be misinterpreted. We will return to these documents.

The years of Beethoven's depression were the years of his increasing dishevelment, economic insecurity, inattention to his person and clothing, and a mounting inability to complete everyday tasks. The composer Louis Spohr, who visited Beethoven on December 8, 1813, wrote in his autobiography of "Beethoven's almost continual melancholy."[31] Rossini wrote: "But what no etcher's needle could express was the indefinable sadness spread over his features."[32] Other visitors' descriptions of Beethoven's melancholy are legion.

Here is the string of mounting disasters to which Beethoven was subjected from age 41 to 49, and some of the failing efforts he took to deal with it:

- His hearing continued to deteriorate from 1812 to 1816 and was all but gone by 1817.
- He gave up on establishing a lasting relationship with a woman after his "Immortal Beloved" letters of July 1812.
- One of his three financial sponsors, Prince Ferdinand Kinsky, died in November 1812. Then Beethoven's sponsor and sometime friend Prince Lobkowitz went bankrupt and had to flee Vienna. Between them, Kinsky and Lobkowitz had promised him 2,500 florins a year for life, beginning in 1809; Beethoven feared losing that income and becoming destitute. This was not paranoia: inflation was raging out of control in Vienna and the costs of the wars against Napoleon were so ruinous that in 1811 Austria declared itself bankrupt. (Kinsky's estate suspended Beethoven's annuities from November. 3, 1812, until March 31, 1815; Lobkowitz from September 1, 1811, until April 1815. Beethoven, typically, threatened litigation against both, and, also typically, showed his consideration and forbearance for his bankrupt benefactor by referring to Lobkowitz in one letter as "Prince Fizlypuzly.")[33]
- In 1813, Beethoven abandoned plans to stage two concerts for his own benefit, though halls were available and he needed the money. This abandon-

ment of money-making propositions is uncharacteristic of Beethoven, who was a stubborn man. It is a sign of depression, and the lost prospect of income exacerbated it—a typical depressive spiral.[34]

• His brother Karl was sick and needed money, which the composer loaned him. Then Karl died in November 1815 and Beethoven took in his nephew, also named Karl, and commenced the long, ugly legal battle with the boy's mother.

• By 1817, he could no longer hear music. In 1818, he had to resort to writing to carry on a conversation.

• At least five of Beethoven's letters from 1813 to 1817 apparently refer to visits to prostitutes; notes in his journal express his remorse.[35]

In letters to his friend Baron Nikolaus Zmeskall von Domanovecz, Beethoven refers to prostitutes as "rotten fortresses" and in other thinly disguised terms. These six letters date from February 1813 through December 1817. In an undated letter, which Emily Anderson places in 1816, Beethoven apparently tries to swear off the habit, writing, "In regard to the fortresses, I fancy that I have already given you to understand that I do not want to spend any more time in marshy districts."[36] Maynard Solomon credits the Sterbas with being the first to note the significance of Beethoven's repeated references to "fortresses."[37] Barry Cooper, in his biography, chivalrously, but not persuasively, defends Beethoven's honor, claiming the Sterbas "patently set out to denigrate Beethoven's reputation" and that "the fortresses could denote the mines that Zmeskall is known to have owned; some of these might well have been shot at or disused during the war, hence 'rotten.'" Cooper suggests that perhaps Beethoven did not want "to visit Zmeskall's mines," or alternatively, that "it would be easier to interpret fortresses as minor government officials, some of whom were under (Zmeskall's) supervision and some of whom were corrupt (were not pure 'virgins' or were 'rotten')."[38] But Solomon cites Beethoven's remorse in a *Tagebuch* entry from 1817: "Sensual gratification without a spiritual union is and remains bestial, afterwards one has no trace of noble feeling but rather remorse." Solomon adds: "There is evidence that Beethoven patronized prostitutes from c. 1811 onwards."[39] This interpretation is more likely. Beethoven's letter renouncing the habit, which Anderson dates from 1816, and his private expression of remorse in 1817, indicate the end of what may have been a long moral struggle.

Thayer believes Beethoven's letters of 1817 show

> the helplessness of their writer in all affairs of common life; also, by implication, the wretched prospect of any good result to his undertaking the supervision and education of a boy more than usually endowed with personal attractions and mental capacity, but whose character had already received a false bias from the equally indiscreet alternate indulgence and severity of his invalid and passionate father and of his froward and impure mother. Moreover, this undertaking rendered necessary a sudden and very great change in the domestic habits of a man nearly fifty years of age, who, even twenty years before, had not been able, when residing in the family of his Maecenas, Lichnowsky, to bear the restraints imposed by common courtesy and propriety.[40]

Here are just a few extracts from Beethoven's letters and journal of those years, in which the composer manages to be depressed even when people send him money:

> I am greatly distressed at receiving the 100 gulden which our poor nuns have sent me. I have put them aside, however, to be used to defray the costs of copying. [April 8, 1813: Beethoven had agreed to send scores for a benefit concert for nuns in Graz.][41]
>
> If I am doing anything wrong or have done so, kindly make allowances for me, for a number of unfortunate incidents occurring one after the other have really driven me into a state bordering on mental confusion. [May 27, 1813, to Archbishop Rudolf.][42]
>
> O God, God look down upon the unhappy B., do not let it last thus any longer. [May 13, 1813, entry in his private journal, or *Tagebuch*.][43]
>
> Perhaps I will go there [Hungary] in any case, since I have nothing to provide for save my own miserable person. . . . I send you all good wishes, beloved brother, and ask you to be a brother to me, for I have no one whom I can really call brother. Do as much good to those around you as these evil times allow you to do— [Summer 1813, to Count Franz Brunsvik. This was written while both of Beethoven's brothers were still alive.][44]
>
> Please do your share and don't let me perish. In everything I undertake in Vienna I am surrounded by innumerable enemies. I am on the verge of despair— My brother, whom I have loaded with benefits, and owing partly to whose deliberate action I myself am financially embarrassed, is—my greatest enemy! [December 18, 1813, to a lawyer in Prague, from whom Beethoven sought advice on whether to sue his financial sponsors.][45]
>
> Peevish about many things, more sensitive than all other mortals, and tormented by my poor hearing I often feel only *pain* in the company of others— [Letter of summer 1815, to Johann Xaver Brauchle, tutor to Beethoven's friend the Countess Anna Marie Erdödy.][46]
>
> Every day I hope to see the end of this distressing condition. Although my health has improved a little, yet it will be a long time apparently before I am completely cured. You can imagine how all this must affect the rest of my existence. My hearing has become worse; and, as I have never been able to look after myself and my needs, I am even less able to do so now; and my cares have been increased further by the responsibility for my brother's child.—Here I have not yet found even decent lodgings. As it is difficult for me now to look after myself, I have recourse now to this person and now to that; and everywhere I am abominably treated and am the prey of detestable people— Thousands of times I have thought of you, dear and beloved friend, and I do so

now; but my own misery has made me feel depressed. [June 19, 1817, to Countess Anna Marie Erdödy.][47]

As for me, I often despair and would like to die. For I can foresee no end to all my infirmities. God have mercy upon me, I consider myself as good as lost. . . . If the present state of affairs does not cease, next year I shall not be in London, but probably in my grave—Thank God that I shall soon have finished playing my part— [August 21, 1817, to Baron Nikolaus Zmeskall von Domanovecz.][48]

Beethoven already had spoken of suicide in his Heiligenstadt Testament of 1802, in his *Tagebuch*, and in letters to friends. A clear example of the extent to which his depression affected his everyday life in those years comes in a letter of October 9, 1813, to his friend Baron Zmeskall: "Don't be annoyed if I ask you to write the enclosed address on the enclosed letter. . . . Yesterday I took a letter to the post and there I was asked to what address the letter was to be sent—So I see that my handwriting can be misunderstood, and perhaps as often as I am—That is the reason for my asking you to help me—"[49]

Here Beethoven is asking his friend, a baron, to address a letter for him. Feeling defeated by the inability to complete a simple everyday task is a hallmark of depression. In a normal mood, Beethoven would have told the postman where the letter was going, or boxed his ears, or simply been a bit more careful in addressing the next letter. In another helpless letter to Zmeskall, of 1817, Beethoven asked the baron to retrieve two pair of his pants from the tailor, because "despite all my efforts I can't make him return them."[50]

Beethoven was living in a mental, emotional, and social cul-de-sac, and it is important to realize that this was not just how he felt—it was an accurate description of how he had to live. He felt misunderstood, and he could not understand people who spoke to him. He longed for social intercourse but felt "only *pain* in the society of others." His family life was a wreck. One of his brothers had died and Beethoven in effect had adopted his child. His surviving brother, about whom Beethoven felt so ambivalent that he could not bring himself to write his name in the Heiligenstadt Testament, was a far from impressive figure. Johann van Beethoven had all the composer's presumption and arrogance, but none of the talent—yet he was rich, having bought a pharmacy just in time to supply the needs of Austrian soldiers wounded in the Napoleonic wars. Inflation was out of control in Vienna; Beethoven believed he had lost two of his three financial sponsors, and even if he did regain his annual stipend, the money was becoming more worthless each day. And through all of this was the problem of earning a living as a deaf musician.

Our understanding of depression has increased tremendously in the past generation. Physicians did not begin to understand depression as a biological problem of brain chemistry until around 1980, when drugs were developed that could manipulate neurotransmitters. These pharmacological discoveries involved the antidepressant drugs known as selective serotonin reuptake inhibitors, which include Prozac, Paxil, and their variations. The biological explanation of depression is interesting in Beethoven's case not because it allows us to dress him up in modern science, but because it explains how depression may incapacitate someone years after the occurrence of the stresses that began the destructive process.

Serotonin is a neurotransmitter, as is norepenephrine, also known as adrenaline, which also is targeted by the modern antidepressants. Adrenaline also has systemic effects—the fight-or-flight response. When young mammals are exposed repeatedly to long periods of stress—be it random electroshocks administered to a lab rat, or random violence and abuse from a drunken father—the body may react, not by shutting down production of adrenaline, but by shutting down the nervous system's receptors for the chemical. The body thus ameliorates the response—the rapid heartbeat, elevated blood pressure, aggression and emotional elevation of the fight-or-flight response—without losing the ability to produce the neurotransmitter, which still serves a biological purpose.

If, after long periods of stress, the stressors are removed, and the person or lab animal is permitted to live a normal life, he may fall into depression anyway. The biological explanation holds that the loss of receptors for the neurotransmitter, or the receptors' loss of efficiency, cause the body to interpret normal levels of the drug as a deficiency, because the nervous system has in effect "turned itself down" during the years of stress. So depression may linger—or become manifest—after its original causes have gone away.

The selective serotonin reuptake inhibitors, or SSRIs, alleviate depression by delaying the body's reabsorption of serotonin, which is released at the synapse at the end of a neuron each time the neuron fires and sends an impulse to the next neuron. The serotonin is rapidly reabsorbed by the neuron that released it, by neurotransmitter pumps that recycle the chemical to be used again. In delaying reabsorption of the serotonin, the SSRIs create a stronger response, comparable to actually increasing the serotonin level. So the drugs effectively reverse, or get around, the process by which the receptors for neurotransmitters were "turned down" under stress.[51]

Most Beethoven scholarship, even Maynard Solomon's standard modern biography, came before these recent medical advances. For centuries—particularly in the years after Goethe published his novel *The Sorrows of Young Werther* in 1774, when Beethoven was four years old—depression was even thought of as a desirable state: a personal indulgence, a romantic mood that people could "snap out of" if only they would try. Today we understand that depression can have biological as well as emotional causes; that it can be induced by long periods of stress, but not manifested until years later; and that it can be a debilitating illness that can interfere with or prevent one from working, and even prevent one from feeling capable of leaving one's house. Whether the suffering induced by depression can make one a better artist is debatable, but is certainly possible, once the artist regains the ability to work. Kay Redfield Jamison, a psychologist and coauthor of the standard medical reference work on bipolar illness, wrote in *Touched with Fire: Manic-Depressive Illness and the Artistic Temperament* that the experience of cycling through periods of intense depression and the exaltation of artistic achievement, and the process of integrating both aspects of the cycle into one's life, may very well contribute to the depth and profundity of one's art. But Jamison, who is bipolar herself, knows that depression itself cannot create the art, but can prevent art from being created until the depression has lifted.[52]

Many biographers do not understand this. Some actually state that depression can *increase* productivity. Here is a typical, uninformed statement about depression and art, from Wolfgang Hildesheimer's 1977 biography of Mozart, in which Hildesheimer attempts to distinguish between the achievements of the "creative genius" and the achievements possible to the rest of us: "Only one thing is certain: depression or psychic suffering does not diminish his productivity, unlike other creative people, but increases it qualitatively and quantitatively."[53] This is nonsense. Anyone who has suffered from a long, deep depression knows it is nonsense, and medical literature confirms that whatever presumed insights depression may bring, neither artists nor anyone else can become productive by it, until the depression lifts.[54]

Evidence of Beethoven's depression is everywhere in his letters, in people's reminiscences of him, in their descriptions of his behavior. Virtually all of Beethoven's biographers have written of his periods of depression, and of the very good reasons he had to be depressed. None of them, however, appears to have believed, or understood, that depression could have stopped him from composing during his barren years, from 1813 to 1819. These years coincided with the struggle for guardianship of his nephew, a struggle whose records reveal all three people involved—Beethoven, nephew Karl, and Karl's mother, Johanna—in the worst possible light. Certainly the guardianship struggle and Beethoven's depression were mutually reinforcing and debilitating. Just as certainly it would be impossible—now or then—to disentangle the causes and effects of these two sources of Beethoven's misery. Both surely contributed to the artistic barrenness of those years. But just as surely, Beethoven's struggle with depression, coming as it did during the guardianship fight, has caused biographers and historians to assign an inordinate amount of blame for Beethoven's declining production to young Karl and the widow Johanna, and to place less emphasis on depression, which had been at least an intermittent problem for Beethoven since he wrote his first preserved letter, when he was sixteen.[55] This misplaced emphasis—on nephew Karl rather than on depression—can be attributed in part not just to lack of understanding of depression but to the nature of the surviving Beethoven documents.

Aside from the Heiligenstadt Testament, the letter to his Immortal Beloved, and a letter from his deathbed to his childhood friends Franz Gerhard Wegeler and Eleonore von Breuning, the only lengthy prose documents of Beethoven's that survive are the long arguments, court appeals, and contracts with his sister-in-law from the guardianship struggle—written by attorneys, with assistance from Beethoven, and signed by him. These fifteen documents, dating from November 28, 1815, to February 18, 1820, occupy 50 pages of Anderson's *Letters*; the final "Memorandum" is 19 pages in itself—by far the longest example of

Beethoven's prose that survives, almost certainly the longest literary effort he ever made.[56] These documents show Beethoven as aggressive and vituperative, and Johanna, in his eyes, as just a few steps above prostitution—or not above it. This tremendous outpouring of bile and vindictiveness is unfortunate, not just for the problems it reveals, but for the historical record.

Only a small percentage of Beethoven's letters reveal anything interesting about him. They are far less interesting as historical documents than the letters of Mozart or Mendelssohn, for instance, who were better writers and more acute social observers. It is unfortunate, but understandable, that biographers have seized upon lengthy documents from the guardianship struggle as a key to understanding Beethoven, his human relationships, and the problems of his artistically barren years. Historians and lay psychologists, however, should tread lightly upon documents from family courts. Custody struggles for children reveal human nature at its worst. Defamation of the opposing adult can be a virtual requirement in this branch of the legal system. The Sterbas' "psychoanalytical" study of Beethoven suffered from many shortcomings—inherent problems with their Freudian approach and the nature of their entire enterprise—but the Sterbas' study also suffers from the two doctors' heavy reliance on documents from the custody fight.

There is no question that the legal struggle for custody of his nephew cost Beethoven time that might have been better spent composing. But it is inaccurate and unfair to all parties involved in a fight for custody of a child to treat legal documents from the dispute as though they reveal the nature of the disputants during the rest of their lives. We can be sure that such documents reveal the worst side of their natures. Biographers have been far too ready to use these 50 pages of Beethoven's rants as though they offer insight into his hidden, or perhaps "latent," feelings, and to suggest that these pages provide clues to the manner in which he went about his daily life. Treating these court documents in this way produces a psychologically distorted picture of Beethoven, casting far too much importance on the custody fight, and far too little on Beethoven's continuing struggle with depression.

[This interpretation of the nature of legal custody fights comes from the author's personal experience, not as a disputant, but during years as editor for Courthouse News Service, which reports and summarizes every civil filing in more than two hundred state and federal courts across the United States. The author has read summaries of more than one million cases, and read the initial filings in thousands of them. These cases deal with every imaginable sort of civil dispute: business collapses, embezzlements, personal injuries, wrongful deaths, racketeering, legal and medical malpractice, sexual predation, accidental poisonings, class-action product liability, and employment lawsuits. Family quarrels, however, produce legal filings of an entirely different nature and intensity: more wantonly vicious, more emotional, more savagely accusatory than any other sort of case. Until recently, defamation of the spouse, as an adulterer or worse, was *required* to get a divorce in many states, and spouses would submit to this defamation, and even stage it, to jump through the hoops of the law. Legal filings in family disputes are inherently unreliable.][57]

Beethoven's biographers have not missed the signs of his depression. They have, however, underestimated the extent to which it undermined his life and eroded his creativity. It's a question of emphasis. Barry Cooper observed that it was rare for Beethoven to start a work and fail to complete it, yet the composer abandoned a piano concerto he began in 1815 and a piano trio in F minor he started in 1816. In trying to explain the "uncharacteristic hiatus" in Beethoven's productivity in 1817, Cooper wrote, "Whatever the root cause of his illness, he had to stay in bed or at least indoors for long periods." Cooper cites a long list of reasons, personal and societal, that might have "caused such depression that he felt unable to compose," but concludes, erroneously, "None of these factors, however, can have affected his composing more than marginally."[58]

Cooper dates Beethoven's years of reduced productivity as 1815 to 1817, followed by a period of "gigantism," during which he wrote the enormous Opus 106 Piano Sonata in B-Flat, called the *Hammerklavier*, and began work on his *Missa Solemnis*. If Cooper's interpretation is correct, and Beethoven's depression was ended, or followed, by his dedication to create giant works, the greater labor and time involved in creating these new masterworks would help to explain why it is difficult to determine precisely when Beethoven's depression lifted and his final period of productivity began, for the fruits of his renewed creativity would not have been revealed for a long time.

Thayer, in his indispensable biography, fell prey to the romantic misconception of depression, writing that Beethoven's ability to compose "saved him from utter despair. Who can say that the world has not been a gainer by the misfortune which stirred the profoundest depths of his being and compelled the concentration of all his powers into one direction?"[59] In fact, depression makes it impossible to concentrate all one's powers, or to give them any direction until the depression has lifted. There is nothing romantic in the way that depression lays waste lives and makes otherwise healthy people utterly unproductive.

Francois Martin Mai, a professor of psychiatry and author of the latest book-length study of Beethoven's medical problems, cites Beethoven's letters to show that the composer met six of nine criteria for major depression. "Although we cannot be certain whether his depressed episodes lasted two weeks or more, in the event they did, the diagnostic criteria for major depression would be met," Mai says.[60] Referring to Axis I of the modern Diagnostic and Statistic Manual of classifying mental illnesses—Axis I being "a diagnosis of the primary psychiatric disorder"—Mai concludes, "The most likely Axis I diagnosis is that of Recurrent Depression."[61] Yet Mai attributes Beethoven's barren years—which he dates as 1812 to 1817—not to depression but to a "creative illness."

Here is how Mai defines creative illness:

> [A] severe neurotic or sometimes psychotic condition in which a creative individual is obsessed by the pursuit of some difficult aim: for a period of three years or more, the artist feels isolated and unproductive, and struggles with at-

> tempts at self-healing; recovery, when it occurs, is spontaneous and is accompanied by euphoria and a transformation of personality—the individual feels as if she or he had gained access to a new spiritual world, and the illness was followed by a burst of creativity. . . . A review of Beethoven's life between 1812 and 1817 reveals that many of his experiences fit the description of a creative illness.[62]

It is baffling why Mai can conclude that Beethoven suffered from a creative illness for five years, characterized by feelings of isolation and struggle and lack of productivity, yet insists that "we cannot be certain whether his depressed episodes lasted two weeks or more."

Even Maynard Solomon, author of the best modern biography of the composer, devotes many more pages to expounding an unconvincing and thinly supported "family romance," by which Beethoven allegedly believed, or wished to believe, that he was the son of a king, than he does to the composer's obvious, long and deep depression. The concept of Beethoven's "family romance" is a major theme of Solomon's biography, which has rightly become the standard modern version of Beethoven's life. Here is how Solomon introduces the subject:

> In the fantasy that Freud and his disciple Otto Rank named the "Family Romance," the child replaces one or both of its parents with elevated surrogates—heroes, celebrities, kings, or nobles. Freud found that this fantasy, which is universal in myth, religion, fairy tales, and imaginative fiction, is widespread in the daydreams of ordinary people, and appears in a more intense and enduring form among the creative and the talented. Usually it is a fantasy that arises during childhood or adolescence and thereafter recedes into amnesia, from which it can be recovered only by analysis. With Beethoven, on the contrary, the fantasy apparently gained in strength and tenacity as he grew to maturity. . . . In Beethoven's Family Romance, as with many others, only the father is replaced by an elevated substitute, while the actual mother is retained.[63]

In support of this Freudian theory, Solomon cites two passages from *The Odyssey* that Beethoven underlined: "My mother saith that he is my father; / For myself I know it not, / For no man knoweth who has begotten him"; and "Few sons are like / their father; most are worse, a very few / Excel their fathers." Solomon points out that Beethoven idolized his grandfather, but not his own father. And he cites "a fantasy of illegitimacy" stemming from the fact that the composer had an older brother, Ludwig Maria, who died shortly after birth. Beethoven's father, Johann, in the attempt to palm off his son as a child prodigy, gave the world, and Ludwig himself, to believe that the future composer was born two years later than he actually had been. By Solomon's reasoning, Beethoven felt that his own baptismal certificate actually referred to his late, elder brother, but that "his own baptismal certificate—the evidence of his birth and the proof of his parentage—either never existed or had been concealed or destroyed. What (he may well have wondered) could have been the reason for this mysterious suppression of the facts of his birth?"[64]

Solomon's arguments for this Freudian "family romance" are unpersuasive. Beethoven had many reasons to dislike his father and little reason to respect him. More to the point, he had much to gain by allowing the Viennese nobility to misinterpret the Dutch particle "van" as analogous to the German "von," and to associate it with noble birth. Otto Erich Deutsch, in his documentary biography of Franz Schubert, states that Beethoven's misunderstood Dutch particle would have been sufficient to exempt him from military conscription, and that "the time of service was fourteen years!" Deutsch provides some half dozen examples from concert reviews, program notes, and other documents, in which singers and musicians of both sexes are referred to as "von" though the particle is not part of their name. "[T]he 'von' is merely a form of politeness," Deutsch says.[65]

The "unearned" noble particle "von" was frequently used in Beethoven's day as a mark of kindness or respect. "Certainly, it was the Viennese custom, often followed by Beethoven himself in his letters, to be very generous with these mildly honorific particles and not to enquire into the exact justification for their use," says Martin Cooper.[66] And Johann Pezzl, commenting upon the Viennese "Thirst for Titles" in his popular *Sketch of Vienna* of 1786, wrote that the title "Frau von" was used for "wives of merchants, wives of lesser government officials, of artists, well-to-do professional men and house officers of great families."[67]

Beethoven, in a good mood, addressed even his lackey Anton Schindler as "Herr von Schindler" in one letter.[68] And Franz Josef Haydn, after returning in glory from two trips to England, objected that his new prince, Nicolaus Esterházy II, son of Haydn's late patron, referred to him in the demeaning third person "Er." Haydn complained to the princess, "and the Prince always called his Kapellm(eister) from then on 'Herr von Haydn,'" Robbins-Landon reports.[69]

The most compelling evidence for Solomon's family romance theory is that Beethoven initiated his lawsuit against his sister-in-law for custody of nephew Karl in the Austrian Imperial and Royal *Landrechte*, a court reserved for the nobility and clergy. The lawsuit was transferred to a lower court, the Vienna Magistrat, when it was revealed that Beethoven was a commoner.[70] But there were reasons other than a Freudian family romance for Beethoven to have sued in the upper court: to pull rank on Johanna; to associate himself in the eyes of the court with the noble class among whom Beethoven, but not his sister-in-law, moved; and for the opportunity it presented to Beethoven to appeal to his patron, sponsor and pupil, the Archduke-Archbishop Rudolph.

Aside from the lawsuit for custody of his nephew, however, there is no evidence that Beethoven tried to pass himself off as noble—other than by letting the Viennese nobility think what they pleased about that "van." There is evidence, though, that Beethoven scoffed at the idea that his father was a king. Here is an excerpt from one of the last lengthy letters he ever wrote, to his childhood friend, Franz Gerhard Wegeler, just after Beethoven had contracted his final illness:

> Unfortunately I cannot write to you today as much as I should like to, for I have to stay in bed. So I shall confine myself to answering a few points in your letter. You say that I have been mentioned somewhere as being the natural son of the late King of Prussia. Well, the same thing was said to me a long time ago. But I have adopted the principle of never writing anything about myself nor replying to anything that has been written about me. Hence I gladly leave it to you to make known to the world the integrity of my parents, and especially of my mother.[71]

Ferdinand Ries related these reminiscences Beethoven told him of his childhood:

> Beethoven remembered his early youth and his friends from Bonn with much pleasure, although in reality those had been difficult times for him. Of his mother he spoke especially with love and affection, and often called her a fine, truly kindhearted woman. He did not like talking about his father, who was mainly at fault for the family misfortunes, but any harsh word about him let fall by a third person made Beethoven angry. In general he was a thoroughly kind person at heart, only his temper and irritability often got him into trouble. And no matter what insult or injustice had been done him by anyone, Beethoven would have forgiven him on the spot, had he met him when crushed by misfortune.[72]

It is simply not necessary to invoke a "family romance" or the theories of Freud and Rank when discussing Beethoven's obvious dislike of his alcoholic father and his love for his consumptive mother, who died young.

Solomon mentions Beethoven's allusions to suicide in the Heiligenstadt Testament of 1802, and in letters to his friends Franz Wegeler in 1810 ("I would have left this earth long ago—and, what is more, by my own hand") and Baron Zmeskall in 1817 ("I often despair and would like to die"), and in his *Tagebuch* in 1814. Solomon writes, correctly, "During this critical period, Beethoven's feelings of impotence and despair had brought him to the very edge of an emotional breakdown, reviving suicidal impulses." And he notes, "In the years 1816-19, Beethoven's productivity declined to the lowest level of his adult life." But like the earlier biographers, Solomon attributes this to "the exhaustion of the middle-period styles" and "The Dissolution of the Heroic Style" (the title of the chapter from which the previous quotes were taken). Solomon concludes, "Now the sense of failure extended beyond Beethoven's deafness and his sexuality. It threatened to derail his creativity."[73] But Beethoven's depression did not merely threaten to derail his creativity; it did derail it.

Depression can have many causes—biological, situational, cultural, psychological, economic, and combinations of all these. In Beethoven's case, none of the causes can be ruled out, and all of them could have contributed. A deaf composer has good reason to be depressed. Beethoven was born in poverty and his economic situation was precarious throughout his life. German culture in the years after Goethe's *Sorrows of Young Werther* accepted and even embraced depression as a noble sort of bearing. And Beethoven seems to have been constitutionally inclined to extremes, in music, in his love for his friends and contempt for them, in exaltation and despair.

Beethoven had every reason to be depressed. It was a natural result of his life. As a child, Beethoven suffered years of randomly inflicted violence from an alcoholic father who drank himself into poverty and death. Family friends wrote to the composer's early biographers that "there were few days" when his father, Johann, did not beat him, and that Johann "sometimes shut him up in the cellar." When the composer was just eight years old, his father "often" came home drunk in the early morning with another musician, Tobias Pfeiffer, whom he had hired to teach his son music. "The father roughly shook him awake, the boy gathered his wits and, weeping, went to the piano, where he remained, with Pfeiffer seated next to him, until morning."[74]

When Beethoven was sixteen, he had to break off his music lessons with Mozart in Vienna to return to Bonn to see his mother die of tuberculosis. Afterward, in the first letter preserved from his life, Beethoven wrote apologetically to an attorney who had loaned him money on his way home:

> Most nobly born and especially beloved friend! I can imagine what you must think of me. That you have well founded reasons not to think favorably of me I cannot deny. However, before apologizing I will first mention the reasons which lead me to hope that my apologies will be accepted. . . . I found my mother still alive, but in the most wretched condition. She was suffering from consumption and in the end she died about seven weeks ago after enduring great pain and agony. She was such a good, kind mother to me and indeed my best friend. . . . Since my return to Bonn I have as yet enjoyed few happy hours. For the whole time I have been plagued with asthma; and I am inclined to believe that this malady may even turn to consumption. Furthermore, I have been suffering from melancholia, which in my case is almost as great a torture as my illness.[75]

After Beethoven's mother died, his father slid deeper into alcoholism. Ludwig became de facto head of his family at age sixteen. Two years later, he had to intercede with the Bonn police to keep his drunken father out of jail. Johann was so far gone in drink that Ludwig, at eighteen, had to ask the Bonn elector to assign to him half his father's salary to support his two younger brothers. The elector granted the request on November 29, 1789, in a document that appears to threaten the father, Johann, with banishment. Johann's alcoholism was so notorious that when he died, the elector-archbishop wrote to the court marshal, "The revenues from the liquor excise have suffered a loss in the deaths of Beethoven and Eichhoff."[76] Johann van Beethoven was sixty-three when he died on December 18, 1792, about six weeks after Ludwig arrived in Vienna for the second time. Beethoven did not return to Bonn for the funeral. Just one of his letters refers to his father in the following year: a reminder to Elector Maximilian Franz in Bonn that Beethoven was to get his late father's salary for the upkeep of his younger brothers.

On his own in Vienna, twenty-two years old, Beethoven began to gain renown, money, and admiration as a piano virtuoso. Then, possibly within one year, and certainly within three years of publishing his first mature works, to acclaim, he came to realize he was going deaf and would lose his career as a performer, and he did lose it. He had virtually no prospects of a regular salary as a *Kapellmeister* because of his deafness, and was forced into the economic uncertainty of life as a freelance composer in a city that loved fads and fashion as much as it loved music. He was unable to form a lasting relationship with a woman. Even if an educated, aristocratic woman did want to be with him she could not, because he was a commoner, and the widows to whom Beethoven often was attracted could have lost custody of their children had they married him. He was physically ill for long periods throughout his life: 71 of the 519 letters in volume one of Emily Anderson's three volumes of collected letters mention illness—letters written when Beethoven was young and in the best health he would ever enjoy—and in the remaining volumes the complaints are virtually continuous. The tremendous effort it must have taken to recover from the suffering he endured almost certainly contributed to the depth of feeling of Beethoven's greatest music. But the suffering also cost him tremendously—it cost him years of productive work.

A few biographers tiptoe to the brink of stating the obvious: that Beethoven's creativity was stifled by depression for several years. William Kinderman wrote, "If Beethoven meant to compensate for shortcomings in his life through creative activity, he failed, at least during 1813. His creativity may have been paralyzed by depression."[77] And Martin Cooper, in *Beethoven, The Last Decade, 1817-1827*, cited a long list of Beethoven's personal problems: his ill health, his still deteriorating hearing, and his inability to maintain a relationship with a woman, and concluded, "These physical and emotional factors brought Beethoven in 1816 very near to what would today be termed a nervous breakdown. This condition is clearly reflected in the reduction of his output, for the years 1816-18 were the most unproductive of his life."[78]

Cooper notes that between completing the two sonatas for cello and piano, Opus 102, in late July 1815, and the *Hammerklavier* Sonata, Opus 106, in the autumn of 1818, "Beethoven concerned himself to an unusual extent with trivialities"—a sign of a man who is having trouble concentrating. And Cooper suggests, perceptively, that Beethoven's periodic depression and hypomania might have affected his metronome markings, many of which seem wildly at odds with a satisfying, and even playable, tempo. "In his case particularly we cannot ignore the part played by the physical-psychological element in his determination of tempi. A man of his temperament and in his physical condition might very well feel in a mood of physical exhaustion and depression that the tempi which he had decided upon in good health and high spirits were too fast, and vice versa."[79] (Beethoven's well-known difficulties with arithmetic probably complicate the problem of his metronome markings.) In a medical appendix to *The Last Decade*, Edward Larkin, a physician, describes Beethoven's behavior after 1815—the years of his struggle to win guardianship of his nephew—as that of "a depressive under stress."[80]

Once again: there is no need to submit Beethoven to psychoanalysis at a distance to make a persuasive case that he was depressed, and that the depression was responsible for the virtual collapse of his artistic production from 1813 to 1819. The evidence is overwhelming: in his behavior, his lost productivity, his relations with the world, in the observations of eyewitnesses, in Beethoven's own handwriting. And though depression is regarded as a mental illness today, there is no need to hypothesize that Beethoven's depression stemmed from any other, underlying, mental illness. Beethoven was a deaf musician. He had no prospect of regular employment, no wife or children, declining prospects of ever being married, and was forced to rely for income upon publishing music in a society that did not respect copyright. In the next chapter we will look more closely at the economic situation Beethoven faced and his problems with publishers. In chapter 3 we will look more closely at Beethoven himself. But in assessing Beethoven's character, it should be kept in mind that depression was a perfectly normal reaction for a man in his situation—and no one else had ever been in Beethoven's situation.

Notes

1. Tim Page, ed., *The Glenn Gould Reader* (New York: Alfred A. Knopf, 1984), 458.

2. Sidney Grew collected epithets used against the piece in "The '*Grosse Fuge*,' the Hundred Years of Its History," *Music and Letters* No. 2 (1931), 141-147; and in "Beethoven's '*Grosse Fuge*,'" *Music and Letters*, Vol. XII, No. 4 (1931), 497-508. The first critical review of the fugue appeared in the *Allgemeine Musikalische Zeitung*, Vol. 28, 1826. Marliave denigrated the work in *Beethoven's Quartets* (London: Oxford University Press, 1928), 222 [page citation from the Dover Press 1991 edition]. Daniel G. Mason called it "irresponsible" and "disappointing" in *The Quartets of Beethoven* (New York: Oxford University Press, 1947), 229, 238. The 1887 review, by an unknown author, and Walker's long out-of-print 1906 book, *Beethoven*, were both cited by Grew. Grew wrote that "so far as it seems possible to learn," violinist Joseph Joachim and his quartet were the first to perform the *Grosse Fuge* in public since Beethoven's death, "and this was not until the late 1880s." George Grove reported in his 1879 dictionary that the fugue was "never played" in Germany, Austria or England. Grew, "Beethoven's '*Grosse Fuge*,'" *Music and Letters*, Vol. XII, No. 4 (1931), 501.

3. Grew, The '*Grosse Fuge*,' 140.

4. Grew, The '*Grosse Fuge*,' 140.

5. Grew, The '*Grosse Fuge*,' 141.

6. William Kinderman, *Beethoven* (Oxford: Oxford University Press, 1997), 301-307.

7. Alexander W. Thayer, *Thayer's Life Of Beethoven*, revised and edited by Elliot Forbes (Princeton, N.J., 1973), 1,100, hereafter cited as Thayer-Forbes.

8. Kinderman, *Beethoven*, 306.

9. Barry Cooper, *Beethoven* (Oxford: Oxford University Press, 2000), 344-345.

10. Barry Cooper, *Beethoven and the Creative Process* (Oxford: Clarendon Press, 1990), 214.

11. Joseph Kerman, *The Beethoven Quartets* (New York: W.W. Norton, 1966), 277.

12. Lewis Lockwood, *Beethoven: The Music and the Life* (New York: W.W. Norton, 2003), 461.

13. Erwin Ratz, *Die Originalfassung des Streichquartettes Op. 130 von Beethoven* (Vienna, 1957), 4. Cited and translated in Lockwood. *Beethoven*, 466.

14. Thayer-Forbes, *Thayer's Life Of Beethoven*, 403; Maynard Solomon, *Beethoven* (New York: Schirmer, 1998), 190.

15. Thayer-Forbes, *Thayer's Life Of Beethoven*, 647; Maynard Solomon, *Beethoven* (New York: Schirmer, 1998), 331.

16. Maynard Solomon, *Beethoven Essays* (Cambridge, Mass.: Harvard University Press, 1988), 166-189. Solomon's chapter, "Antonie Brentano and Beethoven," is an expanded version of his article, "New Light on Beethoven's Letter to an Unknown Woman," *Musical Quarterly* 58 (1972), 572-587.

17. Thayer-Forbes, *Thayer's Life Of Beethoven*, 970, 975-976. The events surrounding Beethoven's agreement to write a new finale for Opus 130, and allow the *Grosse Fuge* to be published separately, also are recounted in Solomon, *Beethoven*, 417, 420-423; Lockwood, *Beethoven*, 452-468 and 545-546; Kinderman, *Beethoven*, 301-307; B. Cooper, *Beethoven*, 337-345; and Martin Cooper, *Beethoven: The Last Decade, 1817-1827* (Oxford: Oxford University Press, 1986), 388-390.

18. Kinderman, *Beethoven*, 303-304, and Thayer-Forbes, *Thayer's Life Of Beethoven*, 974.

19. Lockwood, *Beethoven: The Music and the Life*, 545-546, and Solomon, *Beethoven*, 421. Both cite Wilhelm von Lenz, *Beethoven: Eine Kunststudie*, 5 vols. (Cassel: 1855-60), 218-219. Solomon adds that Beethoven's comment, "Cattle! Asses!" may be apocryphal.

20. Gerhard von Breuning, *Memories of Beethoven: From the House of the Black-Robed Spaniards* (Cambridge: Cambridge University Press, 1995), 96. Von Breuning's memoir was first published in 1874. The 1995 edition was edited by Maynard Solomon and translated by Henry Mims and Solomon.

21. Thayer-Forbes, *Thayer's Life Of Beethoven*, 895-896.

22. Thayer-Forbes, *Thayer's Life Of Beethoven*, 975; Lockwood, *Beethoven*, 460; B. Cooper, *Beethoven*, 338-339.

23. Thayer-Forbes, *Thayer's Life Of Beethoven*, 124, 125, 165.

24. Lockwood, *Beethoven: The Music and the Life*, 54.

25. Lockwood, *Beethoven: The Music and the Life*, 90-91, 337.

26. Emily Anderson, ed., *The Letters of Beethoven* (London: Macmillan, 1961), 804-805.

27. Charles Rosen, *The Classical Style: Haydn, Mozart, Beethoven* (New York: W.W. Norton, 1998), 426.

28. Anderson, *The Letters of Beethoven*, 1,351-354. The idiosyncratic punctuation, with dashes instead of periods, and much underlining, is typical of Beethoven. This letter, however, known as Beethoven's Heiligenstadt Testament, is much more polished and

expressive than Beethoven's typical letters. He evidently wrote and rewrote it with much care.

29. Julia Moore, *Beethoven and Musical Economics* (unpublished Ph.D. dissertation, University of Illinois at Urbana-Champaign, 1987), available through UMI Dissertation Services, Ann Arbor, Mich.; and F. M. Scherer, *Quarter Notes and Bank Notes* (Princeton, N.J.: Princeton University Press, 2004), 112.

30. Editha and Richard Sterba, *Beethoven and His Nephew: A Psychoanalytical Study of Their Relationship* (New York: Schocken Books, 1971), Chapter 5, "Motherhood," 58-76.

31. Sam Morgenstern, ed., *Composers on Music, from Palestrina to Copland* (New York: Pantheon, 1956), 92.

32. Oscar Sonneck, *Beethoven: Impressions by His Contemporaries* (New York, Dover, 1967), 117.

33. Anderson, *The Letters of Beethoven*, 414; Thayer-Forbes, *Thayer's Life Of Beethoven*, 522-526, 552-553, 557-558, 611-612; and Solomon, *Beethoven*, 193-194.

34. B. Cooper, *Beethoven*, 250-254. For Austria's ruinous inflation, see Thayer-Forbes, *Thayer's Life Of Beethoven*, 453-460, 550-557, 590, 611-612; and Moore, *Beethoven and Musical Economics*.

35. Anderson, *Letters of Beethoven*, 407, 408, 527, 596, 619, 638-639.

36. Anderson, *Letters of Beethoven*, 638-639. In Beethoven's letter of Dec. 16, 1816, the analogy is obvious: "Keep away from rotten fortresses, for an attack from them is more deadly than one from well preserved ones." Anderson, 619.

37. Sterba and Sterba, *Beethoven and His Nephew*, 110-111; Solomon, *Beethoven*, 468.

38. B. Cooper, *Beethoven*, 223.

39. Solomon, "Beethoven's *Tagebuch*," in Solomon, *Beethoven Essays*, 283.

40. Thayer-Forbes, *Thayer's Life Of Beethoven*, 663.

41. Anderson, *The Letters of Beethoven*, 412.

42. Anderson, *The Letters of Beethoven*, 420.

43. B. Cooper, *Beethoven*, 223.

44. Anderson, *The Letters of Beethoven*, 421.

45. Anderson, *The Letters of Beethoven*, 430.

46. Anderson, *The Letters of Beethoven*, 519.

47. Anderson, *The Letters of Beethoven*, 683-684.

48. Anderson, *The Letters of Beethoven*, 701.

49. Anderson, *The Letters of Beethoven*, 426.

50. Anderson, *The Letters of Beethoven*, 741. This letter bears no date or recipient; Anderson places it in 1817 and believes it was written to Baron Zmeskall.

51. Selected writings about depression and brain chemistry include Andrew Solomon, *The Noonday Demon: An Atlas of Depression* (New York: Scribner's, 2002); Frederick K. Goodwin and Kay Redfield Jamison, *Manic-Depressive Illness* (Oxford: Oxford University Press, 1990); Peter D. Kramer, *Listening to Prozac* (New York: Penguin, 1997); and first-person narratives of depression: William Styron, *Darkness Visible* (New York: Vintage, 1990); and Kay Redfield Jamison, *An Unquiet Mind* (New York: Vintage, 1995). The author thanks his brother, Dr. Richard A. Kahn, professor of biochemistry at Emory University, for assistance with this synopsis.

52. Kay Redfield Jamison, *Touched with Fire: Manic-Depressive Illness and the Artistic Temperament* (New York: Free Press, 1994).

53. Wolfgang Hildesheimer, *Mozart* (New York: Vintage, 1983), 55.

54. Francois Martin Mai, *Diagnosing Genius: The Life and Death of Beethoven* (Montreal: McGill-Queen's University Press, 2007). Mai's chapters 4 and 5, "The Interpretation" and "Illness and Creativity," directly address Beethoven's depression, with dozens of citations from medical literature and Beethoven sources. See too Jamison's *Touched with Fire*. Both Mai and Jamison are professors of psychiatry.

55. Anderson, *The Letters of Beethoven*, 3-4: "I have been suffering from melancholia, which in my case is almost as great a torture as my illness."

56. Anderson, *The Letters of Beethoven*, 1,360-409. Selected documents are in Sterba and Sterba, *Beethoven and His Nephew*, 309-334.

57. The Courthouse News Service Web page is www.courthousenews.com.

58. B. Cooper, *Beethoven*, 254.

59. Thayer-Forbes, *Thayer's Life Of Beethoven*, 282.

60. Mai, *Diagnosing Genius*, 161.

61. Mai, *Diagnosing Genius*, 164.

62. Mai, *Diagnosing Genius*, 191.

63. Solomon, *Beethoven*, 28.

64. Solomon, *Beethoven*, 28, 30. Parentheses in original.

65. Otto Erich Deutsch, *The Schubert Reader: A Life of Franz Schubert in Letters and Documents* (New York: W.W. Norton, 1947), 742, for the "von" particle as a form of politeness. For Deutsch's other examples of advantages to be derived from interpreting the Dutch "van" as the noble, German, "von," see 84, 595, 836-838.

66. Martin Cooper, *Beethoven: The Last Decade* (Oxford: Oxford University Press, 1986), 25.

67. H. C. Robbins-Landon, *Mozart and Vienna* (New York: Schirmer, 1991), 80-81. Robbins-Landon translated an abridged version of the 1786 edition of Johann Pezzl's popular guidebook *Skizze von Wien* (Sketch of Vienna) in *Mozart and Vienna*, 53-191.

68. Anderson, *The Letters of Beethoven*, 1,058.

69. H. C. Robbins-Landon, *Haydn: Chronicle and Works, Vol. IV, The Years of "The Creation," 1796-1800* (Bloomington: Indiana University Press, 1973), 43.

70. Anderson, *The Letters of Beethoven*, 1,360-361, 1,371-380.

71. Anderson, *The Letters of Beethoven*, 1,321-322.

72. Franz Wegeler and Ferdinand Ries, *Beethoven Remembered: The Biographical Notes of Franz Wegeler and Ferdinand Ries* (Arlington, Va.: Great Ocean Publishers, 1987), 109-110.

73. Solomon, *Beethoven*, 283, 296.

74. Thayer-Forbes, *Thayer's Life Of Beethoven*, 61; and Solomon, *Beethoven*, 22.

75. Anderson, *Letters of Beethoven*, 3-4.

76. Thayer-Forbes, *Thayer's Life Of Beethoven*, 53-57, 136; and Solomon, *Beethoven*, 13-17, 41-42. Thayer quotes from the court document of Jan. 1, 1793.

77. Kinderman, *Beethoven*, 168.

78. Martin Cooper, *Beethoven: The Last Decade*, 13-14.

79. Martin Cooper, *Beethoven: The Last Decade*, 14, 468.

80. Dr. Edward Larkin, "Beethoven's Medical History," in Martin Cooper, *Beethoven: The Last Decade*, 458.

Chapter 2

Beethoven the Freelance Musician

As a freelance musician, Beethoven could expect to die in poverty. In fact, he was a rare exception because he did not die "destitute or nearly so," as Julia Moore wrote after studying thousands of Viennese estate inventories for her 1987 Ph.D. thesis, *Beethoven and Musical Economics*.[1] Even musicians who were not disabled by deafness, and who once had been as popular as Beethoven, died in destitution, among them Luigi Boccherini, Karl Ditters von Dittersdorf, Carlos Ordoñez, Johann Vanhal, Emanuel Förster—who died in 1823 with a net worth of 82 florins—and Josef Czerny, whose net worth was 6 florins when he died in 1831. Michael Haydn, longtime *Kapellmeister* in Salzburg, had to borrow money from his more famous brother, and lived his final years "with the spectre of poverty close to him, partly due to the various French invasions but mostly because of growing inflation."[2] Michael Haydn was earning just 600 gulden a year when he died in 1806. Mozart too apparently died in poverty, though he presents a special case. Profligacy and debts—possibly to gamblers—may have driven him to write the series of alarming letters in the last three years of his life, begging money from his friend, the wealthy merchant Michael Puchberg.[3]

All these men had been popular composers, sometimes wildly so. Even Franz Josef Haydn, the most famous composer in Europe, and for thirty years an employee of an unusually generous line of princes, had only 2,000 florins in savings when he went to London in 1791 for the series of concerts that made his fortune. But in 1806, three years before he died, Haydn told Princess Caroline Esterházy that despite his yearly salary and pension of 1,700 gulden, he had had to "dip into capital to the extent of 2,000 fl." Princess Caroline had her husband, Nicolaus II Esterházy, immediately grant Haydn a pay raise of 600 gulden.[4] But Haydn was a fortunate exception in a profession characterized by economic misery.

Common musicians and copyists, who could not appeal directly to princes, lived close to destitution even when they were paid. In a 1763 letter to Prince Nicolaus Esterházy, copyist Anton Adolph begged for a raise from 12 gulden a month, on which he had to support his wife and family and pay for wood, rent, and candles. Adolph had copied 3,328 pages for the prince in the past four months. Saying he was

> crushed with work, . . . I beg Your Serene Princely Highness on my knees, in humility and submissiveness, that in your graciousness (known to the whole world) you grant me some improvement in my monthly salary, or something towards lodgings, wood, or candles; for which act of grace God the Almighty will reward you richly, but I with my poor wife will pray to God every day in our prayers to grant rich blessings to Your Serene Princely Highness.[5]

Prince Esterházy refused, so Adolph fled from his service—a crime—and "yet one more ghastly reminder . . . of the dire poverty in which most musicians lived in those days."[6]

Widows and orphans had to survive on even more pitiful pensions, if they were lucky enough to have a pension at all. Joseph Elssler, brother of Haydn's longtime servant and copyist Johann Elssler, in begging Prince Nicolaus II Esterházy for a job as oboist in 1800, wrote that his mother—widow of another longtime Esterházy musician—"is surviving on a pension of 4 kreutzers a day." A kreuzer was about a penny. At 60 kreuzers to a florin, the widow's pension came to 24 florins a year.[7]

Inflation in Vienna

To understand the financial pressures upon Beethoven, a short detour into the Austrian state's disastrous economy is necessary. Mozart wrote in 1782 that on 1,200 florins a year, "a man and his wife can manage in Vienna if they live quietly and in the retired way we desire."[8] In 1789, the then-unmarried writer G. Friedrich Schiller declared "that it was possible to live 'reasonably well' on an income of 1,400 florins."[9] So when three noblemen—Princes Franz Joseph Lobkowitz and Ferdinand Kinsky, and Archduke, later Archbishop, Rudolph—promised Beethoven 4,000 florins a year for life, beginning in 1809, it was a generous offer—but one that was ruined almost immediately by hyperinflation.

Beethoven's sharp dealings with publishers, particularly for his *Missa Solemnis*, have led some biographers to say that he was obsessed with money, particularly toward the end of his life. This is misleading. Beethoven's thirty-five years in Vienna coincided with the Austrian emperors' disastrous experiments with paper money, which produced a long period of inflation. From 1796 to 1823, the cost of renting an apartment in Vienna increased thirtyfold. The other necessities of life rose accordingly.[10]

Haydn cited the "greatly increased living costs—felt by everyone" in an 1801 letter to Prince Nicolaus II Esterházy. That year Carl Rosenbaum, a diarist and acquaintance of Haydn—who later paid grave-robbers to steal the composer's head—calculated the daily depreciation of government bonds and currency in his diary:

> Friday, 8th October . . . the government bonds are sinking day by day; today the 5% banknotes at a loss of 10½%. The 12 Kreuzer notes are often exchanged for 10 Kreuzer, but only until 20th Oct., then they go down to 9 Kreuzer. Un-

> pleasant prospects!—The inflation becomes greater every day, and with it the lack of ready money.—With the metamorphosis of the 12 Kreuzer notes down to 7 they are scarcely able to cover the most basic needs.[11]

Austria's economic disaster was caused not just by the empire's long, losing effort in the Napoleonic wars, but because Emperor Franz Josef chose to print paper money rather than alienate the aristocracy by taxing them. Disaster came in 1809, when Napoleon's armies occupied Vienna for the second time, and the French emperor demanded 40 million florins in war reparations. This set off a period of hyperinflation: 31 percent in 1810, a cumulative 348 percent by 1814, and a total inflation rate of 1,212 percent from 1809 to 1817.[12]

"What a destructive, disorderly life I see and hear around me," Beethoven wrote during the 1809 occupation, "nothing but drums, cannons, and human misery in every form." In November he wrote that the city had suffered "every hardship that one could conceivably endure." By June 1810, "the cost of living in Vienna has risen still further and . . . the amount of money one needs is terrifying."[13] And the hyperinflation was just beginning.

The Austrian state declared bankruptcy in 1811. "In 1816, crop failures pushed prices to their highest levels of the entire bankruptcy period. There occurred a second, officially unacknowledged state bankruptcy, and starvation in Vienna as well as in outlying areas of the monarchy was a serious problem."[14]

During this accelerating economic catastrophe, one of Beethoven's sponsors died, one went bankrupt, and both suspended payments of his stipend. Prince Kinsky died in 1812 after falling from a horse; Beethoven threatened to sue his estate for payment. Prince Lobkowitz went bankrupt in 1814 and fled Vienna to avoid debtor's prison. By that year, had Beethoven been receiving his promised annuity, inflation would have reduced it to one-half of its original value.

By December 1815, Beethoven had worked out settlements with Lobkowitz and with Kinsky's estate, to be paid in the new currency. But inflation had "destroyed the value of Beethoven's (1809) stipend," Moore says, "and if no one then stepped forward to lend assistance, it was because his financial difficulties were altogether unremarkable."[15] To cite just one more example, in 1823, Beethoven's old friend and financial sponsor, Count Ferdinand Waldstein, died bankrupt.[16]

The most acute years of Vienna's economic disaster, 1814-1817, coincided with Beethoven's first long, dry creative period. He was unable to perform in public due to his deafness, and now he was not writing music either. "Beethoven's financial situation was characterized by an overall decline throughout his life in keeping with the increasingly severe crises of the Austrian economy as a whole," Moore wrote.[17] The years of financial stress contributed to his depression, which in a vicious circle reduced his creativity still more, exacerbating the financial and personal stresses.

Deaf, unemployed save for the music he could write and sell in a system that did not respect copyright, Beethoven had good reason to worry about money. The only thing he knew how to do was make music. He had enough self-knowledge, and frankness, to tell one of his publishers, "Everything I do apart from music is badly done and is stupid." Beethoven's friend, the piano maker Johann Andreas Streicher, cited that statement in a March 5, 1825, letter to the publisher Carl Friedrich Peters, with whom Beethoven had negotiated, less than honestly, for the *Missa Solemnis*: "But what am I to say about Beethoven's behavior to you and how can I endeavor to excuse it?" Streicher wrote. "This I can only do by letting you have his own opinion of himself which he expressed in my home: 'Everything I do apart from music is badly done and is stupid.'"[18] It is unclear when Beethoven made the remark to Streicher, whom he had known since 1796, but it sounds like the remark of a depressed man.

When economic disaster hit Vienna, Beethoven could no longer earn money by teaching—which he never liked anyway—or by performing. And even at his most prolific, it would have been difficult to make a living by composing, for Europe had no effective copyright laws, so as soon as a piece was published it was free to be stolen. That is why Mozart published so little when he was alive—because when a piece was published it became de facto public property. Mozart, though, could earn money as a pianist. Beethoven could not.

Mozart and Beethoven were among the first men who tried to survive as freelance musicians in Vienna. That these two men had such difficulty surviving as freelancers indicates that the system was rigged against it. In fact, freelance musicians had been treated so badly for so long that one wonders why Mozart or Beethoven would even want to do it.

The Social Status of Musicians

The musician has always been treated as a dangerous fellow. Franz Liszt summed it up in an 1854 article about Beethoven: "We have not yet ceased viewing musicians as rare, curious phenomena, half angels, half donkeys, who bring heavenly songs to mortals, but who, at the same time, in their day-to-day life, are to be treated in the most ambiguous manner or with the most unambiguous scorn."[19]

Throughout Western history, society has attributed to musicians a dangerous intimacy with both God and the devil. Much of Western Europe's fear and loathing of the musician emanated from the Catholic Church, but the prejudice predates Christianity. In Homer's *Odyssey*, the Sirens would have lured Odysseus to destruction had he not had his crew lash him to the mast—he could not resist the temptation of hearing their song, though the crew was not allowed to hear it. Plato banned most musical modes from his Republic, and the Greek God Pan, the piper, was half goat. Yet since Pythagoras, Greek philosophers thought music the summation of all the arts and sciences, a key to the nature of the universe. Music continued to be considered the capstone of philosophy, science, and art, through Boethius (480-524) whose threefold classification of music—the music of the spheres, the harmony of the human body and spirit, and vocal and instrumental music—influenced philosophers for more than one thousand years. Music's strange powers are the basis of the folk tale of the Pied Piper of

Hamelin, which medieval Europeans apparently believed actually happened in that German town in 1284. The piper performed a useful function—he rid the town of rats—but he also lured away its children, who were never seen again.

"Society . . . seemed then, as it still seems today, prepared to accept (musicians) either as idols or as undeserving fools," wrote Walter Salmen, editor of the splendid book *The Social Status of the Professional Musician from the Middle Ages to the 19th Century*.[20] Because music was dangerous it had to be regulated, and from the Middle Ages through the Classical Period and beyond, the Church dictated not only the words and instruments appropriate to musical performances, but which rhythms and harmonic intervals were allowed, and when. In 1324, less than two centuries after composers of the Notre Dame school began writing two-part vocal music that would develop into polyphony, Pope John XXII declared that "some concords, such as the octave, fifth, and fourth, that enrich the melody and which may be sung above the simple ecclesiastical chant, in such manner however that the integrity of the chant itself shall remain undisturbed" would be permitted "on festal days."[21] And the Church famously banned the interval of the tritone, or diminished fifth, which it called the *diabolus in musica*—the devil in music. (If the Church was correct, the devil has been behind four hundred years of Western music, as the resolution of the tritone, accompanied by a descending fifth in the bass, was the driving harmonic force behind Baroque, Classical, and Romantic music, and remains so in Western popular music.) Through the centuries, the church has banned polyphony, duple time, triple time, most harmonic intervals, the organ, in fact all the instruments, for performances of sacred music. Even into the Classical period, separation was maintained between vocal music, which was for God and the angels, and instrumental music, which could be of the devil. Beethoven was denied permission to perform his *Missa Solemnis* in Vienna in 1824 because a public theater was not a fit place for sacred music, so he had to offer only selections from it, and call them "hymns." Even tuning systems for string and keyboard instruments were made subjects of fierce theological dispute.[22]

Exploring the "multiple personalities" of music, or of our reactions to it—its sacred and demonic aspects, its relation to number, to human emotions, to the nature of the heavens and the universe—would take us far afield, and though the enterprise would be interesting, it's unnecessary. No one, from composer to virtuoso to academician to a teenager plugged in to earphones would deny that this sacred-demonic split exists, if not in music itself, then in Western society's estimation of it. Western society's perennial worship of a few, selected musical gods, or a few select pieces of music, combined with its deprecation of the general run of musicians—particularly freelance musicians—indicates that the subject is as deeply ingrained as it is irrational. In fact, fear of the irrational had much to do with the multiple layers of fear, adoration, misunderstanding, and resentment of freelance musicians through the centuries.

"In Europe, where an alien Christianity was superimposed upon traditional religions, the clergy saw the *Spielmann* (itinerant, or folk musician) as 'the continuing carrier of paganism, previously considered to have been defeated,'" musicologist Dieter Krickeburg wrote.

> The medieval European concept of ignominy was characterized by the rejection from society of certain occupational groups. . . . This critical, obdurate vilification was . . . [partly] based . . . on the circumstance that these professions, accorded a sacral dignity in paganism, were demonized by Christianity. The musician was the successor of the medicine man, the magician, the singer of heroic sagas. Though the imperial laws of 1548 and 1577 proclaimed that members of the majority of the then-disreputable professions, including pipers and trumpeters, as well as their children, were eligible to become guild members, the stigma of infamy remained for a long time.[23]

The thirteenth-century tale of the Pied Piper came at a time when "the disparagement of secular musicians had reached a high point" in Northern Germany, when peasants had been Christianized but had not been "completely pervaded by the spirit of Christianity." The *Spielmann* was an easy target to be prosecuted and burned as a witch during the witchcraft trials of the coming centuries. "The witch craze obsessed all strata of society, and the *Spielmann* was involved through the witches' dances," Krickeburg wrote. The devil was thought to take the form of a *Spielmann* and seduce village boys and girls while they danced. "The dishonorable burial of musicians outside the churchyards led to a harvest-time expression which persisted even into the nineteenth century: whenever the reapers came upon large ant or molehills it was said, 'There a musician lies buried.'"[24]

The oldest known European freelance musicians of whom we have records are the *jongleurs*, or minstrels, of the tenth century, and the Goliards of the eleventh and twelfth centuries—disreputable all. The Goliards, wandering students or friars who claimed to be followers of a mythical patron, Bishop Golias, were "deprecated by respectable people," Donald Jay Grout wrote in his *History of Western Music*. And no wonder—their songs were "drawn largely from the eternal trinity of youthful masculine interest: wine, women, and satire." Petrarch called them "people of no great wit, but with amazing memory, very industrious, and impudent beyond measure."[25] Their descendants, the *troubadours* of southern France and the *trouvères* of the north, belonged to, or helped create, a courtly tradition, and sometimes were members of the nobility themselves. This split endured throughout Europe through the centuries: between the tolerated, though still suspicious, musician attached to a court (much of the troubadours' music, after all, was about seducing other men's wives—"Burney gives an account of a celebrated troubadour named Anselm Faiditt, married to a beautiful *nun*, who followed her lord from court to court, singing his songs as she went"[26] in about the year 1100) and the musician unattached to any court, and therefore unprotected, reprehensible and reviled—and, perhaps, envied.

By Beethoven's day, freelance musicians had been subjected to more than one thousand years of legal prohibitions that made them, in effect, non-persons, lower on the social scale, and with fewer legal rights, than farm animals. The *Spielmann* could not own land or inherit it, or inherit money—though he could inherit debts. He could not be a witness, juror or judge, or carry a weapon, or bring a lawsuit for damages—even for homicide. He was denied burial in sanctified ground. He could not join a trade guild.[27] In England, "As early as 747 the

Council of Cloveshoe had forbidden the [Benedictine] monks to admit the 'sportive arts; that is, of poets, harpers, musicians, and buffoons.' . . . As a consequence, a priest was forbidden to be 'an eala-scop or an ale-poet, or to any wise gliwege, or play the gleeman with himself or with others.'"[28] In continental Europe, musicians were barred by law from entering through the town gates of some cities, among them Montpellier, which enacted its law in 1321. "And, according to the statutes of Siena, a person who violently attacked a *Spielmann* would not be punished."[29] Even sons and grandsons of musicians were prohibited from guild membership.

Yet while feudal society inflicted this treatment upon musicians, it acknowledged its need for music. Until around 1600 in many places a wedding was not legal unless it was celebrated with music, and a feudal landlord could be required by law to provide music for his peasants. But the system Europe devised to provide its common people with music was as riddled with class and caste prohibitions as the rest of society. The *Spielmann*, the roaming rural musician, was almost outside the human pale. Next up the scale were the town musicians, who, due to their precarious perch and their fight for a place in a small social niche, could be counted on to lead the fight against freelancers. Church musicians had the highest status. There were grades within grades, including *Ratsmusiker*, or town musicians; and *Kunstgeiger*, or trained violinists; and this miserable pecking order inspired longtime rivalries between cantors, organists, and town schoolteachers, who also were expected to teach, and write, music. Arno Werner classified the "ascending order" of musicians, from the Middle Ages to the nineteenth century, in this order: minstrel, performer, town piper, organist, cantor, court musician, concert master, conductor, director of music. These musicians fought for scraps from the cash-poor economic system.[30]

There were no more than 150 noble families in Germany in the thirteenth century, and 43 episcopal sees. These were the patrons who might be able to offer musicians regular employment, though wealthy patrons might hire them occasionally, and independent cities hired musicians as watchmen to blow their *hautbois* upon the approach of strangers or at the sight of fire. These watchmen-musicians organized their own guild and became known as town pipers.[31] In England, Henry III established the system of watchmen in 1253 in London, where they were known as waits.[32]

A body of custom and law grew up granting some rights, but still heaping obloquy, execration, and legal prohibitions upon town pipers—who did not play just pipes, but all the instruments—and the legal prohibitions extended even to the instruments. Music with trumpets and drums was reserved for the upper classes because of their martial association, but even within the armies there were prohibitions, trumpets being reserved for the cavalry, while the infantry had to content itself with bagpipes.

The town piper system was a poor cousin to the trade and craft guilds, from which musicians were excluded. The post of town piper existed as early as 1355 in Lüneburg, and in 1375 in Basel, according to town records. A 1343 document from Wismar lays out "Rules for Musicians," which set an upper limit on how much musicians may be paid, but no lower limit. Itinerant musicians, who belonged neither to the church, court, or town systems, had no rights, and could stay in town only so long as they obeyed the citizens' wishes. The only "right" that musicians had was that those who lived in the city could be hired to play at weddings—itinerant musicians could not. Lüneburg enacted similar rules in 1430.[33]

Weddings and funerals were prized sources of revenue, and town musicians ruthlessly excluded freelancers from working these occasional gigs, which were called *Accidienten*. But musicians above the first three levels of Arno's scale—those with regular jobs, however poorly paid, at church or court—were often forbidden from playing at commoners' festivities, and even if they were permitted to play for weddings or funerals, they had to think twice about it, as doing so would degrade them in the social scale. And the gradations of the social scale were unbelievably petty and rigid.

"Trade guilds required a so-called proof of lineage in which one had to prove non-descent from a musician," Salmen wrote.[34] "After 1652 in the duchy of Braunschweig the baptismal certificate required for acceptance into a craft omitted the remark that the applicant was not the son of a piper. It still appears, however, in birth certificates in Hildesheim in 1681."[35] In Hildesheim in 1674 there were "protests and a (futile) law suit of the shoemakers' guild against one of their masters whose father-in-law had been observed as 'a fieldpiper playing before the regiment.'"[36] So the stain of being a musician passed unto the daughter, and the man she married.

Records of medieval lawsuits present a picture of musicians' dreary social status. In a misdemeanor complaint from Flensburg in 1685, a businessman's wife complained that the wife of a musician had entered church before her, and so had "laid claim to superior status." The musician, Lorentz Schwensen, defended his wife by saying that the businessman's wife had "in public spoken disparagingly of them, saying, 'Who do this *Spielmann's* wife and her husband consider themselves to be?,' not to mention her other insinuations." Schwensen claimed that "having been classified by the Council, in view of his upright calling, not as a *Spielmann* but as a town musician, he had consequently been accepted as a Master, dedicated to the liberal arts." The citizens of Flensburg seem to have had it in for musicians. Musicologist Heinrich Schwab cites another complaint from that town, of 1646, in which "the wife of the town musician Heinsen was denounced because she 'had draped her bed with taffeta curtains, which were above her station.'"[37]

Musicians resented their dismal status and struggled to improve it. Watchmen-musicians often were assigned the job of conducting annual chimney inspections, an onerous and dirty job in a time when there was no defense against fire. They sought to free themselves from such work, and from the obligation to work as watchmen; an applicant for the job of town musician rejected an offer from Delitzsch in 1658 for that reason. Musicians in Kiel in 1726 refused to "beat the drums" for the erection of a gallows until they were given "a warranty to assure them that his was, 'in fact, honorable work and that none, now or later, could make reproach.'"[38]

Liberalization of these rules came slowly, and the social stigma of being a musician could not be erased by princely decree. Feudal rules dictated well into Beethoven's day even the fabrics from which men and women of different social classes were permitted to make their clothes; such prohibitions extended to their musical instruments. A 1726 law in Lübeck stated that "shawm players must refrain from playing string instruments in all social gatherings. They may, however, play their shawms or *hautbois* (oboes) for entertaining the common soldiers."[39] That year in Leipzig, common people who were married were allowed to hire trumpets and drums for the ceremony, which formerly had been reserved for the aristocracy.[40]

If a town musician died, his replacement was expected to marry the man's wife or daughter, so the town would not have to support them for the traditional "widow's year." In 1704, the young George Friedrich Handel refused a job in Lübeck because he did not want to marry the daughter of the organist Dietrich Buxtehude, who had got the job by marrying the daughter of his predecessor. Johann Sebastian Bach's famous 200-mile walk to hear the great Buxtehude play the organ may have been motivated as well by a desire to see the woman he would have to marry if he sought that job. When Bach made his long walk to Lübeck in 1706, Buxtehude was 69; he would die the next spring. His daughter was 30—nine years older than Bach, who returned from Lübeck to Arnstadt, where he married his cousin.[41] But musicians with less talent and ambition than Handel and Bach were not above marrying into regular work. In Kiel in 1724, the town's new 26-year-old music director became the fourth husband of the town musician's wife, who was 50.[42]

Town musicians must have been of wildly varying quality, but Johann Joachim Quantz, whose music is still occasionally played today, left a record of the rigorous training he received during his seven and one-half years of apprenticeship under a town musician. "The first instrument which I had to learn was the violin . . . followed by the oboe and the trumpet," Quantz wrote in 1754. Apparently, it was still unusual in those days that a town piper would be permitted to learn the trumpet, as the translator or editor inserted an exclamation point after the word. "I was also not spared learning other instruments such as cornet, trombone, French horn, recorder, bassoon, bass viol, cello, viola da gamba, and God knows how many others, which a piper has to be able to play. It is a fact that because one has to learn so many different instruments, one always remains a bungler on each."[43]

Through Haydn's day, musicians received at least half their pay in kind—food, wine, clothing, candles, firewood, even hair powder.[44] So scarce were the jobs that musicians often had to work for years for no pay at all, waiting for a town or court musician to die, in hopes of getting his gig. There was a name for these poor wretches, the *Expektanten*. Richard Petzoldt describes the system:

> Until the nineteenth century there existed a well developed system of exploitation of apprentices and journeymen called the *Stadtpfeifer* (pipers' training system). The apprentices usually received more beatings than nourishment, and by the time a trainee was released after a total of eight years (five years as a jour-

neyman) he had experienced much hardship. The complaints over the miserable conditions continued and as the guild system, inherited from the Middle Ages, slowly gave way to a more independent life for musicians, the economic struggle for survival became more and more intense.[45]

The violinist Augustin Uhlig wrote in 1733 that he had served in a court orchestra for fifteen years, the first four without pay. Another violinist, Franz Xaver, in a petition to the Munich court for a raise in 1785, wrote that he had served it for seventeen years, the first four without pay. Ignatius Albert, a contrabass player, asked for a "regular post" in 1766, after working six years without pay. And in 1801, the widow of court musician Plebs wrote that her late husband had gone into debt while serving his first nine years without pay. She begged for an increase in her pension. She was 65. Her request was denied.[46]

Nor were musicians allowed to quit a job once they had secured it. Johann Sebastian Bach was thrown in prison for daring to tell the Duke of Weimar that he was leaving his service to take a job in Cöthen. Duke Wilhelm Ernst kept his *Kapellmeister* locked up for a month, in the worst of the duke's three prisons, "to drive home to Bach that . . . he was nothing more than a rebellious lackey," Klaus Eidam wrote in "The True Life of J. S. Bach." Eidam cites this splendid document, written by the Weimar court secretary:

On Nov. 6th [1717] the heretofore concertmaster and court organist Bach was detained at the ducal judge's chamber because of his stubborn testimony and his too forceful demand of dismissal. Finally on December 2nd the dismissal was accorded to him by the court secretary with express disfavor, and at the same time he was freed from detention.[47]

Mozart had to beg repeatedly to be allowed to leave the service of Archbishop Colloredo in 1781, and was finally dismissed with a kick in the behind. Mozart mentioned this twice in a letter to his father of June 9, 1781, complaining of his treatment from Count Arco, the archbishop's secretary:

So that is the way to persuade people and to attract them! To refuse petitions from innate stupidity, not to say a word to your master from lack of courage and love of toadyism, to keep a fellow dangling for four weeks, and finally, when he is obliged to present the petition in person, instead of at least granting him admittance, to throw him out of the room and give him a kick on his behind. . . . Well, that will be the last time. What is it to him if I get my discharge? And if he was really so well disposed towards me, he ought to have reasoned quietly with me—or have let things take their course, rather than throw such words about as "clown" and "knave" and hoof a fellow out of the room with a kick on his arse; but I am forgetting that this was probably done by order of our worthy Prince Archbishop.[48]

Children who fell into the musical system of the church and the courts were subjected to far worse treatment, including abduction and castration, which ostensibly was illegal, but which produced the greatest opera stars for two centuries. The church and nobility began abducting young boys with good voices during the Middle Ages, particularly if they were attractive and could read music.

In England, Richard II (1367-1400) began the custom of abducting boys to sing in his Chapel Royal. King Richard empowered John Melynek "to take and seize for the king all such singing-men expert in the science of music as he could find and think able to do the king's service, within all places of the realm, as well as cathedral churches, colleges, chapels, houses of religion, and all other franchised or exempt places, or elsewhere."[49] In 1456, Henry VI established a commission to take charge of the abductions. And an exchange of testy letters between King Henry VIII and Cardinal Wolsey survives in which Henry's Dean of the Chapel Royal, Richard Pace, remonstrates with Wolsey, who had complained that the king had stolen a choirboy from him. Pace wrote: "My Lord, if it were not for the personal love that the King's Highness doth bear Your Grace, surely he would have out of your chapel not children only, but men also."[50]

By the fifteenth and sixteenth centuries on the mainland, when the Netherlands school of polyphony was the most advanced on the continent, boys were regularly abducted and dragged them from one end of Europe to the other. Roland Lassus, better known as Orlando di Lasso, "was three times abducted from Mons (in the Netherlands), where he was a treble in the choir of St. Nicholas Church. Lassus was born in 1532, and the third abduction, when he was nine years old, succeeded, for his parents agreed to allow Ferdinand Gonzaga, regent of Sicily . . . to keep the boy and eventually to take him first to Palermo and then to Milan," Henry Raynor wrote in *A Social History of Music from the Middle Ages to Beethoven*. Lassus, who was taken to Munich in 1556 and became *Kapellmeister* there in 1563 for the Archduke of Bavaria, recruited choirboys for the archduke from Italy in 1574, where he also bought instruments; and "three Spanish choirboys" arrived in Munich in 1582. During the 1580s, the archduke began to employ *castrati*, whom he found in the Netherlands and Germany.[51]

Castration of boys with good voices may have been practiced in Eastern Orthodox churches as early as the 1100s; it became increasingly common in the West during the 1500s, due to the Church's need for male soprano voices. Rome had decreed that women could not sing in church because of St. Paul's injunction: *Mulier taceat en ecclesia*. The Roman Church, as so often during the history of Western music, took an equivocal position. Anyone connected with a castration was subject to excommunication—Burney says it was punishable by death—yet "every church in Italy, including the Pope's own private chapel, had castrati on its staff—in the 1780s, there were reckoned to be over 200 of them in churches in the city of Rome alone," according to Angus Heriot, author of a history of the castrati.[52]

Clement VIII (pope from 1592 to 1605) cleared the way for the spread of castration for musical purposes. He admired the castrati's voices, and publicly acknowledged the presence of castrati in Roman churches in 1599. (The first surviving complete operas, by Giulio Caccini and Jacopo Peri, date from 1601 in Florence.) Surely it was no coincidence that the papacy's semi-official tolerance of castration occurred simultaneously with the rise of a new art form that provided the venue for the West's first international musical superstars.

"The castrati were born, as a rule, of humble parents, for only those in fairly pressing need of money would have consented to the mutilation of their children," Heriot says.[53] Castration, followed by years of rigorous training, preserved great range and flexibility in voices of boys who were put to the knife while anesthetized by opium or alcohol—ether was not introduced into medical practice until the 1840s. Mortality from the operation varied wildly, from 10 to 80 percent, "depending upon the competence of the surgeon."[54] Many boys had no one to defend them from castration, for the church often recruited the members of its boy choirs from state-run orphanages. Leopold Mozart visited these orphanages and singing schools on tours with his son, who studied voice in London with a famous castrato, Giovanni Manzuoli, when Wolfgang was nine, and five years later befriended the greatest castrato of them all, Carlo Broschi, known as Farinelli, on the castrato's estate outside Bologna.

Boys whose voices were not good enough to warrant castration might be sent to university when their voice broke, if their local church or court leaders were kind, but were just as likely to be simply dumped from the choir and left to fend for themselves. Such was the fate of Franz Joseph Haydn, who had been recruited at age eight for the choir at St. Stephen's Cathedral in Vienna, managed to fight off his own castration, then was cast adrift, penniless, in 1749, when he was seventeen.

Perhaps this narrow escape had a hand in inspiring Haydn, the great musical innovator, to become one of the first to demand that his prince not treat him like a lackey. Historians generally do not credit Haydn with fighting to improve the status of musicians, because Haydn was a quiet diplomat and a courtier, but documents from the Esterházy princes reveal decades of his quiet work on behalf of his musicians. When his new prince, Nicolaus II, recalled him in 1794 from London, where Haydn had earned the equivalent of 24,000 florins in four concert seasons, Haydn dutifully returned. But when the prince addressed him in the customary, and demeaning, third person "*Er*," used with servants, Haydn "was impelled to remind his Gracious Lord that he was a Doctor of Oxford and not to be treated like a lackey."[55] But Haydn, once again, was an exception. Musicians were expected to work as servants, as many ads in the *Wiener Zeitung* indicate. Anton Neumann was *Kapellmeister* for the Bishop of Olmutz—and also his valet. Even Haydn's friend Karl Ditters von Dittersdorf, a popular opera composer who boasted of his independence, had to wait on tables every other night for his prince.[56]

Such were the customs, the social status, and the economic conditions awaiting Beethoven when he arrived in Vienna to stay in 1792, and he did not bother to disguise the resentment he felt for it. Like Mozart before him, Beethoven wanted regular, salaried work as a *Kapellmeister* or court composer, and like Mozart he would be denied it, whether from jealousy, intrigue, personal unsuitability or the simple dearth of such jobs, which became available, as they had been since the Middle Ages, only through death of the occupant. Beethoven's letters are full of imprecations against his "enemies" in Vienna, and though he was famously suspicious and irascible, the letters of Leopold and

Wolfgang Mozart report similar plots and intrigues against Wolfgang from courts and musicians throughout Europe.

Musicians fought for space in a tiny socioeconomic niche. By the 1780s, only ten noble families kept full-time orchestras in Vienna, and the financial disaster of the Napoleonic wars forced many of these to be disbanded. The liberal reforms of the Emperor Franz Josef probably contributed to musicians' economic displacement, as the emancipation of the peasants reduced the incomes of the great landed estates. The nobility retained small, cheaper wind ensembles known as *Harmonien* to keep up appearances, but even Nicolaus II Esterházy, one of the wealthiest princes in Europe, fired his *Harmonie* in 1798 to save money.[57] Life for musicians, never easy, was becoming even more difficult at the very time that Beethoven was establishing his reputation and trying to live as a freelance musician.

The complicated arrangements for the publication of Beethoven's Opus No. 1, the three trios of 1795, illustrate the musical economics of the time. The trios brought Beethoven a profit of 735 florins—enough to live frugally for six months, before inflation. This money did not come from sales in a free marketplace, but from subscriptions from generous sponsors: 123 subscribers, most of them nobles, subscribed for 245 copies of the trios. Countess Thun ordered 22 copies, Prince Lobkowitz and Baron Stroganoff ordered six apiece. The young Beethoven had collected an impressive list of sponsors, as Vienna held only about 140 extended families of nobles.[58]

It must be understood, however, that neither Beethoven nor the publisher, Matthias Artaria, could expect any profit from sales after the subscription. Here is how it worked: Beethoven paid Artaria one florin per copy, and sold each one for a ducat, or 4.5 florins—yielding profit of 735.5 florins for Beethoven. But Beethoven had to pay Artaria 212 florins for cost of the plates, which Artaria repurchased for 90 florins after the subscribed copies were delivered. Artaria then could print more copies for foreign sales—outside of Vienna—and he could sell the trios in Vienna after Beethoven's sponsors had had them for two months.[59] But unless Artaria had a deal with other publishers in distant cities, he was not likely to realize any profit from foreign sales. Europe had no copyright system, so once a piece was published it was free to be stolen and republished in cheaper editions, as the pirate publishers did not need to pay the composer.

Beethoven's subscription list is all the more impressive as it came just seven years after Mozart had had to withdraw a proposed edition of three string quintets for lack of subscribers. The Viennese tired quickly of their musical idols, and though Beethoven in 1795 was the city's new and rising musical hero, Mozart's fate foretold what lay ahead for him. Neither Mozart, Beethoven, nor anyone else in those days could survive by his publications alone. Within ten years of the publication of his Opus No. 1, Beethoven's hearing was failing and his performing career was over. He could not make a living through concerts, for outside of London a tradition of public concerts, to which anyone could gain admission by buying a ticket, barely existed in Europe until after Beethoven was dead. Aside from the occasional gift or commission from foreigners, and whatever he could wring from the cutthroat publishing system, Vienna's 140 noble families and the city's small middle class were the patrons—the "market"—from whom Beethoven, with his hearing failing and his performing career over, had to wrest his living, in competition with every other musician in Vienna.

Beethoven's Sources of Income

Beethoven had six ways to earn money: from private lessons, from commissioned works, from gifts given in gratitude for a dedication, from performing, from charging admission to public concerts of his music, and, at the tail end of the process, from publishing. But Beethoven hated to give private lessons, which paid only a pittance in Vienna, and when he lost his hearing he no longer could give them.[60] Nor was he temperamentally suited for it. As a favor to his old counterpoint teacher Johann Albrechtsberger, Beethoven agreed to give harmony lessons to the man's grandson, Karl Hirsch, but during one lesson Beethoven became so enraged with the boy that he *bit him on the shoulder*.[61] He also pinched the child and hollered at him in fury, particularly for parallel fifths and octaves.

Beethoven would accept charming young countesses as students, but often refused to accept money for this, in accord with the tradition dating back to the Middle Ages, by which musicians would accept money if it were given as a gesture of appreciation from an equal, but not as payment, which was considered demeaning. This is graphically illustrated in a Beethoven letter of January 1802, which was not published until 1971. Rather than thank Countess Susanna Guicciardi for a gift she had sent to thank him for instructing her daughter, Giulietta, (or Julia) Beethoven wrote:

> I think you should know, dearest countess, that you would have received your present back yesterday morning almost on the spot if my brother hadn't happened to be with me; he did his very best to stop me. . . . I'm not exaggerating when I say that your present gave me a shock. . . . It immediately put the little I had done for dear J. on a par with your present, and it seemed to me that you wanted to humble my pride by wanting to show me that you wished far rather to put me in your debt than to have the appearance of being in mine. What, after all, did I do to deserve anything like this? . . . I'll never, never again be so openhearted toward you as before this. But now for my warning. I accept this present; but should it ever occur to you to let yourself think up anything even remotely similar, I swear by everything that I hold sacred that you will never see me again in your house.[62]

He signed the letter, "Your greatly upset Beethoven."

The class distinctions that riddled every element of society made Beethoven's daily life a social, economic, and personal minefield. Socially and economically, he was willing to blow himself up in his stubborn insistence to be treated as an equal. He did this at great personal cost. But unpleasant and peculiar as Beethoven could be in society, he clearly suffered more psychological pain than he inflicted upon his social betters.

Patrons who commissioned a piece of music were given exclusive right to play it, or to have it played, generally for six months.[63] After that, the patron kept the music but the composer could sell it for publication. But commissions, even for great works, were barely sufficient for Beethoven to make a living. He received 500 florins from Count Franz von Oppersdorf for his Fourth Symphony in 1807. Had Viennese currency suffered no inflation since Schiller estimated in 1789 that a bachelor could live on 1,400 florins a year, then, the commission for the Fourth Symphony might barely have supported Beethoven for the time it required him to write it.

Oppersdorf was delighted with the symphony and offered another 500 florins for another one, but Beethoven, in financial straits, blew the deal by selling the Fifth Symphony to Breitkopf & Härtel for 100 ducats—450 florins. This was because, in a convoluted financial arrangement distressingly typical of Beethoven, he had promised Breitkopf & Härtel the Fourth Symphony in 1806, then put them off "because a gentleman of quality has taken it from me, but I have the privilege of publishing it in half a year."[64] Having sold Oppersdorf the symphony he had promised Breitkopf & Härtel, Beethoven then sold Breitkopf & Härtel the symphony he had promised Oppersdorf. He tried to salvage Oppersdorf's commission—some of which he had already accepted—by putting off publication of the Fifth Symphony, but Oppersdorf quite reasonably refused to pay the rest of the 500 florins. For the Count was paying not just for the pleasure of hearing the music, but for the prestige of having it while no one else did.

These dealings may show that Beethoven was an unscrupulous businessman, though it's just as likely that he was simply incompetent. He had no high regard for publishers—with reason, as we shall see—so he accepted Oppersdorf's money, thinking he could put off Breitkopf & Härtel for six months, or write them a new work, which he did. What the frantic deals clearly indicate are Beethoven's pressing need for money. In 1808, when his commission for the Fifth Symphony was dissolving, poverty had forced Beethoven to move in with Countess von Erdödy, and accept, briefly, an offer to leave Vienna to become *Kapellmeister* for Jerome Bonaparte in Cassel—an offer that led Beethoven's sponsors to offer him the yearly pension that kept him in Vienna.

For his Ninth Symphony, Beethoven received a commission of 50 pounds sterling in 1824 from the Philharmonic Society of London—550 florins. This symphony, however, had cost Beethoven two years of intensive work, and years more in its conception and evolution. The 550 florins, while a good sum of money, was not enough to support Beethoven for two years. Unlike Mozart and Haydn, Beethoven could not, or would not, knock out a symphony in a few days or weeks. Commissioned works required a steady flow of inspiration, which Beethoven could not always depend on. As he aged, he wrote even more slowly.

Dedications were an even more uncertain source of income, dependent wholly upon the goodwill of the dedicatee, and Beethoven often dedicated pieces out of friendship rather than for hope of money. In fact, he became furious if a titled friend sent him money in return for a dedication he had made from friendship. "I am angry, angry, angry," he wrote his friend Nikolaus Zmeskall von Domanovecz, an official in the Hungarian royal court, after Zmeskall had paid him, or sent a present, in return for the dedication of the Opus 95 String Quartet in F Minor. "I cannot tell you in writing how much this present pains me," Beethoven wrote, in an echo of the letter he had sent Countess Susanna Guicciardi.[65]

By tradition, payment for a dedication might take the form of a watch or a snuffbox, which the grateful composer, as often as not, would sell. But Johann Sebastian Bach received nothing for dedicating six concertos to the Elector of Brandenburg, who did not even bother to acknowledge receiving them, and may never have had the works performed.[66] Nor did Frederick the Great give Bach so much as a pfennig for his *Musical Offering*—not even travel expenses for the elderly Bach's trip to Potsdam. After Beethoven dedicated *Wellington's Victory* to the Prince of Wales—later George IV—it required ten years for him to extract thanks for it. When the present finally arrived, in 1824, it was kingly—600 pounds sterling, or 6,600 florins—surely worth the wait. The King of Prussia was not so generous that year after receiving the dedication of the Ninth Symphony. He sent Beethoven a ring with a "reddish" stone that Beethoven hocked for 300 florins in devalued currency.[67] So earnings from dedications were a chancy proposition.

After a piece was published, it was out of the composer's hands and he would get no more income from it.

During his first years in Vienna, Beethoven earned most of his income by performing in salons.[68] He did not publish his Opus 1 trios until his third year in the city. Despite his fame as a performer, this was a relatively brief phase of his career, cut short by deafness and by Beethoven's discomfort at being treated like a servant. Mozart encapsulated the problem a virtuoso faced, in an April 28, 1781, letter to his father: "After the concert yesterday the ladies kept me at the piano for an hour. I believe that if I had not stolen away I should be sitting there still. I thought I had really played enough *for nothing*."[69]

The demands of making a living as a musician conflicted with the musician's need to acquire, or maintain, social status. Mozart, a celebrity since childhood, was comfortable demanding payment for performing for the nobility, thinking it commensurate with, rather than degrading to, his social situation. After Archbishop Colloredo refused to let him play at a charity concert for the widows and orphans of Viennese musicians, Mozart wrote an enraged letter to his father, in which he praised the oboist and cellist Joseph Fiala, a member of Colloredo's Salzburg orchestra.

> Fiala has risen two thousand times higher in my estimation for refusing to play for less than a ducat. Has not my sister been asked to play yet? I hope she will *demand* two ducats. For, as we have always been different *in every way* from the other court musicians, I trust we shall be different in this respect too. If they won't pay, they can do without her—but if they want her, then, by Heaven, let them pay.[70]

If Mozart or Beethoven performed gratis, it cheapened their music. But Beethoven, less at ease with the aristocracy, and probably, with himself, was more likely to reject payment, as a way of proclaiming his equal social status. Beethoven felt far more acutely than Mozart that it cheapened him as a man to accept payment for playing for people he considered friends and equals. "(E)ven in late 1802 he was already uncomfortable in the social setting of aristocratic salons, which diminished his desire to perform there," Julia Moore wrote. "He tended to find it difficult . . . to accept payment from aristocratic patrons from whom he was on friendly terms."[71]

Virtuosi had to create their audience by playing for the nobility, but had to tread a fine line between playing too seldom, and having a small following, and playing too often and wearing out their welcome—and their material—and becoming passé. Beethoven apparently walked that line very well.[72] But the commissions he received came from the reputation he had built in private concerts for the nobility—not from public concerts. In Beethoven's day, few towns outside of London and the free cities of Northern Germany had a tradition of regular public concerts. No one had yet charged money for a public piano recital, possibly because the pianos were not yet powerful enough for their sound to fill a hall, but also because a single piano was not considered adequate to provide music for an entire concert. Vienna did not have a building dedicated to concerts—as opposed to opera—until 1831, four years after Beethoven died.[73]

During his thirty-four years in Vienna, Beethoven was paid for performing in just fifteen public concerts, eight of which he arranged for his own benefit.[74] Such concerts were called academies, and Beethoven's last two academies for himself, during which he presented his Ninth Symphony, were financial disasters. To present a concert for his own benefit, Beethoven had to write the music, rent the hall, pay for the candles, pay the copyists, and sometimes pay the musicians, though the amateurs, who made up the bulk of the orchestra, generally donated their service. (Candles could be a major expense. It cost 230 florins for candles to light the Redoutensaal for a performance of Haydn's *The Creation* in 1802, and a year later the cost to light the same hall for a performance of *The Seven Words* had risen to 250 fl.)[75] For the premiere of the Ninth Symphony, on May 7, 1824, Beethoven paid 1,000 gulden to rent the Karntnerthor Theater and pay some members of the chorus and orchestra, plus another 800 gulden for the copyists. The receipts of 2,200 gulden brought him only 420 gulden profit for years of work, and at the repeat performance on May 23, the theater management claimed it lost 800 gulden.[76]

Even a grand public concert could draw only from the aristocracy and the city's small middle class, which Moore estimates as no more than 2.5 percent of Vienna's 200,000 to 250,000 residents.[77] The standard price for a concert ticket was two gulden, or one thaler, which was more than a week's salary for a laborer.[78] Musicians could not give academies in the summer, when the nobility fled the dust and heat of Vienna to their country estates, and during the fall and winter the theaters were given over to rehearsals and performances of operas, the highest status form of musical production. The only time available for academies was during Advent and Lent, when operas were forbidden. During these six weeks, competition for halls was fierce, and theater managers could and did refuse nights to Beethoven in favor of mediocrities.

The abbreviated concert season was responsible for the disappointing returns from Beethoven's first two concerts for his own benefit, in 1803 and 1808. Haydn gave concerts on the same nights, and "Beethoven was forced to take the left-over musicians, all the best that Vienna had to offer having been engaged in the huge band . . . that played Haydn's music."[79] This scheduling conflict, which was no fault of Haydn's, ruined what might have been one of the world's great evenings of music, at the *Theater an der Wien* on December 22, 1808, where Beethoven presented his Fourth Piano Concerto, the Choral Fantasy, and the first public performance of his Fifth and Sixth Symphonies. Johann Friedrich Reichardt, a composer and writer, attended this four-hour concert on a bitterly cold night:

> Poor Beethoven, who from this, his own concert, was having the first and only scant profit that he could find in a whole year, had found in the rehearsals and performance a lot of opposition and almost no support. Singers and orchestra were composed of heterogeneous elements, and it had been impossible to get a single full rehearsal for all the pieces to be performed, all filled with the greatest difficulties.[80]

Little has been written about rehearsal practices in Classical Vienna, which almost certainly were far from adequate to present acceptable renditions of Beethoven's difficult music. A single rehearsal, if any, appears to have been standard. Haydn rehearsed Prince Esterházy's orchestra once a week at Eisenstadt,[81] and though that may have been sufficient for an ensemble that played together for years, it would have been inadequate for the pick-up orchestras that performed Beethoven's concerts. "Rehearsals were almost invariably held the day of the concert," according to Mary Sue Morrow[82]—the halls were available for rehearsals those days because concerts were held only on days that the theaters were closed.

Haydn, customarily generous in providing music for concerts to benefit widows, orphans, and the poor, refused to conduct one of his symphonies in London because he was not allowed to rehearse it. "On 30th March 1795 I was invited by Dr. Arnold and his associates to a grand concert in Free Maisons [*sic*] Hall," Haydn wrote, in English, in one of his London notebooks. "One of my big symphonies was to have been given under my direction, but since they wouldn't have any rehearsal, I refused to cooperate and did not appear."[83] In a letter of 1789, referring to his difficult "Paris" Symphonies, No. 90-92, Haydn wrote, "Now I would humbly ask you to tell the Princely *Kapellmeister* there that these 3 symphonies because of their many particular effects, should be rehearsed at least once, carefully and with special concentration, before they are performed."[84]

When Haydn was granted an honorary doctorate from Oxford in 1791, he was allowed to rehearse his Symphony No. 92—now known as the Oxford—in the morning. In reviewing one of Haydn's Oxford concerts from that weekend, the *Morning Herald* reported: "A new Overture by Pleyel led on the second act.

The composition was much admired and the Band played it with very great correct[n]ess and spirit, though they never saw it till that evening."[85]

These were not exceptions, but the rule. Mozart wrote so quickly that many of his works were performed with no rehearsal at all.[86] Beethoven often was still composing and having parts copied on the day of a performance. Ferdinand Ries found him writing the trombone parts for his oratorio, *Christ on the Mount of Olives*, on the morning of performance day. Yet oratorios require coordinating a chorus with an orchestra. For this reason, Morrow says, "Oratorios usually had two [rehearsals] on the days immediately preceding the performance. Since many of the oratorios were completely new works, the rehearsals must have been both crucial and hectic."[87]

Complicating the rehearsals was that the tradition of the master conductor had not yet been established. Orchestras had two leaders, the first violinist, also called the *Musik Direktor*, and the *Kapellmeister*, who presided at the keyboard. Personal and professional rivalries between them ruined many a concert. A contemporary critic, Johann Schonfeld, "even went so far as to suggest that it would be good if the two in charge would go over a piece together beforehand to settle on a common tempo. He then observed that if all members of the orchestra could rely on the *Musik Direktor* (i.e., the concert master) for the proper tempo, things would improve even more."[88] When a pianist conducted from the keyboard, Charles Rosen says, he played chords "to keep the orchestra together." Rosen adds: "In 1767, Rousseau complained that the conductor of the Paris opera made so much noise beating a sheet of rolled-up music paper on the desk to keep the orchestra in time that one's pleasure in the music was spoiled."[89]

Rehearsals, when they occurred, may have been what we would call "run throughs." Mozart described for his father the preparation for his "Paris" Symphony, K. 297: "I was very nervous at the rehearsal, for never in my life have I heard a worse performance. You have no idea how they twice scraped and scrambled through it. I was really in a terrible way and would gladly have had it rehearsed again, but as there was so much else to rehearse, there was no time left."[90]

Beethoven's supremely difficult Quartet in A Minor, Opus 132, apparently was rehearsed just twice before its first performance. English conductor George Smart, who attended one rehearsal, wrote in his journal that it was played twice, and each time lasted for 45 minutes.[91] As the A minor quartet requires about 45 minutes to perform, the rehearsal Smart attended in 1825 must have consisted of playing the piece through two times.

Beethoven's music, particularly his symphonic work, relies far less than was customary upon passage work, and far more upon long-term dynamics, contrast, and control of the orchestra. Many of his works received hostile critical reception. Some of the hostility stemmed from the music's length and complexity, which strained the listening capacity of his public. But some of the hostility must have sprung from inadequate performances caused by lack of rehearsal. "It's clear that compositional style and institutional structure were out of sync at the beginning of the 19th century," Mary Sue Morrow wrote.[92] To hear any quartet in the world attempt the *Grosse Fuge* after only two rehearsals would be horrifying.

The Development of the Public Concert

The custom of presenting concerts of instrumental music for the general public did not exist through most of Germany and Austria until Beethoven was dead. The musical traveler Charles Burney barely mentions public concerts in the four volumes he wrote on his continental travels of 1769 to 1772. Mozart, who arrived in Vienna in 1781, and Beethoven, who arrived eleven years later, were the first freelancers to try to wrest a good part of their living from public concerts in continental Europe. If Mozart was more successful at this, for a while, it was partly because he had the assistance of an impresario, Philipp Martin, who organized Vienna's first series of public concerts, in a public park, the Augarten, in 1782. But Martin had left Vienna by the time Beethoven arrived.

Northern Germany had an earlier tradition of public concerts than did Vienna, possibly due to its political ties and proximity to England, where regular series of public concerts predated the tradition in Austria by more than a century. Northern Germany also was the realm of the free cities, where merchants and the relatively wealthy professionals and civil servants had to fulfill the patronage functions that elsewhere were carried out by the nobility. The first public concerts in Germany were given by Frankfurt's *collegium musicum* in 1712, despite the opposition of the Church, and in Hamburg in 1721. Leipzig businessmen underwrote a Grand Concert of weekly concerts in 1743 by combining two *collegia musica*, but the onset of the Seven Years' War in 1756 interrupted those experiments.[93]

Economists William and Hilda Baumol believe the Seven Years' War precipitated the replacement of the old *Kapelle* system, in which "the demands of a noble household were supplied by a cadre of household servants led by a *Kapellmeister*, who was little more than a servant himself," with the cheaper system of hiring professional musicians as they were needed.[94] It may have been one of the earliest historical examples of a professional class being replaced by contract labor. This did not happen overnight; the Baumols call it a "gradual replacement." Both systems survived through Beethoven's day, though by then the old *Kapelle* system was dying. "Probably all of Vienna's standing orchestras were disbanded during the 1809 occupation of the city by Napoleon's armies," Moore says, though the fabulously wealthy Esterházys were able to revive their orchestra until the revolutionary year of 1848.[95]

Austria lagged as far behind northern Germany in establishing public concerts as Leipzig and Hamburg lagged behind London, where the tradition began far earlier and proliferated more rapidly than elsewhere in Europe. John Bannister became the first promoter known to give regular public concerts, in the 1670s, at a "nasty hole in Whitefriars. . . . A shilling a piece, call for what you please, pay the reckoning and 'Welcome, Gentlemen.'"[96] Bannister, a colorful character who was a violinist for King Charles II, started his concerts to protest the king's giving Bannister's first violin chair to a foreigner (though there had been complaints that Bannister had skimmed money he was supposed to pay the rest of the section). Other promoters soon followed, including Bannister's own son, who continued the concerts after his father died in 1679.

Why England established the concert tradition so much earlier, and why it continued for more than a century without spreading to the rest of Europe, is something of a mystery. It surely was due in part to England's mercantile spirit and more prosperous middle class—a class that barely existed in the hundreds of petty principalities in Germany and Austria. In his German travels of the early 1770s, Charles Burney lamented "the terrible poverty of the common people" compared to "the splendor and luxury of the numerous courts, where music flourished so ostentatiously."[97] English Puritan hostility to church music may have driven sponsorship to the middle class. In the two decades after the revolution that began in 1642, Puritans removed organs from churches and destroyed them—but some of the instruments were taken to taverns, which became venues for public concerts.[98]

Also curious is why no great English composers arose to benefit from the concert tradition, while Germany and Austria, which provided the great composers, took so long to emulate England in providing public concerts. The Baumols contend that "the political fragmentation of Germany and Italy provided opportunities for musicians which France and England did not offer. . . . France and the United Kingdom had no secondary cities with a thriving musical life. Lyons and Rouen were not Mannheim, and York or Glasgow were not Berlin."[99] Musicians' starvation wages in Germany, and their status as bound, feudal-type servants, allowed German courts and bishoprics to compete against one another relatively cheaply in music, and in the illustriousness of their composers. Vienna benefited too from its proximity to Italy, Bohemia, and Hungary.

By this reasoning, the social and economic conditions and the wide class divisions that made possible the astonishing flowering of Viennese Classical music, culminating in the music of Haydn, Mozart, Beethoven, and Schubert, also inhibited the establishment of public concerts, which were unaffordable for an impoverished citizenry. "(W)hile suitable economic circumstances are, in themselves, hardly sufficient to elicit an abundance of musical genius, they may constitute a necessary condition for this result," the Baumols say. "(E)conomics can hardly be the entire story, but neither can its role be denied altogether."[100]

Economist F. M. Scherer, however, found mixed evidence on the Baumols' theory of political fragmentation. He found employment of composers relative to population highest in Austria, Germany, Italy, and Czechoslovakia, but no evidence to support the theory in Germany, which was the most politically fragmented of all, with the most independent courts.[101] Scherer, in his excellent book, prudently declined to enter the debate about the influence of economics upon genius.

The impoverished state of the German and Austrian peasants and laborers surely reduced the demand for public concerts, but the rise of the institution was delayed as well because the upper classes actively suppressed it. Just as Count von Oppersdorf and other nobles who could afford to commission works wanted the prestige of having them performed privately for a few selected friends, the upper classes throughout Europe tried, and succeeded, in preserving the exclusivity of public concerts for the prestige of their class. Even in London, Europe's greatest venue for public concerts, the aristocracy purposely limited attendance through high ticket prices, pushed prices even higher by selling tickets only by subscription to a series of concerts rather than to single concerts, and prohibited ticket-holders from giving their tickets to others.[102] Even those who could afford a subscription might not be admitted: advisory committees, often of upper-class women, were created for the purpose of "vetting audience credentials."[103] The English government restricted the spread of public concerts by requiring licenses for them, until four string players from the Philharmonic Society, frustrated at being unable to present a chamber music series, challenged the licensing requirement in court, and "proved that the Office of the Lord Chamberlain had no basis for demanding the licenses and thereby cleared the way for many other kinds of cheap concerts."[104]

In Paris the situation was more complicated due to the competing factions of Bourbons and Orleanists and the elite bourgeoisie, but the government and its upper-class clients monopolized public concert-giving there, too, through control of the *Concerts Spirituels* and the Conservatory Concerts. Conservatory students and members of its orchestra were prohibited from performing elsewhere without permission, and the Conservatory hall was not made available for other performers. The government crippled the first attempt to establish independent concerts, the *Gymnase Musical*, in 1835, by refusing to allow vocal music to be performed, "a stipulation which no other series had ever been given." Songs and arias from the latest opera were an essential part of any concert, and the government's restriction helped bring those concerts to an end in six months. The public and the popular press didn't like it. Press attacks that called the Conservatory Concerts "a veritable musical oligarchy" fed the increasing social hostility between the classes and forced the government to allow a second low-class series, the Concerts St. Honoré, which lasted from 1837 to 1841. With a ticket price of one franc, this series did not actually compete with the established concerts—no upper-class music lover would care to be seen at a one-franc concert. "Its clear low-status orientations may very well have been the reason why the government did not impose as rigid programming restrictions upon it as upon the earlier series," William Weber says.[105] Music was a tool for the besieged upper classes to hold themselves aloof from the moiling masses. Large-scale, low-cost public concerts in London and Paris did not proliferate until after the revolutionary year of 1848.

Public concerts developed later in Vienna than in the two other great European capitals, partly due to Vienna's smaller size and its later rise to importance, but above all because music in Classical Vienna was a participatory art. The professionalization of music, which, for good and ill, split the art into performers and listeners, proceeded more slowly and less thoroughly in Vienna than in London or Paris. In 1763, a Vienna newspaper reported on a performance of

Gluck's opera, *Il Parnasso Confuso*, with thirteen members of the high nobility in the cast, including Archduke Leopold, an archduchess, and three "serene highnesses."[106]

Many, perhaps most, of the aristocrats who commissioned works from Mozart or Beethoven hoped to perform it themselves, or to play in the orchestra or chamber group that would perform it. It was an upper-class German tradition. In Prussia, Frederick the Great did not employ Johann Quantz to write hundreds of flute concertos for Frederick to listen to, but for the emperor to play every night. Mozart's subscription concerts during the 1780s were not aimed at the public, but, like all music in Classical Vienna, at the aristocratic dilettante—the word did not have the pejorative value we give it today. As late as 1838, an English visitor to Vienna wrote that "a gentleman wishing for a quartet or quintet in the evening walks out in the morning for the purpose of inviting any friends he may chance to meet; and as the slightest acquaintance is sufficient, no difficulty occurs." William Weber continues: "We should not, however, exaggerate the point. . . . (A) writer in a popular magazine said in 1849 that he was having increasing difficulty finding evenings when four of his regular friends were all free to play quartets."[107]

When German and Austrian commoners finally did establish associations to give regular public concerts, in the 1820s and afterward, these groups, primarily choral, were founded for the delight and edification of their participants, not for the concertgoing public. Berlin (1791), Leipzig (1802), Lübeck (1805), Erlangen (1806), and Frankfurt (1818) established choral societies during Beethoven's lifetime. More choirs of amateur sprang up in the 1820s, in Halle, Cassel, Mannheim, and elsewhere, and in Paris and London. But in Austria, Metternich wanted to ban the choral societies, feeling they were a cover for conspiracies and fearing any organization not conceived and organized by the state. The choruses he did not suppress he infiltrated with spies, though they operated with police permits and under police supervision.[108]

Weber insists that the choral societies *were* politically subversive, and that the nobility in Vienna, Paris, and London had good reason to fear them.

> A striking similarity in the development of choruses in London, Paris, and Vienna was that in all cases it was a product of social discontent. In London and Paris numerous choral societies sprang up during the political upheavals of the early 1830s; in Vienna one came with the pre-revolutionary social ferment of the 1840s. It was the choruses rather than the orchestras which were involved with the protest movements because they required little formal training and could therefore draw upon a much wider range of people for their members.[109]

Most of these societies, though, developed after Beethoven was dead. And all of them were devoted primarily to vocal music, rather than to the orchestral music in which Beethoven specialized.

Beethoven, then, faced nearly insuperable problems in trying to earn a living. The few composers who earned large sums from public concerts—Johann Christian Bach, George Friedrich Handel, and Franz Haydn—could have done so only in London. Haydn wrote in his London journal: "On 4th May 1795, I gave my benefit in the Haymarket Theater. . . . The whole company was pleased and so was I. I made four thousand Gulden on this evening. Such a thing is possible only in England."[110] Haydn's financial success surely is one reason that Beethoven always thought highly of the English and dreamed of going to England. But in his day, on the continent, "Public concerts did not yet provide a reliable source of income, even for a musician of Beethoven's stature," Julia Moore wrote.[111]

According to the cliché, independent artists, such as Mozart and Beethoven, brilliant though they may be, are unfit for the demands of commerce. The truth is that the social and economic system of Europe was not yet set up so that independent musicians such as Mozart or Beethoven could prosper in it. It was the demand to hear the music of Mozart and Beethoven that helped create the European concert tradition from which later generations of composers and performers benefited.

"It was Mozart, and even more decisively Beethoven, both living as freelance musicians in Vienna, dependent on their earnings from as wide a variety of sources as they could create for themselves, who made the public concert into a vehicle for important new music, and they did so rather in spite of than because of the complex musical situation of Vienna," Henry Raynor wrote.[112]

Beethoven's only other hope was publishing. This too was beset with problems, including lack of copyright protection and a tradition of outright theft by publishers, with encouragement from the state.

The Business of Music Publishing

The early history of music publishing can be traced from surviving manuscripts, but we know less about the economics of the business. Our knowledge of the musical economics of even the relatively recent nineteenth century is still "fragmentary and limited," according to William Weber.[113] Until recently, musicologists, for obvious reasons, tended to focus on the music itself or on its social reception, rather than the economics of the business. But the records that do exist indicate that making a living from selling instrumental compositions was an all but hopeless task for Beethoven. For its first three centuries, music publishing was not a money-making proposition for any composer. Composers had their music published for glory, not for profits. In fact, it cost composers money.

In the 1570s, when Archduke Wilhelm of Bavaria was spending 2 million gulden a year on his court's music, and his *Kapellmeister* Orlando Lassus was rounding up child singers in Italy, Lassus presented a book of his Masses, *Patrocinium Musices*, to the Pope. This brought honor to Lassus and to Archduke Wilhelm; whether it brought them any money is unlikely. "(I)f [publications] meant anything to the composer, it was only that his work had somewhat increased in international status; they brought him no material advantage," according to Henry Raynor.[114]

After Gutenberg published a Bible from movable type in about 1454, it took printers nearly fifty years to figure out how to use the new technology to print music. The man who did this, Ottaviano de Petrucci, received an exclusive license to print music in Venice in 1498, and became the first great music publisher. (Queen Elizabeth granted England's first exclusive license to print music, and music paper, in 1575.) Composers, facing a monopoly on printing, were not likely to profit from sale of their works, unless the composers happened to be the ones who got the printing monopoly. But even if they did—as Thomas Tallis and William Byrd did in England—there was little or no profit in it for them, as composers. After enjoying their monopoly for two years, Byrd and Tallis had to ask Elizabeth for a subsidy, saying they had lost 200 marks on the business.[115] Printing was expensive. And to whom were they to sell?

The clergy were the most likely buyers, not just because the church was wealthy—so was the nobility—but because the chants and ceremonies of the liturgical days and year provided the only system already established that required cycles of musical compositions. By 1501—two generations after Gutenberg—nearly 270 books of liturgical music had been published throughout Europe.[116] But church music, being for the glory of God, was "usually sold at a price which represented only the copying costs."[117] A publisher who sought profit would have to seek it through secular music. Petrucci, the first great music publisher, printed thirty-four collections of liturgical music and twenty-seven collections of popular music. His slightly later Parisian contemporary, Pierre Attaignant, one of the first to publish popular music from movable type, published more popular music than sacred: thirty-five volumes of *chansons*, containing more than 1,000 songs, plus seven books of Masses and thirteen of motets, a hybrid form that could be sacred or secular or have elements of both.

After the last of the art-loving popes, Leo X, died in 1521, the courts took an increasing role in promoting and preserving new music. This sprang from noblemen's love of music, surely, but also from the competitive urges of families such as the Medicis in Florence, the Gonzagas in Mantua, and of dukes and princes throughout Europe—lending credence to the Baumols' theory that the political fractionation of Germany, Austro-Hungary, and Italy spurred the musical competition among rival courts that helped create the great Viennese Classical period. Whether they could admit it or not, the great courts used music to compete with Rome, and the courts were more likely to encourage the production and preservation of new styles of music than was the conservative Church. By the mid-sixteenth century, secular music was being printed and sold in relative abundance, especially for voice with lute accompaniment—madrigals, motets, and songs—usually in anthologies, from which the composers did not benefit.

Our knowledge of the early history of Western music comes overwhelmingly from Church sources, for the Church was the chief, and generally the only, preserver of written music before Gutenberg and Petrucci. The extent of the influence of popular songs and dances upon early sacred and courtly music is impossible to determine, though surely it was great—greater, in fact, than musicologists can possibly know, for popular music was not written, so its survival depended upon being adapted, and transformed, by musically literate composers. We can deduce the influence of popular music from the church's never-ending struggle to repress and control it, and from the proliferation of parody Masses written throughout the Middle Ages, based on secular tunes such as the popular *L'Homme Armé*, which was set by dozens of composers.

Music publishing developed slowly for a number of reasons: the limited market of musically literate people who could afford to buy it, the great expense of publications of all types, and the technical difficulties involved, for Gutenberg's system of movable type could not be transferred directly to music. Petrucci did not print his first book of music, the *Odhecaton*, until 1501, three years after he received his monopoly, evidently requiring that time to figure out how to cut and manufacture the type and to lay out and print that anthology of secular music. Petrucci's system required three impressions for each page—one for the staves, one for the notes and a third for the words. They were high quality, expensive publications—so expensive that they probably were not used in performance, but as reference works from which scribes copied pieces to be sung as needed. Music printing remained so expensive for more than a century that composers expected to lose money at it, which must have repressed some of the interest they may have had in publication.

Alfonso Lobo, *Maestro de Cappella* at the Toledo Cathedral, paid five years of his salary—5,936 *reales*—to have 130 copies printed of nine books of his vocal music and one book of his organ music in 1605. Tomás Luis de Victoria, one of the great composers of the Spanish renaissance, paid about half as much in 1603 to publish 130 copies of a collection of his music. To pay for publication he sold rights to part of his annual income from the Empress, and he recouped his losses slowly by selling the works to those who could afford them—cathedrals in Spain and Lima. He earned back 14 ducats (about 480 *reales*) this way in 1606.[118] It would have required six years of sales at that rate for Victoria just to break even.

Even Giovanni Pierluigi de Palestrina, choirmaster at St. Peter's in Rome and editor of the ecclesiastical chant, the most famous, among the best paid, and the highest-ranking musician in Europe, found it difficult to publish. Palestrina lamented in a dedication to Pope Sixtus V in 1588: "I have composed and published a good deal. I have much more music in my possession but this I cannot publish because of the lack of money which I have already described. To publish this work would require the spending of sums which I cannot afford, especially of the large print which music naturally requires [to be] used for it."[119]

Ecclesiastical music was primarily for the voice, as the church demanded that music be an adjunct to worship—a servant of the words. Instrumental music may have been a wanton luxury of the devil, but the church could not keep instruments out of sacred music, though it fought that battle for centuries. The first instruction book for instrumentalists was published in 1511, aimed at working musicians. Donald J. Grout considered this a sign of the "improvement in the status of instrumental musicians, who, in the Middle Ages, had been regarded for the most part with contempt or condescension."[120]

It took more than a century before the first keyboard works were printed. *Parthenia, or the Maydenhead of the first musicke that ever was printed for the Virginalls*, published in London in 1611, was also one of the first English music books published from engraved plates. Engraving the plates was the expensive part of the process, but it produced higher quality prints than could be turned out by all but the most talented publishers who used movable type. Keyboard pieces are particularly troublesome for movable type because of the need to print multiple vertical notes on a staff, and because the early solutions for musical type involved short segments of staff attached to stems and note heads. This required keeping an enormous number of dies—as many as 450 of them, each bearing a different figure—a tremendous difficulty and expense.[121] The *Parthenia* was followed in about 1620 by the famous *Fitzwilliam Virginal Book*, an anthology of 297 pieces, many of them dance forms. But keyboard works would make up only a tiny fraction of the publishing business for another century. Harpsichords and clavichords were expensive. The keyboard craze would not consume German and Austrian society until the price of instruments came down and the middle class expanded in the late eighteenth and nineteenth centuries. Even in 1830, with Austria's economy reviving after the disasters of the Napoleonic wars, the cost of a piano exceeded the total estate of about half of the citizens of Vienna.[122]

For the first two centuries of music publishing, then, there was little or no tradition of publishing orchestral music, and no reason to publish it. Only courts had orchestras at their disposal. Even in the early Viennese period, most musicians were so poor that their musical instruments were generally owned by the court. Publishing music for large instrumental ensembles did not make economic sense: the expense would be great and the circulation minuscule. In 1823, at the height of the Viennese Classical period, just 11 percent of Breitkopf & Härtel's inventory was devoted to orchestral music; nearly two-thirds of its inventory consisted of sonatas, songs, and chamber music. Choral music accounted for about 20 percent.[123] Small circulation, greater expense of publication, and the dearth of opportunities for performance all contributed to the tendency for publishers to keep inventory reduced to small stocks, but the underlying reason was the nature of musical composition in the last days of a feudal society. From the pre-Baroque through the Classical period, music was written for an occasion, for a court or church. It generally was performed once, perhaps twice if the prince liked it. When more music was required, the court composer would write something else.

The businesses of music publishing and public performance had to grow together if they were to grow at all: public concerts to make the works popular, and publishers to provide the music to the performers and to the public. Profits for publishers lay in wider circulation, so businessmen with an eye on the ducat preferred popular music such as songs accompanied by a single instrument, or music for small groups of voices, which might be sold to literate commoners, of whom there was a greater supply than noblemen. Instrumental music, to the extent it was published at all, was more saleable for solo instruments, duets, or trios, than for large groups. The nature of the market prompted publishers to prefer smaller works to great ones—and to offer more money for a piano sonata than for a symphony. Beethoven received 50 ducats for his three string trios, Opus 1, in 1798, but only 10 ducats for his First Piano Concerto in 1801, and 20 ducats for his First Symphony that year. His Piano Sonata in B-Flat, Opus 22, brought him another 20 ducats in 1802.[124]

Beethoven was not a special case. Haydn offered three new symphonies to a Paris publisher for 15 ducats—or 67.5 florins—apiece in 1784. Four years later, Haydn asked Viennese publisher Matthias Artaria for 100 ducats for six string quartets—75 florins apiece—and he asked 300 florins for three piano sonatas (trios)—100 florins apiece—though piano trios, which in those days were expected to contain a simple continuo part for the bass instrument, were much easier to write than string quartets or symphonies.[125] Prices in Paris and Vienna may not be strictly comparable, but it's clear that Haydn's asking price was not based upon his labor or the length of time spent in composition, but upon the expected demand for the music.

Music publishing developed as a business without regard for the composer. It was Beethoven's teacher Haydn—who once traded a string quartet for a good pair of razors[126]—who began to fight back against publishers in the 1760s, when he found that publishers all over Europe were printing his works without paying him. Every publisher was a pirate who stole from every other publisher, and they all stole from composers. H. C. Robbins-Landon insists that by the 1770s, publishers were "printing more spurious Haydn than genuine Haydn in Paris." In researching his monumental biography, Robbins-Landon found 160 phony Haydn symphonies, written by 47 composers, and even more phony Haydn Masses were on the market.[127]

Haydn didn't like it any more than Beethoven would. The miserably paid copyists were a primary source of stolen works. When Haydn's first published works appeared in 1764 in Paris, then the center of the music publishing world, there were no music presses in Vienna. "(E)very thing is more dear in Vienna, and nothing more so than music, of which none is printed," the musical traveler Charles Burney wrote in September 1772. "As there are no music shops in Vienna, the best method of procuring new compositions, is to apply to copyists."[128]

After centuries of slow evolution, the business of music publishing grew, and changed, so rapidly during Beethoven's lifetime that though Beethoven took music lessons from Haydn, the two composers lived in different economic worlds. "Haydn died in 1809, having lived within a system unchanged since music had first been recognized as a social necessity," Henry Raynor wrote. "Beethoven, who died eighteen years later, lived as a modern composer lives, on the earnings of his work in a free market." Rapid changes in European society, "combined with the social and political results of the Napoleonic War . . . turned the composer from a humble functionary whose one advantage was his close contact with an audience which found his work socially necessary into a freelance whose life was one of inevitable insecurity."[129]

Beethoven, unlucky in so many aspects of his life, was fortunate in this: that music publishers were opening for business all across Germany and Austria just in time to help him eke out a living. Some founded their printing—or copying—shops after losing their jobs when the court orchestras disbanded. That's how Nikolaus Simrock, a French horn player, entered the trade in 1792, after the Cologne electoral orchestra was dissolved. He decided to become a full-time music dealer, and also sold musical instruments, stationery, prayer books, and carpets.

Music publishing in Germany and Austria began as a crude business. Publishers in German-speaking lands lagged behind England, Italy, and France, technically and as businessmen. Many publishers got their start by having employees copy scores by hand. That's how Breitkopf & Härtel established their publishing business in Leipzig. From 1762 to 1787 Breitkopf & Härtel published a six-part thematic catalogue, with sixteen supplements, offering more than 1,400 musical works for sale, "available for copying at a fixed rate per page."[130]

All of Beethoven's German and Austrian publishers established their businesses during his lifetime. Bernhard Schott founded his printing firm in Mainz in 1768 and began publishing music in 1770—and also sold writing materials, violin strings, and wine. The Artaria brothers opened their music publishing house in Vienna in 1778. Franz Anton Hoffmeister set up shop there in 1784. Hoffmeister opened the *Bureau de Musique* in Leipzig with a partner in 1800; it grew into one of the world's largest music publishers, C. F. Peters. By 1833, a "General Directory of the German Book Trade" listed 333 music dealers or book dealers who also sold music in Central Europe, and "most likely this represented scarcely half of the actual music dealers," Klaus Hortschansky wrote in "The Musician as Music Dealer in the Second Half of the 18th Century."[131]

It took more than three hundred years for music publishing to grow into a flourishing business, and its rapid growth during the Viennese period was due as much to social and economic factors as to the presence of masters such as Haydn, Mozart, and Beethoven. Perhaps the most important economic fact driving the growth of music publishing during Beethoven's lifetime, however, was the systematic abuse of composers through piracy. Publishers issued cheaper editions of new compositions from popular composers as soon as they appeared, for Europe had no copyright system, and the pirates obtained the "rights" to their "editions" by buying a copy from the original publisher—or from a copyist—without paying the composer a kreuzer.

"Those Arch Villains"

In trying to earn a living from having his music published, Beethoven was attempting a thing that no one had ever done. Commercial publishing of instrumental music was growing rapidly during his lifetime, and was much further advanced as a business in Germany and Austria than public concerts, but with no copyright laws, and piracy the rule rather than the exception, publishing was a complicated, difficult, and chancy operation for a composer. Publication actually decreased the value of a work to its composer, for once a composition was published, and the composer received a one-time fee, the piece was in effect given away forever to the pirate publishers and to other musicians. That is almost certainly why Mozart sold only eighteen pieces with opus numbers for publication during his lifetime.[132]

Intellectual theft was a way of life. Second-rate composers and publishers stole tunes from new operas and rushed chamber arrangements into print. Composers had to defend themselves from this or suffer the financial hurt. While preparing *Abduction from the Seraglio* in 1782, Mozart wrote to his father from Vienna, "Well, I am up to the eyes in work, for by Sunday week I have to arrange my opera for wind-instruments. If I don't, someone will anticipate me and secure the profits."[133]

If a piece became popular, copyists often made more money from it than its composer. Mozart's letters are full of complaints about this. He made copyists work under his direct supervision to prevent them from sneaking extra copies to sell on their own, which then would be copied again. Leopold Mozart wrote from Milan, when Wolfgang was fourteen and rehearsing his first opera, *Mitridate, Re di Ponto*, that the Italian copyist "is absolutely delighted, which is a good omen in Italy, where, if the music is a success, the copyist by selling the arias sometimes makes more money than the *Kapellmeister* does by his composition."[134] This system reduced costs for the courts, and may have been the only way they could retain their copyists on starvation wages.

Wolfgang Mozart complained in a 1784 letter to Leopold that

> the Salzburg copyists are as little to be trusted as the Viennese. I know for a positive fact that Hofstetter made two copies of Haydn's music. . . . And as no one but myself possesses these new [piano] concertos in Bb and D [K. 450 and 451], and no one but myself and Fraulein von Ployer (for whom I composed them) those in Eb and G [K. 449 and 453], the only way in which they could fall into other hands is by that kind of cheating. I myself have everything copied in my room and in my presence.[135]

Copyright evolved out of censorship laws, which were enacted to suppress treason and sedition. The laws evolved to protect the rights of publishers to *reproduce* original works; composers and authors were not granted inherent rights to their creations until late in the twentieth century. The first copyright law, England's Statute of Anne, which took effect in 1710, gave publishers the "sole right and liberty of printing" a manuscript for fourteen years. For the next three hundred years, publishers, not creators, remained the principal beneficiaries and had the most powerful influence upon copyright laws, which retain feudal elements to this day.[136] The roughly three hundred minor German states of the eighteenth century actually encouraged the pirating of literature from other states, feeling it would encourage home industry.[137] So did the United States, whose Copyright Act of 1790 encouraged piracy of foreign works, for the scientific and cultural benefit of the nation, an encouragement that was repeated in the 1831 Copyright Act.[138] For its first four centuries, to the extent that music publishing was regulated at all, it was done to grant monopolies to printers and protect the rights of publishers, not of composers or authors.

Publishers tended to view composers as upstarts and pirates themselves, for composers—until Beethoven—were not expected to make a living from publishing. Composers earned their living by writing for the noble and ecclesiastical authorities who employed them. They might be paid again for dedicating a piece to an admirer. If they sold their work through subscription, they could be paid a third time. Publishers thought Beethoven was being unreasonable in begrudging them a chance to earn their own living.

(The first work for which copyright was granted for all of Germany was the collected edition of Goethe's work, which was begun in 1828—the year after Beethoven died. German states did not adopt a general copyright law, however, until the Prussian Act of 1837, which, ironically, was enacted after a long campaign, including at least six lawsuits, by one of Beethoven's publishers, Adolph Martin Schlesinger, who was losing money by unauthorized reprints and arrangements of Carl Maria von Weber's operas *Der Freischütz* and *Oberon.*[139])

Pirates dominated the publishing business. They not only stole music outright, they altered it, forged it, misattributed it, bribed copyists to steal it, pasted their own name over copies they bought from the original publisher, left entire movements out of stolen symphonies, inserted other composers' misattributed work into symphonies, asked composers to proofread the music that the publishers had stolen from them, and refused to allow composers to dedicate their work so the publisher could wring a few more florins from it by dedicating it to someone else. Royalties, of course, were out of the question. Pirates had a stranglehold on the business at every stage of operations. Robbins-Landon's exhaustively documented five-volume biography of Haydn describes in detail the problems composers faced in trying to make a living from publishing.

The first compositions Haydn sold on the market were copied by hand, but he could sell only a few, for if his own copyist did not steal it, the purchasers' copyists would. Haydn's music was stolen from the moment his first pieces were published by a Parisian pirate, in 1764. "Parisian publishers made a fortune on his music which, at least until the early 1780s, was mostly published without his approval and with no financial benefit to him whatever."[140] At least eleven publishers in Paris alone were publishing pirated Haydn pieces by the early 1770s. Haydn was so popular in Paris that the publishers sent buyers to scour Vienna and the Austrian provinces to purchase anything that sounded even remotely like Haydn, to be published under his name: "favorites proved to be Haydn's brother Michael in Salzburg, Dittersdorf, Ordoñez, Leopold Hoffman and Vanhal."[141]

Theft and forgery of Haydn's work was so widespread that when the Bohemian composer Adalbert Gyrowetz brought three of his own symphonies to Paris, the orchestra refused to believe that one was his—it had already been published in Paris under Haydn's name. Gyrowetz convinced them by showing them his handwritten score. Longman & Broderip in London "published" the parts to Haydn's Symphonies Nos. 90, 91, and 92 by simply pasting its own name over the Paris publisher's name, until Longman could run off its own copies. The Dutch publisher Johann Julius Hummel not only stole Haydn's quartets from a Parisian publisher, which had stolen them first, he changed Haydn's nine-bar theme into eight bars, and "revised" other movements as well. London publisher William Forster printed a pirated edition of Haydn's Symphony No. 62 without its first movement, and inserted the second subject of the opening movement of Haydn's Symphony No. 53 into a separate overture. "There are other examples too numerous to elaborate. Haydn must have been horrified."[142] (Beethoven suffered the same treatment from the Zurich publisher Hans Georg Nägeli, who inserted four bars into Beethoven's Piano Sonata Op. 31, No. 1.[143])

Haydn protested to his Viennese publisher, Artaria, that he wanted to thank the King of Prussia for giving him "a beautiful ring . . . by dedicating these six (Opus 50) Quartets to him; but you won't be satisfied with that, because you want to dedicate the works yourself, and to someone else. But to make amends for this loss, I promise to give you other pieces free of charge."[144]

Haydn's biographer George A. Greisinger—who was also Breitkopf & Härtel's agent in Vienna—wrote to his home office in 1802 that the Paris publisher Le Duc had sent Haydn a "wretched edition" of symphonies that Le Duc had stolen: "[H]e could hardly understand how one could send him such a corrupted and falsified piece of bungling [*Machwerk*], for he is ashamed to place such product among his music."[145]

Piracy was so widespread that there were distinctions between relatively honest pirates and dishonest ones. Honest pirates worked out deals with publishers in other cities, on the noble concept that one thief should not steal from another one. Matthias Artaria in Vienna had an arrangement with Longman & Broderip in London, so that when one publisher bought a piece, he would send it to the other, who would bear some of the cost of buying it from the composer, and would have the piece ready for publication before the other pirates got it. George Smart of London toured Germany and Austria in 1825 trying to work out similar deals—which would be of no benefit to composers, who got no extra money from the sister publishers, but lost them as possible sources of foreign sales.

Robbins-Landon believes the widespread forgery of Haydn's work and its publication in stolen, botched editions was primarily responsible for the rapid decline in the popularity of his music that set in immediately upon Haydn's death. These blatant thefts hurt Haydn economically, but he was on the Esterházy payroll from 1761 until he died in 1809, except for his years in London, where he made more money than he ever did on the mainland. Piracy was a much more serious and a more crippling economic problem for Beethoven, for in the last two decades of his life he could neither teach, perform, nor conduct.

Artaria did not like it when Beethoven resold a piece to a competing publisher in London, rather than letting Artaria split the cost of acquiring the composition with Longman & Broderip, but it's hard to blame Beethoven for this. His correspondence, particularly in his later years, is full of complicated plans to arrange simultaneous publication in several cities so he could receive multiple payments. Historians do not present Beethoven, who never learned how to multiply, as a pioneering businessman—they tend to represent his complaints against publishers as grousing. But Beethoven, as we would say today, had no "business model." He had to invent it. In the end, he favored the system of offering his works through subscription: to get money from subscribers before copyists and rival publishers stole his works. Printing costs were reduced, too, by knowing in advance the size of the press run. Then he could sell the piece again to the publisher, who might as well buy it since he already had the plates, and could keep it in his stock forever.

Publishing pressures affected Beethoven's art for good and ill. The works for which he is most widely remembered today, the symphonies and concertos, were a drag on the market: the most expensive to print, for the smallest circulation. Publishers preferred easier works for small groups from which they could expect greater sales. Publishers earned greater profits from Beethoven's "lesser" works, such as trios, violin sonatas, or his less-difficult piano pieces, than from his grander, symphonic works or difficult piano sonatas, which were beyond the ability of most amateurs, and most professionals, by the end of his life.

It is to Beethoven's credit that he wrote so many great orchestral works, whose creation required so much more time and labor, and for which there was less economic demand or reward than there was for solo or chamber pieces. It was his inborn urge to create art—not musical economics—that drove Beethoven to write his great orchestral works, and he often had to offer additional, more saleable, smaller works as a package to induce publishers to print his major works.[146]

Aside from love of art, vanity, or a sponsor's request, there was little motivation for composers to write "great works" for publication. One of the works of which Haydn was most proud, the oratorio *The Seven Words*, for which he received 10 guineas from the English publisher William Forster in 1787, did not sell out for thirty years, though Haydn was wildly popular in England, and Forster's press run had been only fifty copies.[147]

Fees from publication had always been an adjunct—fortunate when a composer received them, but not a way to make a living. While Beethoven was still playing in salons, he did not publish his first two piano concertos until he had worn them out in performance and had a new concerto ready. But Beethoven's deafness, which forced him to give up performing, changed everything for him. Publishing had to become his main source of income—along with the annual stipend his three sponsors began paying him in 1809.

Beethoven's publishers, and later biographers, accused him, with some justice, of sharp dealing in his compositions, particularly the *Missa Solemnis*. During the more than four years it took him to finish the Mass, Beethoven sold it through subscription to nine noblemen across Europe and also offered it to at least six publishers. He even took money from one publisher before giving the Mass to another, while promising to deliver to the first publisher a second Mass, in C sharp minor, of which, so far as we can tell, he never wrote a note. But Beethoven is hardly to be blamed for having to claw his living from a system that gave composers no rights whatsoever. In fact, one of Beethoven's publishers, Breitkopf & Härtel, printed a public apology to "connoisseurs and amateurs of music, and even to composers themselves" for mistakes that appeared in works it had printed without the "assistance" of the composer—in other words, had stolen. In a somewhat stunning lament, Immanuel Breitkopf wrote that he hoped the public understood how hard it was to "wrest them [the compositions] from certain musicians."[148]

But the *Missa Solemnis* came at the end of Beethoven's life, by which time his international reputation, and hard experience, had given him something like an equal footing with the businessmen with whom he had been quarreling for more than twenty years. His war with publishers was well under way by 1802, when one of his Vienna publishers, Artaria, tried to rush into a print a quintet in C major that Beethoven had sold to Breitkopf & Härtel in Leipzig. Beethoven wrote to Breitkopf & Härtel on November 13:

> Well, I must tell you that during the time when I was in the country for the sake of my health, those arch-villains Artaria & Co. asked Count Fries to lend them the quintet to copy, stating that theirs was imperfect and that the work had already been engraved and published here, and—they did in fact try to delight the public with it a few days ago.[149]

Beethoven wrote that he managed to head this off by making Artaria—"those scoundrels"—promise to publish its pirated version based on Breitkopf & Härtel's correct copy. But in January 1803, he had the *Wiener Zeitung* publish an announcement stating that Breitkopf & Härtel had published the correct edition in Leipzig, and that he had had "nothing whatever to do with the edition of this quintet produced at the same time by Herren Artaria and Mollo in Vienna," which he called "extremely faulty, inaccurate and quite useless for the performer."[150] This led to a lawsuit that dragged on for more than two years, because the publisher Mollo actually had had nothing to do with the edition. Yet despite this quarrel, Beethoven went on to have good relations with Artaria—as good, anyway, as he would have with any member of the publishing "family of scoundrels."

It is ironic, then, that by the end of Beethoven's life, financial considerations may have been a driving factor for him when he created his greatest, late period works. "Until the final decade of his life, Beethoven usually composed whatever he wanted without regard for profit," Julia Moore wrote. During most of his life, Beethoven sold publication rights when a piece was done, or after the six months had expired from a commission. "During the 1820s, however, he reversed the process: first he negotiated prices, then he composed. The fees he received during the 1820s were many times higher than those of earlier years."[151] So in a self-feeding, escalating cycle, Moore says, Beethoven's financial problems caused him to demand more money for his work, which caused him to write grander, more massive works—such as his *Missa Solemnis*, the Ninth Symphony and the late quartets—to justify the fees he charged.

Moore says financial pressures could have been a factor in both major turning points in Beethoven's stylistic development, citing "the watershed year 1803, when Beethoven initiated his middle-period style, and when he first began to suffer the effects of inflation." And she adds, "The last decade of Beethoven's life, when his financial difficulties were most severe, his compositional decisions were most influenced by financial considerations, and financial considerations assumed significance at an early stage in his compositional plans."[152]

Beethoven's artistic response to the economic pressures upon him is far from a simple subject. It is not true, as one legend has it, that he was ignored and his music reviled during his lifetime. Though his music was harshly, often vehemently criticized throughout his life, Beethoven was a professional, and he could take it, and sometimes managed to be unexpectedly magnanimous to his critics. He wrote to the impresario Johann Peter Salomon in London 1815, "Ries, my former pupil, wrote to me a short time ago that [the pianist, composer and publisher Johann Baptist] Cramer *had spoken in public against my compositions*, for no other reason, I trust, than to *promote the art* of music. Hence I have no objection to raise."[153] And in a typical, and revealing letter to Breitkopf & Härtel, publishers of the influential *Allgemeine Musikalische Zeitung*, Beethoven commented on the journal's review of his Third Symphony. "If you fancy that you can injure *me* by publishing articles of that kind, you are very much mistaken. On the contrary, by so doing you merely bring your journal into disrepute." But he added, "Be so kind as to give my compliments to *Herr von Rochlitz* [the editor of the *AMZ*]. . . . Tell him *that I am not quite so ignorant about foreign literature as not to know that Herr von Rochlitz has written some very fine articles* and that, should I ever go to Leipzig, I am convinced that we should certainly become quite good friends."[154] Nor is it necessarily true, as another cliché would have it, that economic forces degraded Beethoven's art. As Moore argues, it may have stimulated him to create greater works: "His personality was more inspired than daunted by seeming insurmountable obstacles."[155]

Biographers, and even Beethoven's contemporaries—particularly in England—have drawn harsh, perhaps hasty conclusions, based on Beethoven's relations with his publishers. Beethoven could be rude, abrasive, crudely manipulative, resentful, and unfair. But Beethoven faced obstacles of every sort—physical, personal, legal, economic, traditional, and societal—in virtually every aspect of earning a living in the only way he knew how, the music business: in teaching, performing, concertizing, and publishing. Any honest estimation of the conditions he faced must conclude that Beethoven really did have a difficult life, that he really did have enemies, and that from a composer's standpoint, publishers really were scurrilous villains. Trying to draw conclusions about Beethoven's character from his relations with publishers is just as dangerous as trying to draw conclusions about him from his relationship with his nephew and sister-in-law.

The final word, or perhaps the final excuse, for Beethoven's attitude toward publishers was provided by J. W. N. Sullivan, who wrote that the composer's greatness "is not in the least incompatible with artfulness and unscrupulousness in dealing with publishers. That a man should write the *Missa Solemnis* and at the same time fail to fulfill certain commercial contracts may or may not be an interesting psychological fact. It only becomes a moral problem and the *Missa Solemnis* a paradox if it be assumed that the creation of the *Missa Solemnis* implies a reverence for contracts. . . . We may wish that to his other virtues he had added 'a nice sense of honor and honesty in his dealings with publishers,' but it seems evident that the virtues he had were even more rare and more valuable."[156]

Notes

1. Julia V. Moore, *Beethoven and Musical Economics* (unpublished Ph.D. dissertation, University of Illinois at Urbana-Champaign, 1987), 413-418.

2. H. C. Robbins-Landon, *Haydn: Chronicle and Works: Vol. II, Haydn at Esterháza, 1766-1790,* 390; *Vol. IV, The Years of "The Creation,"* 491; *Vol. V, The Late Years, 1801-09*, 253, 333; and Moore, *Beethoven and Musical Economics*, 413.

3. Mozart's apparent destitution in his final days is an enduring mystery, as he earned a large income—much larger than Beethoven did—and Mozart died before Vienna was troubled with inflation. Mozart's biographers have laid the blame on his wife, Constanze; on Mozart's presumed free spending and inattention to his finances; on his generosity to rapacious and unscrupulous friends such as the clarinetist Anton Stadler; or on other unspecified problems. The desperate tone of many of Mozart's letters begging Puchberg for money indicate that the composer was in some sort of trouble. We suggest, admittedly without evidence, that he may have run up gambling debts to titled gamblers, or to aristocrats who ran the casinos and who could have ruined Mozart with a few words to his creditors' noble peers. Emily Anderson, *The Letters of Mozart and His Family* (New York: Norton, 1989), 914, 915, 917, 928, 932-957; Volkmar Braunbehrens, *Mozart in Vienna: 1781-1791* (New York: Grove Weidenfeld, 1990), 321-336.

4. Robbins-Landon, *Haydn: Chronicle and Works, Vol. V*, 348.

5. Music copyist Anton Adolph's letter to Prince Esterházy is cited in Robbins-Landon, *Haydn: Chronicle and Works, Vol. II*, 646-647.

6. Robbins-Landon, *Haydn: Chronicle and Works, Vol. II*, 648.

7. Robbins-Landon, *Haydn: Chronicle and Works, Vol. II*, 566.

8. Anderson, *The Letters of Mozart*, 795.

9. Braunbehrens, *Mozart in Vienna*, 128.

10. Julia Moore, "Beethoven and Inflation," in *Beethoven Forum, Vol. 1*, ed. Lewis Lockwood and James Webster (Lincoln: University of Nebraska Press, 1992), 198, 241-251.

11. Robbins-Landon, *Haydn: Chronicle and Works, Vol. V*, 87, 235.

12. Moore, *Beethoven and Musical Economics*, 267.

13. Anderson, *The Letters of Beethoven* (London: Macmillan, 1961), 234, 245, 276.

14. Moore, *Beethoven and Musical Economics,* 23.

15. Moore, "Beethoven and Inflation," 222.

16. Thayer-Forbes, *Thayer's Life Of Beethoven*, 747.

17. Moore, *Beethoven and Musical Economics*, 375.

18. Anderson, *The Letters of Beethoven*, 1,154.

19. Sam Morgenstern, ed., *Composers on Music* (New York, Pantheon, 1956), 167.

20. Walter Salmen, "Preface," in *The Social Status of the Professional Musician from the Middle Ages to the 19th Century*, ed. Salmen (Stuyvesant, N.Y.: Pendragon Press, 1983), iii.

21. Paul Henry Lang, *Music in Western Civilization* (New York: Norton, 1941), 127.

22. Stuart Isacoff, *Temperament: The Idea That Solved Music's Greatest Riddle* (New York: Knopf, 2001).

23. Dieter Krickeburg, "On the Social Status of the *Spielmann* ('Folk Musician') in 17th and 18th Century Germany, Particularly in the Northwest," in *Social Status of the Professional Musician*, 99.

24. Krickeburg, "On the Social Status of the *Spielmann*," 99, 115.

25. Donald Jay Grout, with Claude V. Palisca, *A History of Western Music* (New York: Norton, 1980), 64-65.

26. Edmondstoune Duncan, *The Story of Minstrelsy* (New York: Scribner's, 1907), 46.

27. Heinrich W. Schwab, "The Social Status of the Town Musician," in *Social Status of the Professional Musician*, 31-59.

28. Duncan, *The Story of Minstrelsy*, 37-38.

29. Salmen, "The Musician in the Middle Ages," 25.

30. Schwab, "The Social Status of the Town Musician," 34.

31. Salmen, "The Musician in the Middle Ages," 5-6.

32. Duncan, *The Story of Minstrelsy*, 109.

33. Schwab, "The Social Status of the Town Musician," 36, 44, 49, 50.

34. Salmen, "The Musician in the Middle Ages," 25.

35. Krickeburg, "On the Social Status of the *Spielmann*," 118.

36. Werner Braun, "The 'Hautboist': An Outline of Evolving Careers and Functions," in *Social Status of the Professional Musician*, 145. Parentheses in original.

37. Schwab, "The Social Status of the Town Musician," 33, 57.

38. Schwab, "The Social Status of the Town Musician," 50.

39. Braun, "The 'Hautboist,'" 137.

40. Richard Petzoldt, "The Economic Conditions of the 18th-Century Musician," in *Social Status of the Professional Musician*, 181-182.

41. Christopher Hogwood, *Handel* (London: Thames & Hudson, 1984), 23; and Klaus Eidam, *The True Life of J. S. Bach* (New York: Basic Books, 2001), 48-51.

42. Schwab, "The Social Status of the Town Musician," 54.

43. Christoph-Hellmut Mahling, "The Origin and Social Status of the Court Orchestral Musician in the 18th and Early 19th Century in Germany," in *Social Status of the Professional Musician*, 261.

44. Moore, "Beethoven and Inflation," 221.

45. Petzoldt, "The Economic Conditions of the 18th-Century Musician," 182. Parentheses in original.

46. Mahling, "The Origin and Social Status of the Court Orchestral Musician," 244.

47. Eidam, *The True Life of J. S. Bach*, 113-114.

48. Anderson, *The Letters of Mozart*, 740-741.

49. Duncan, *Minstrelsy*, 85, 106, citing Harleian manuscript No. 433, from the reign of King Richard II, and a commission established in 1456 "for impressing youths to supply vacancies among the king's minstrels. Care was to be had that those chosen should be graceful and attractive no less than well-skilled in music, for the better diversion of his Majesty Henry VI."

50. Henry Raynor, *A Social History of Music from the Middle Ages to Beethoven* (New York: Taplinger, 1978), 52.

51. Raynor, *A Social History of Music*, 52, 92

52. Angus Heriot, *The Castrati in Opera* (New York: Da Capo Press, 1974), 10, 25.

53. Heriot, *The Castrati in Opera*, 38.

54. Heriot, *The Castrati in Opera*, 44; F. M. Scherer, *Quarter Notes and Bank Notes* (Princeton: Princeton University Press, 2004), 97; and Harold Schonberg, *The Virtuosi* (New York: Vintage Books, 1988), 6. We may be permitted to doubt Schonberg's statement: "The operation itself seems to have been relatively painless." The mortality figures

alone cast that statement into doubt. According to Heriot, "The operation, as described by d'Ancillon in the '*Traite des Eunuques*,' was usually performed as follows: the child, often drugged with opium or some other narcotic, was placed in a very hot bath for some time, until it was in a state of virtual insensibility. Then the ducts leading to the testicles were severed, so that the latter in the course of time shriveled and disappeared." Heriot, *The Castrati in Opera*, 44.

55. Robbins-Landon, *Haydn: Chronicle and Works, Vol. I*, 38-39, 60; *Vol. III*, 319; *Vol. IV*, 22.

56. Moore, *Beethoven and Musical Economics*, 66, 110-111; and H. C. Robbins-Landon, *1791: Mozart's Last Year* (New York: Schirmer, 1988), 25.

57. Scherer, *Quarter Notes and Bank Notes*, 25-26, 92-94; Moore, *Beethoven and Musical Economics*, 89-118; and Robbins-Landon, *Haydn: Chronicle and Works, Vol. IV*, 314. Moore found twenty-six aristocratic *Kapellen* working during 1770-1790, but only five surviving by 1796.

58. Robbins-Landon, *Beethoven: A Documentary Study* (New York: Macmillan, 1970), 64-65; and Mary Sue Morrow, *Concert Life in Haydn's Vienna: Aspects of a Developing Musical and Social Institution* (Stuyvesant, N.Y.: Pendragon Press, 1989), 22.

59. Thayer-Forbes, *Thayer's Life Of Beethoven*, 177; and B. Cooper, *Beethoven*, 55-92.

60. Robbins-Landon reports that the sums earned for music lessons in Vienna were pitiful. After a lesson with Haydn in December 1792, Beethoven noted this expense in his diary, "Haidn 8 Groschen." Robbins-Landon, *Haydn: Chronicle and Works, Vol. III*, 205.

61. Thayer-Forbes, *Thayer's Life Of Beethoven*, 664.

62. Alan Tyson, "Beethoven to the Countess Susanna Guicciardi: A New Letter," in *Beethoven Studies*, ed. Tyson (New York: Norton, 1973), 9-10; Sonneck, *Beethoven: Impressions of His Contemporaries* (New York: Dover, 1967), 33.

63. Robbins-Landon believes that Haydn may have been responsible for insisting that this system of payment, which formerly gave the noble sponsor rights to the work for "a number of years," be reduced to six months. *Haydn: Chronicle and Works, Vol. IV*, 257-258.

64. Anderson, *Letters of Beethoven*, 157.

65. Anderson, *Letters of Beethoven*, 655-656.

66. Scherer, *Quarter Notes and Bank Notes*, 55.

67. Anderson, *Letters of Beethoven*, 1,145; and Moore, *Beethoven and Musical Economics*, 367.

68. Moore, *Beethoven and Musical Economics*, 367. Prince Karl Lichnowsky underwrote Beethoven with 600 florins a year from 1800 until an uncertain date. Anderson, *Letters of Beethoven*, 58; Moore, *Beethoven and Musical Economics*, 323-326, 331-333.

69. Anderson, *Letters of Mozart*, 726-727.

70. Anderson, *Letters of Mozart*, 718.

71. Moore, "Beethoven and Inflation," 206.

72. Tia DeNora, *Beethoven and the Construction of Genius: Musical Politics in Vienna, 1792-1803* (Berkeley: University of California Press, 1995), esp. chapter 3, "Beethoven and Social Change," 37-59.

73. Raynor, *Social History of Music*, esp. chapter 18, "The Rise of the Public Concert," 314-330; Arthur Loesser, *Men, Women & Pianos* (New York: Simon & Schuster, 1954), 289; Morrow, *Concert Life in Haydn's Vienna*, 65.

74. Moore, *Beethoven and Musical Economics*, 297.

75. Robbins-Landon, *Haydn: Chronicle and Works, Vol. V*, 240, 273.

76. Thayer-Forbes, *Thayer's Life Of Beethoven*, 908-913; Martin Cooper, *Beethoven: The Last Decade* (Oxford: Oxford University Press, 1986), 276-279.

77. Julia Moore, "Mozart in the Market Place," in *Journal of the Royal Musical Association*, 1989, 34.

78. Morrow, *Concert Life in Haydn's Vienna*, 110-111.

79. Robbins-Landon, *Haydn: Chronicle and Works, Vol. V*, 377.

80. Thayer-Forbes, *Thayer's Life Of Beethoven*, 448; Robbins-Landon, *Haydn: Chronicle and Works, Vol. V*, 377.

81. Robbins-Landon, *Haydn: Chronicle and Works, Vol. V*, 292.

82. Morrow, *Concert Life in Haydn's Vienna*, 184.

83. Robbins-Landon, *Haydn: Chronicle and Works, Vol. III*, 299.

84. Charles Rosen, *The Classical Style* (New York: Norton, 1998), 145.

85. Robbins-Landon, *Haydn: Chronicle and Works, Vol. III*, 90.

86. Anderson, *Letters of Mozart*, 557; and Susan Kagan, *Archduke Rudolph, Beethoven's Patron, Pupil, and Friend* (Stuyvesant, N.Y.: Pendragon Press, 1988), 28-31.

87. Morrow, *Concert Life in Haydn's Vienna*, 180-181.

88. Morrow, *Concert Life in Haydn's Vienna*, 180-181, citing Johann Ferdinand Schonfeld, *Jahrbuch der Tonkunst von Wien und Prag*, Vienna, 1796.

89. Rosen, *Classical Style*, 192, 196.

90. Anderson, *Letters of Mozart*, 557.

91. Anderson, *Letters of Beethoven*, 1,246-247.

92. Mary Sue Morrow, email to the author, Nov. 10, 2006.

93. Raynor, *Social History of Music*, 314-330.

94. William and Hilda Baumol, "On the Economics of Musical Composition in Mozart's Vienna" (New York: C.V. Starr Center for Applied Economics, 1992), 7-8.

95. Moore, *Beethoven and Musical Economics*, 88.

96. Raynor, *Social History of Music*, 258.

97. Roger Lonsdale, *Dr. Charles Burney* (Oxford: Oxford University Press, 1965), 115; and Charles Burney, *The Present State of Music in Germany, the Netherlands and United Provinces* (London: Travis & Emery, 2003), 319-320.

98. Raynor, *Social History of Music*, 243.

99. Baumol & Baumol, "On the Economics of Musical Composition in Mozart's Vienna," 17-18.

100. Baumol & Baumol, "On the Economics of Musical Composition in Mozart's Vienna," 17.

101. Scherer, *Quarter Notes and Bank Notes*, Chapter 5, "The Geography of Composer Supply and Demand," 117-141.

102. William Weber, *Music and the Middle Class* (New York: Holmes and Meier, 1975), 67.

103. Simon McVeigh, "An Audience for High-Class Music," in *The Musician as Entrepreneur, Managers, Charlatans and Idealists, 1700-1914*, ed. William Weber (Bloomington: Indiana University Press, 2004), 165.

104. Weber, *Music and the Middle Class*, 98-99.

105. Weber, *Music and the Middle Class*, 100.

106. Robbins-Landon, *Haydn: Chronicle and Works, Vol. I*, 403.

107. Weber, *Music and the Middle Class*, 96-97.

108. Raynor, *Social History of Music*, 317.

109. Weber, *Music and the Middle Class*, 101.

110. Robbins-Landon, *Haydn: Chronicle and Works, Vol. III*, 309.

111. Moore, *Beethoven and Musical Economics*, 114.

112. Raynor, *Social History of Music*, 321.

113. William Weber, "The Musician as Entrepreneur and Opportunist, 1700-1914," in *The Musician as Entrepreneur*, 15.

114. Raynor, *Social History of Music*, 102.

115. A. Hyatt King, *Four Hundred Years of Music Publishing* (London: The British Museum, 1968), 13-14; Raynor, *Social History of Music*, 105-106.

116. King, *Four Hundred Years of Music Publishing*, 8.

117. Robbins-Landon, *Haydn: Chronicle and Works, Vol. V*, 91.

118. Raynor, *Social History of Music*, 102-104.

119. Raynor, *Social History of Music*, 105, citing Palestrina's preface to his "Lamentations," dedicated to Pope Sixtus V in 1588.

120. Grout, *A History of Western Music*, 221-222.

121. Scherer, *Quarter Notes and Bank Notes*, 160, 238.

122. Moore, *Beethoven and Musical Economics*, 64; Loesser, *Men, Women & Pianos*.

123. Scherer, *Quarter Notes and Bank Notes*, 190.

124. Moore, *Beethoven and Musical Economics*, 323.

125. Robbins-Landon, *Haydn: Chronicle and Works, Vol. II*, 495, 708-709.

126. Robbins-Landon, *Haydn: Chronicle and Works, Vol. II*, 604.

127. Robbins-Landon, *Haydn: Chronicle and Works, Vol. I*, 297-299; *Vol. II*, 603.

128. Burney, *The Present State of Music in Germany*, 352, 363.

129. Raynor, *Social History*, vii.

130. Klaus Hortschansky, "The Musician as Music Dealer in the Second Half of the 18th Century," in *The Social Status of the Professional Musician*, 208-209.

131. Hortschansky, "The Musician as Music Dealer," 207-213.

132. Alfred Einstein, *Mozart: His Character, His Work* (New York: Oxford University Press, 1945), 110.

133. Anderson, *Letters of Mozart*, 808.

134. Anderson, *Letters of Mozart*, 174.

135. Anderson, *Letters of Mozart*, 876-877.

136. Martin Kretschmer and Friedemann Kawhol, "The History and Philosophy of Copyright," in *Music and Copyright*, ed. Simon Frith and Lee Marshall (Edinburgh: Edinburgh University Press, 2004), 21-53; and Kretschmer, "Intellectual Property in Music: A Historical Analysis of Rhetoric and Institutional Practices," in *Culture and Organization, Vol. 6, No. 2* (Bournemouth: Routledge, December 2000), 197-223.

137. W. H. Bruford, *Germany in the Eighteenth Century: The Social Background of the Literary Revival* (London: Cambridge University Press, 1965), 275-280. The enormous forces arrayed against international copyright are presented in James J. Barnes, *Authors, Publishers and Politicians: The Quest for an Anglo-American Copyright Agreement, 1815-1854* (London: Routledge & Kegan Paul, 1974).

138. Section 5 of the U.S. Copyright Act of 1790 states, "Nothing in this act shall be construed to extend to prohibit the importation or vending, reprinting, or publishing within the United States, of any map, chart, book or books, written, printed, or published by any person not a citizen of the United States, in foreign parts or places without the jurisdiction of the United States." The 1831 Copyright Act allowed any U.S. citizen to import from abroad any sort of work, without exception. Kretschmer and Kawhol, "The History and Philosophy of Copyright," 14-15.

139. Bruford, *Germany in the Eighteenth Century*, 275; Kretschmer and Kawhol, "The History and Philosophy of Copyright," 24.

140. Robbins-Landon, *Haydn: Chronicle and Works, Vol. II*, 590.

141. Robbins-Landon, *Haydn: Chronicle and Works, Vol. II*, 591.

142. Robbins-Landon, *Haydn: Chronicle and Works, Vol. I*, 579-599; *Vol. II*, 663-664; *Vol. III*, 42; *Vol. IV*, 142.

143. Wegeler-Ries, *Beethoven Remembered*, 77-78.

144. Robbins-Landon, *Haydn: Chronicle and Works, Vol. II*, 693-694.

145. Robbins-Landon, *Haydn: Chronicle and Works, Vol. V*, 223.

146. Moore, *Beethoven and Musical Economics*, 323-329.

147. Robbins-Landon, *Haydn: Chronicle and Works, Vol. III*, 82.

148. Raynor, *Social History of Music*, 333.

149. Anderson, *Letters of Beethoven*, 77-80.

150. Anderson, *Letters of Beethoven*, 1,434-435, citing a notice in the Jan. 22, 1803, *Wiener Zeitung.*

151. Moore, *Beethoven and Musical Economics*, 194.

152. Moore, *Beethoven and Musical Economics*, 194.

153. Anderson, *Letters of Beethoven*, 512.

154. Anderson, *Letters of Beethoven*, 150-151.

155. Moore, *Beethoven and Musical Economics*, 217.

156. J. W. N. Sullivan, *Beethoven: His Spiritual Development* (New York: Vintage, 1960), 128.

Chapter 3

Beethoven's Character

There is evidence to support practically any statement one cares to make about Beethoven's character, so long as the statement is extreme. He was magnanimous, noble, and petty; wise, forbearing, and violent; gallant and boorish; high-minded, ill-educated, and vindictive. He was charismatic, repulsive, and eccentric; simple and complex; capable of inspiring tremendous love and devotion from people even after he had treated them badly for a long time. He had trouble dealing with people, even people he liked and who liked him. He drew tears from his friends and patrons with his piano playing, then laughed at them and called them spoiled children. In society, Beethoven had no defenses—or he had nothing but defenses. Lewis Lockwood wrote that Beethoven had "the irascible outward manner of a proud, uncompromising artist forced to come to grips with a barely comprehending world,"[1] but it is also true that Beethoven had difficulty understanding the world, and the rules by which other people live in it.

An artist's personality may be reflected in his works, but how it is reflected, and what bearing a creator's character has on his works are questions we will not address. Beethoven's life and character are worth studying in their own right. He overcame deafness to write some of the greatest music the human race has produced, or ever will produce. His life will always be worthy of study, not just because he was a great artist, but because despite his great unhappiness, and the unhappiness he inflicted upon others, he tried hard throughout his life to be a good man.

But Beethoven was peculiarly ill adapted for dealing with other people and with practical aspects of the world. This social maladroitness almost certainly contributed to his recurring bouts of depression. It may have affected the nature of his music. His isolation, misery, and absolute lack of alternatives may have driven him to concentrate more intensely upon composing, so that humanity, in the end, received great joy from Beethoven's misery.[2] Though if that is the case, it is hard to see how or why this knowledge should provide any more consolation for humanity than it did for Beethoven.

Bohemians were famous for their musicality long before Beethoven's day. Bohemian musicians were granted special permission to wear their traditional clothing and to roam to summer resorts to perform for aristocratic vacationers, despite local regulations that protected local musicians from foreign competition. Bohemia produced more composers per capita than any other European state but Austria in the eighteenth century—and more composers per capita than Austria from 1650 to 1750—though Bohemian nobles and churchmen employed fewer composers than practically all other European states, according to economic historian F. M. Scherer.[3] Bohemia has always been a net exporter of music and musicians.

Thackeray introduced into English the modern sense of Bohemian—"an artist or litterateur who, consciously or unconsciously, secedes from conventionality in life or art"—in his 1848 novel *Vanity Fair.* But the expansion of meanings, from a geographic region to a way of life, had begun in France by the fifteenth century, when the term was applied to Gypsies, who were believed to have come from Bohemia, though they probably only had entered France from that direction. The true origin of the Gypsies remains obscure and controversial.[4] India, Egypt, the Basque region of northern Spain, or "Romany"—one of whose meanings is "from the Roman Empire"— all have been suggested. Whether the anathema that, rightly or wrongly, has attached to Gypsies, and to musicians, for centuries, derived from the Gypsies or the Bohemians or from musicians, or from a fourth source, is unanswerable, though the problem probably poses more questions about Western society in general than it does about Bohemians, or Gypsies, or musicians.

As a term of opprobrium, "Bohemian" eventually was adapted as a badge of honor by those who proudly set themselves against the social order, though they eventually rejected the term in favor of words they devised themselves, which they also rejected once the words had come into common use. (In modern America, Bohemians became beatniks, then hippies, which failed to produce a successor term, possibly because America's genius for commercializing absolutely everything made the production of a successor term pointless—anathema to the anathematized—and possibly because mainstream society, whether it would admit it or not, adopted some of the values of Bohemianism: the glamour of living outside the law and beyond social controls, the exotic dress, and above all, the glorification of music. Modern America in this way recapitulated a centuries-old process during which Bohemians, as skilled, colorful, wandering musicians, were given privileges for their talents, then excoriated for the talent and the privileges, always with an undertone of envy.)

One can be Bohemian, or find oneself a Bohemian, in the modern sense, in at least three slightly, but significantly, different ways. One can consciously adopt a Bohemian bearing as a social or political statement. Franz Schubert, a more thoroughgoing Bohemian than Beethoven, presents an example of this in a letter in which he laments the breakup of his artistic circle. Schubert, then 26, wrote to his friend, the visual artist Franz von Schober:

> Our circle, as indeed I had expected, has lost its central focus without you. Bruchmann, who has returned from his journey, is no longer the same. He seems to bend to the formalities of the world, and by that alone he loses his halo, which in my opinion was due only to his determined disregard of all worldly affairs. . . . What is the good of a lot of quite ordinary students and officials to us?[5]

A key element of this form of Bohemianism is that the artist, or pretender, *must be seen* rejecting society and "determinedly disregarding worldly affairs." This has become a rite of passage for Western artists and, during this writer's generation, for virtually all Western youths.

Beethoven was not a Bohemian in this sense.

One may also become a Bohemian by truly rejecting social conventions, actively or passively, which may lead society to believe that one has "determinedly disregarded all worldly affairs," when in fact one simply sees no point in obeying social conventions, or one has other things in mind. Or one may become or appear to be a Bohemian because one does not understand social conventions, and therefore cannot follow them.

Beethoven was a Bohemian in these senses.

In the first two senses, in which one stands outside of society because one finds its rules obnoxious or encumbering, one may at least be granted, like Schubert, a real or imagined society of like-thinking fellows. But if, like Beethoven, one finds oneself a Bohemian in the third sense—because one finds society's rules not only pointless but mystifying—then one may become, like Beethoven, particularly subject to loneliness, alienation, frustration and depression.

To some extent, Beethoven was a Bohemian in all three senses. But unlike many artists, who are able to drop the pose when it suits their convenience or when it works to their advantage, Beethoven truly did not understand some social conventions. His naiveté and directness, and his inability to "play the game" caused him particular anguish in his relationships with women. This is not to say that Beethoven did not understand and could not abide by simple social customs and rules of deportment—though often he did not. He surely understood intuitively, as Mozart said directly, that in Vienna, "Whoever is *most impertinent* has the best chance. . . . One must not make oneself cheap here—that is a cardinal point—or else one is done."[6] But subtler social rules often escaped Beethoven, and he had no tolerance for official ceremony.

The classic instance of this was related by Beethoven's friend and student, Ferdinand Ries.

> Beethoven was a stranger to rules of etiquette and all that they imply; he never concerned himself about such things. Thus he often acutely embarrassed the entourage of Archduke Rudolph when he first started to frequent that circle. Attempts were made to coerce Beethoven into behaving with the proper deference. This was, however, unbearable for him. He did promise to mend his ways, but that was as far as it went. One day, finally, when he was again, as he termed it, being "sermonized on court manners," he very angrily pushed his way up to the Archduke and said quite frankly that though he had the greatest possible reverence for his person, a strict observance of all the regulations to which his attention was called every day was beyond him. The Archduke laughed good-naturedly about the incident and gave orders to let Beethoven go his own way in peace; he must be taken as he was.[7]

Proper behavior with high nobility included keeping one's distance, letting the lord direct the conversation, and speaking only when spoken to.[8]

Beethoven was not above posing as a young rebel, but in his case it is difficult to unravel the pose from the man. Frau Elizabeth von Bernhard lived at the home of a secretary of the Russian Embassy in Vienna from 1796 to 1800 and had access to Count Andreas Razumovsky and his circle, which included Prince Joseph Franz Lichnowsky. She left this reminiscence of a scene at Prince Lichnowsky's: "I still remember distinctly how both Haydn and Salieri sat on the sofa on one side of the little music-room, both most carefully dressed in the old-fashioned style with bag-wig, shoes and silk stockings, while Beethoven used to appear even here in the freer ultra-Rhenish garb, almost carelessly dressed."[9]

H. C. Robbins-Landon suggests that Beethoven's dress was a fashionable pose, inspired by Goethe's Romantic novel, *The Sorrows of Young Werther*.

> This "Werther" mode also became the rage in France: blue frock, yellow waistcoat, boots. After Louis XVI's execution, the radicals also dictated masculine mode: powder was synonymous with Royalist, male clothing became simpler than ever: the men renounced "beautiful" clothing and looked for the "practical." It is interesting to observe that Beethoven was completely under the sway of this "Werther" mode: in the Horneman miniature of 1803 . . . we see the composer in the obligatory blue frock-coat with yellow buttons; in the Waldmuller portrait of 1823, the composer is wearing the yellow waistcoat . . . which we may also see Prince Lichnowsky wearing. . . . Beethoven's nonchalant way of dressing ("the other side of the Rhine" mode) was, then, simply the progressive expression. Haydn appeared stiff in his old-fashioned dress, with powdered wig and knee-breeches with stockings (not white, however: Haydn had his principles, too, and white stockings meant *Capellmeister-Dienst* and a servant's status).[10]

Christian Horneman's miniature, however, portrays the most handsome Beethoven of all the images ever recorded from life. Horneman presented Beethoven in the *Werther* mode for the same stylistic reasons that Willibrod Josef Mähler painted the composer with a lyre, under a stormy sky, at about the same time. And there is no reason to believe that Ferdinand Georg Waldmüller did not do the same in the portrait he made after Beethoven threw him out after a single sitting in 1823, and refused to sit for him again.[11]

A peculiar story tells how Beethoven may have acquired the blue frock coat with yellow buttons in the Waldmüller portrait. Louis Schlösser, violinist and later conductor at Darmstadt, befriended Beethoven in 1822-23, when Schlösser was in Vienna to study with the composer Joseph Mayseder. One day, Schlösser wrote, he met Beethoven on the street and was "surprised . . . to find Beethoven, usually so careless about his attire, dressed with unwonted elegance, wearing a blue frock coat with yellow buttons, impeccable white knee-breeches, a vest to match, and a new beaver hat, as usual on the back of his head." Schlösser continued:

> I could not resist telling my teacher Mayseder, who lived in the neighborhood, about the striking metamorphosis of Beethoven's elegant appearance, an event which, however, caused Mayseder far less surprise than it had caused me, for he said with a smile: "This is not the first time that his friends have taken his

old clothes during the night and laid down new ones in their place; he has not the least suspicion of what has happened and puts on whatever lies before him with entire unconcern."[12]

Dozens of eyewitnesses have attested to Beethoven's disregard and ignorance of style and clothing. "As a rule, Beethoven was shabbily dressed," Countess Gallenberg told Otto Jahn in 1852. And his pupil Carl Czerny thought it worth remarking, "About the year 1813-14, when Beethoven looked well and strong, he also cared for his outward appearance." Another contemporary, Dr. W. Christian Müller, described Beethoven as he knew him in 1820:

> How little he knew of the world, and how little care he paid to conventional forms and earthly things, is shown by his outward appearance during the period when he was composing most prolifically. He did not know, for example, of the fashion of wearing frilled shirts. So that he would look more presentable when giving lessons to his female pupils, a woman friend of his had shirts made for him, with frills added as an embellishment. "What is this for?" he asked her when he saw them. "Ah, yes, to keep me warm," he said, answering his own question, and stuffed the frills under his waistcoat.[13]

Beethoven knew nothing about fashion in clothes and had no interest in it. So complete was his lack of interest that when he believed he had a chance of marrying Therese Malfatti, in 1810, Beethoven asked his friend Baron Ignaz von Gleichenstein to buy clothes for him: "Since I understand so little about these things as it is all so against my nature, please buy for me linen or Bengal cotton for shirts and at least half a dozen neckties.—Use your good judgment but don't delay, you know how I need them." Beethoven then was visiting the Malfatti household with Gleichenstein, who was courting Therese's sister, Anna. In those days Beethoven twice asked to borrow a looking glass from his friend Nikolaus Zmeskall—an item Beethoven would not have had to borrow had he truly cared about his appearance.[14]

Therese Malfatti rejected Beethoven, who probably asked her that summer to marry him. The rejection must have hurt all the more because Gleichenstein succeeded in marrying Anna the next year. A heartbreaking letter to Gleichenstein shows that Beethoven, socially inept, needed the baron to intercede for him and to interpret his chances:

> Your news has again plunged me from the heights of the most sublime ecstasy into the depths—And why did you add the remark that you would let me know when there would be music again? Am I then nothing more than a music-maker for yourself or the others?—At any rate, your remark can be interpreted thus. Therefore only in my own heart can I again find something to lean upon; and so for me there is to be no support outside. No, friendship and emotions of that kind only spell wounds for me. Well, so be it. For you, poor B, no happiness can come from outside. You must create everything for yourself in your own heart; and only in the world of ideals can you find friends.[15]

It is unlikely that Therese's father, Dr. Giovanni Malfatti, a famous surgeon who owned an estate at Mödling, near Vienna, would have allowed his daughter to marry the unkempt, half-deaf composer with an uncertain income. (She married a baron in 1816.) But Beethoven appears to have committed a social blunder, possibly by his too frank speech. In the sad letter in which he asks Gleichenstein if he is "nothing more than a music-maker," Beethoven also asks, "I beseech you to set my mind at rest by letting me know whether I was to blame yesterday. Or if you cannot do that, tell me the truth. I am as glad to hear it as I am to speak it—There is still time; truths can still be of use to me."[16]

The great sadness of Beethoven's life was not that he did not find a woman who loved him, but that he never found a woman who would let him love her, openly. There were many reasons for this. Beethoven was not handsome, he was not wealthy, he did not play cards, he was a terrible dancer, he was clumsy, stubborn, and peculiar. One woman to whom he proposed, the singer Magdalena Willman, refused to marry him "because he was so ugly, and half crazy." Willman, we may assume, did not say this to Beethoven's face; Thayer heard the story from her niece, who "had often heard her father speak of it."[17]

Beethoven longed for an intellectual companion as well as a physical one, and such a woman could be found only among the nobility or among Vienna's rising bourgeoisie. But in a day when parents arranged or could veto their daughter's marriage, the odds were against Beethoven. He could bring neither wealth nor stability to a daughter of the middle class, and the noble widows to whom he was so often attracted could lose their title, and their children, for marrying beneath their class. And Beethoven had no talent for or interest in the social games that consumed the lives of—and were all that were permitted to—the upper-class women in whose circles he moved.

Beethoven's personal problems, though, extended beyond social prohibitions. He had great difficulty abiding by simple social conventions that most people find almost instinctive. He did not do this (always) to insult people or to strike a pose; he simply lacked some of the social instincts that most of us take for granted. He was capable of pretense if there was something to be gained by it, or if he worked himself up to it—this appears in some of his letters. But, as the incident with Archduke Rudolph showed, he had no talent, patience, or interest in what passed for normal social intercourse. Some of this may be attributed to his simplicity, honesty, and lack of pretense. (Interestingly, he shared this trait with another composer, whose character was as different from Beethoven's as can be imagined. Béla Bartók also offended people, inadvertently, because of what Bartók's wife called his lack of "any conception of what an everyday conversation is."[18])

Beethoven was so socially awkward, so incapable of assuming a polite veneer, and "his dislikes were so strong, that to avoid speaking to persons to whom he was not well affected, he would actually increase his pace in the street to a run," the English composer Charles Neate wrote of Beethoven's behavior in 1815.[19]

The dramatist Franz Grillparzer called him "naïvely savage," though in a "good-natured way," recalling that when he visited Beethoven in Hetzendorf, the composer brought five bottles of wine from an adjoining room. "One he set down by Schindler's plate, one before his own and the remaining three he stood up in a row before me, probably to tell me, in his naïvely savage, good-natured way that I was at liberty to drink as much as ever I wished."[20]

Grillparzer's tale dates from 1823, when, the writer says, "so thoroughly had Beethoven's manner of life estranged him from all the habits and customs of the world." But Beethoven was a stranger to conventional behavior long before that. Frau von Bernhard wrote that when Beethoven visited the Razumovsky circle before the turn of the century, "he would usually stick his head through the door to make sure that no one was present whom he disliked. . . . [H]e was unmannerly both in demeanor and behavior."[21] This behavior, which predates Beethoven's deafness, seems more asocial than anti-social, and indicates great social unease, rather than a wish to offend people or strike a pose.

In 1809, Beethoven indignantly moved out of rooms that Countess Anna Marie Erdödy had offered him, when he found that the countess had been secretly paying his servant a few florins a month to keep the man from abandoning Beethoven, who was notoriously rough on servants. Beethoven moved directly from the Countess's apartments into a whorehouse. This was less than a month after Countess Erdödy had taken the lead in arranging for three noblemen—Archduke Rudolph, Prince Lobkowitz, and Prince Ferdinand Kinsky—to promise to pay Beethoven 4,000 florins a year, for life, on the far from onerous conditions that he live in Vienna and compose whatever he like. Beethoven apologized to the Countess, in a letter written, apparently, from the whorehouse, and proceeded to dedicate three pieces to her—two of them in that year.

From his room in the bordello, Beethoven then wrote a savage letter to his friend, Baron Ignaz von Gleichenstein, which began: "My rooms are on the Walfischgasse No. 1087, on the second floor. (It's a b[rothe]l, you will know it)—Is it true? Are you really here? Detestable, false, faithless, treacherous, thoughtless friend!"[22] This insulting outburst came because Gleichenstein had returned to Vienna and had not yet sent his regards to Beethoven, or thanked him for the dedication of his Opus 69 Cello Sonata.

Yet Beethoven continued to be friends with Countess Erdödy and Baron Gleichenstein, which shows considerably more noble forbearance than members of their privileged class were accustomed to show to commoners. These incidents and others led Beethoven's student Carl Czerny to write, "It has sometimes been said abroad that Beethoven was neglected and oppressed in Vienna. The truth is that he enjoyed, even as a young man, all possible support and an encouragement and respect on the part of our high nobility which has rarely been the portion of a young composer."[23]

Though Beethoven's resentfulness, violent temper, and lack of control were legendary, he also was capable of great acts of kindness. In the most touching example of this, he managed to do so without speaking. The Baroness Dorothea von Ertmann, a pianist, lost her youngest son in 1807. Years later, she told the visiting Felix Mendelssohn

> the loveliest anecdotes about Beethoven, how, in the evening when she played for him, he used the candle snuffers as toothpicks, etc. . . . She related that when she lost her last child, Beethoven at first did not want to come into the house; at length he invited her to visit him, and when she came he sat himself down at the pianoforte and said simply: "We will now talk to each other in tones," and for over an hour played without stopping, and as she remarked: "he told me everything, and at last brought me comfort."[24]

Beethoven had trouble with words—with speaking, and even more difficulty with writing. At the beginning of his final illness, in the last long, and revealing, letter he ever wrote, he apologized to his childhood friends, Franz Wegeler and Eleonore Wegeler, née von Breuning, for failing to answer their letter for nearly a year. "I am rather slack about writing letters, for I believe that the best people know me well in any case. Often I think out a reply in my head; but when it comes to writing it down, I usually throw away my pen, simply because I am unable to write as I feel."[25]

Beethoven was socially inept even before he became deaf, but his inarticulateness transcended the limits which nearly everyone feels from time to time, at "not finding the words." At times, he seemed unable to decode universally understood social behavior. An incident in early March 1807, when Beethoven was hard of hearing but not yet deaf, demonstrates the difficulty he had in negotiating social conventions. The entire affair is told and recapitulated in three letters that Beethoven wrote to Marie Bigot and her husband, from which we quote at length, to illustrate the depths of Beethoven's incomprehension.

Marie Bigot, a talented pianist, was eighteen in 1804, when her husband brought her to Vienna, where he was librarian for Count Razumovsky. Haydn and Beethoven both admired her playing. "The first time that she played in the presence of Haydn, the old gentleman was so moved that he clasped her in his arms and cried: 'O, my dear child, I did not write this music—it is you who have composed it!' And upon the printed sheet from which she had played he wrote: 'On February 20, 1805, Joseph Haydn was happy.'" Beethoven, too, could not resist her playing. "One day she played a sonata which he had just composed, in such a manner as to draw from him the remark: 'That is not exactly the character which I wanted to give this piece; but go right on. If it is not wholly mine it is something better.'"[26] During the social disaster of March 1807, then, Marie Bigot was about 21, talented, beautiful—and married.

Beethoven quarreled with the Bigots because he asked Marie to go for a carriage ride with him while her husband was at work. Her husband had forbidden this only the day before—whether from jealousy or simple propriety is beside the point. For on the next day—March 4—Beethoven repeated his offer, in the first of his ill-advised letters, which began like this:

> My Dear and Much Admired Marie: The weather is so divinely beautiful—and who knows whether it will be like this tomorrow? So I propose to fetch you about noon today and take you for a drive—As Bigot has presumably gone out already, we cannot take him with us, of course—

After assuring her that her husband would surely not want to deny them this pleasure, Beethoven continues, improvidently:

> It would be quite alien to the outlook of our so enlightened and cultured Marie if for the sake of mere scruples she were to rob me of my greatest pleasure—Oh, whatever reasons you may put forward for *not accepting* my proposal, I shall ascribe your refusal to nothing else but your distrust of my character—[27]

Marie Bigot refused to go, and told her husband straightaway of Beethoven's invitation. This must have led to a face-to-face confrontation between M. Bigot and Beethoven, that day or the next, at which Beethoven said—nothing. On March 5, he wrote his second letter, to M. Bigot, stating that he would not apologize for his behavior because Beethoven is the one who feels "very much hurt."

Beethoven began the second letter without a salutation:

> Thursday, March 5, At four o'clock in the afternoon. Hardly have I arrived home when the first thing I do is to write to you, dear Bigot. I can well believe that my strange behavior has startled you—I am not apologizing for it, for then I should be assuming that you *attach great value to me* and that *what I did must have hurt you*—I feel too keenly how little I still mean to you—At the same time you would be wrong to think that my behavior was prompted by my displeasure *at the refusal of my request to Marie*—True enough, I cannot deny it, I felt very much hurt; and the reason why I did not speak to you was in order not *to display my feelings*.[28]

This is all rather too much: to be forbidden the privilege of going out unescorted with a man's wife; to repeat the invitation to her the next day, and be caught at it; then to walk away from the husband without a word when confronted about it. But Beethoven's social dundering was just beginning. "It occurred to me," he wrote to M. Bigot,

> that our kind and excellent Marie might possibly think that my invitation of yesterday was connected with the conversation about it of the day before yesterday.—But that is certainly not the case—And I still cannot understand why it would have been improper if Marie and Caroline [the baby] had come out driving with me—But we shall talk about this—Do let me know quickly in two words whether my behavior has offended you. You cannot conceive the pain it causes me merely to think that I have given you an unpleasant moment—If I have done so, then I have been sufficiently punished for it, seeing that *at table* the thought constantly tortured me—Owing to some exceedingly pressing business it is impossible for me to call on you—I have to go out and I shall not be home until a late hour, when I hope to find a few lines from you which will comfort me—At the same time I cannot conceal the fact that this incident has affected my emotions and that I shall always hesitate to look forward with pleasure to anything I may expect to receive from you—[29]

So many of these statements are so clumsily put and so unbelievable that one scarcely knows where to begin:

• that the Bigots "might possibly think" Beethoven's invitation "was connected to the conversation" less than 24 hours old in which he had been told no the first time;

• that he cannot understand why it would be improper to take a carriage ride with a married woman, despite her husband's prohibition;

• that he still is not sure "whether my behavior has offended you";

• that he has been "punished" for this "at table"—presumably, while dining with the Bigots—because he feared that he might have given them an "unpleasant moment";

• that "some exceedingly pressing business" prevents him from resolving this face to face;

• that it is up to the Bigots to "comfort" him, because he had violated the husband's orders, courted the wife, and when the husband called him on it, walked away from him without a word;

• and finally, Beethoven has the brass to try to transfer his unease to the Bigots, saying, "I shall always hesitate to look forward with pleasure to anything I may expect to receive from you."

Beethoven concludes the fiasco in his third letter, addressed to both Bigots, by telling them, "you have hurt me very deeply—but your action will only serve to strengthen our friendship more and more." Among the statements in this letter that we may be permitted to doubt are that Beethoven actually felt, again, that the Bigots should apologize for misunderstanding him, and that he believed he was not contravening M. Bigot's instructions not to go out alone with his wife—because he had also invited the baby.

After beginning, "Dear Marie, Dear Bigot! Not without experiencing the deepest regret have I been made to realize that the purest and most innocent feelings can often be misunderstood—" Beethoven explains his pure and innocent motives:

> As for my invitation to take you and Caroline for a drive, it was only natural that since on the previous day Bigot had objected to your coming alone for a drive with me, I should think that both of you considered it perhaps unsuitable or improper—and when I wrote to you, all I wanted to make clear to you was that I saw nothing improper in it. And if I added emphatically that I attached great importance to your not refusing my invitation, I did so merely in order to induce you to enjoy the *beautifully fine day.* I was thinking far more of your and Caroline's pleasure than of my own. And in this way, namely, by stating that *distrust on your part or a refusal would be really offensive to me*, I thought I could almost compel you to yield to my entreaties.—Well, surely you ought to consider how you can make amends to me for—having spoilt for me—that lovely day, both on account of my frame of mind and also on account of the lovely weather—

Then, incredibly, Beethoven attempts to instruct the Bigots on proper behavior:

> If I said that *something dreadful* would result from my going to see you, that was certainly meant rather as a jest, the purpose of which was to show you that everything concerned with you attracts me more and more, so that my dearest wish is to be able to live with you both for ever. Then supposing that there were some deeper meaning in my statement, why, even the most sacred friendship can often have other secret implications, but—on that account *to put a wrong construction* on your friend's secret—because you cannot fathom it at once—that you should *not* do, dear Bigot and dear Marie. For *never, never* will you find me dishonorable. Since my childhood I have learned to love virtue—and everything beautiful and good—Indeed you have hurt me very deeply—But your action will only serve to strengthen our friendship more and more—

Lamentable though these protests be, Beethoven preceded them with comments that, considering the situation, were even more ill-advised:

> Possibly once or twice I did indulge with Bigot in some jokes which were not quite refined. But I myself told you that sometimes I am very naughty—I am extremely natural with all my friends and I hate any kind of constraint. Now I count Bigot among my friends; and if something about me annoys him, friendship demands that both of you should tell me so—

Of course, the Bigots already had told him so, more than once. Yet the most alarming statement in this letter to a married couple—which Beethoven underlined—is so confusing it is impossible to interpret, except equivocally:

> [D]ear M[arie], I never dreamt of reading anything more into your behavior than the gift of your friendship—You must think me very mean and petty if you assume that the friendliness of so excellent a person as yourself might lead to my believing that—I had immediately won your affection—Besides, it is one of my chief principles *never to be in any other relationship than that of friendship with the wife of another man. For I should not wish by forming any other kind of relationship to fill my heart with distrust of that woman who some day will perhaps share my fate*—[30]

This last sentence defies innocent interpretation.

The entire series of letters demonstrates Beethoven's ineptitude at social intercourse. He understood that men and women play social games, but he did not know how to play. He did not understand the rules. He may not have understood the point, and he surely did not understand that often, in the game between men and women, the game itself is the point. Yet despite the sputtering pretense and transparent dodges, the letters contain an enormous amount of truth.

Beethoven *was* misunderstood, but as the third letter indicates, he seemed incapable of explaining his feelings clearly enough to understand them himself. His suspicion of others—which, when he became profoundly deaf, came to dominate his character—is apparent: ("whatever reasons you may put forward for *not accepting* my proposal, I shall ascribe your refusal to nothing else but your distrust of my character—"). He was so inarticulate that he was unable to speak when M. Bigot confronted him. Beethoven was telling the truth when he told the husband that the entire fiasco left him feeling "very much hurt; and the reason why I did not speak to you was in order not *to display my feelings.*" And it was true that the Bigots "cannot conceive the pain it causes me merely to think that I have given you an unpleasant moment"—for Beethoven felt pain in virtually all social interactions, as he wrote, clearly, for once, in his Heiligenstadt Testament.

Beethoven's emotional states may have been more intense than others'—not an unusual trait among creative artists—but they were not so qualitatively different as to estrange him from his fellows. What estranged him was his inability to express himself in a medium other than music. He despised pretense, and though his natural manner could be disarming, still, he lacked an intuitive understanding of social conventions, even when addressing a little girl. When a young pianist, Emilie M., eight to ten years old, sent him a present of a wallet she had made herself, along with a letter she wrote with help from her governess, this is how Beethoven responded from Teplitz, a spa outside Vienna: "My Dear, Kind Emilie, My Dear Friend! My reply to your letter to me is late in arriving. My excuse must be a great amount of business and persistent illness. The fact that I am here for the recovery of my health problems proves the truth of my excuse."

This is odd; it is baffling, that a composer of European fame feels he must justify the truth of his "excuse" to a little girl. Beethoven's entire letter, written without a trace of condescension, surely was from the heart. After thanking Emilie for the wallet, which "will be treasured among other tokens of a regard which several people have expressed for me, but which I am still far from deserving," Beethoven continued:

> Persevere, do not only practice your art, but endeavor also to fathom its inner meaning; it deserves this effort. For only art and science can raise men to the level of gods. If, my dear Emilie, you should ever desire to have anything, do not hesitate to write to me. The true artist has no pride. He sees unfortunately that art has no limits; he has a vague idea how far he is from reaching his goal; and while others may perhaps be admiring him, he laments the fact that he has not yet reached the point whither his better genius only lights the way for him like a distant sun. I should probably prefer to visit you and your family than to visit many a rich person who betrays a poverty of mind. If I should ever go to H., then I will call on you and your family. . . . When I find people of that sort, there is my home.[31]

Perhaps Beethoven's protest to Emilie was simple force of habit; in dozens of other letters he protested that his addressee did not believe him. His suspiciousness of others increased as he aged—a common trait associated with deafness. But Beethoven's protests that his friends did not believe him began appearing in his letters in 1796, before he became deaf. His letter to Emilie reveals many of Beethoven's defining traits: his simplicity, his good heart, his idealism and artistic sincerity, but with it all, a seriousness of intent so undisguised it comes off as a bit strange. Not every adult is able, or willing, to address a child as an equal. Beethoven's statement that he would feel more at home with Emilie and her family than he would with "many a rich person" we must take as the truth.

But Beethoven's friends would have smiled—out of his presence, of course—at his statement, "The true artist has no pride." Lions and peacocks are grovelers next to Beethoven. His pupil Ferdinand Ries relates that when Muzio Clementi, the virtuoso pianist, composer, and publisher came to Vienna, "Beethoven wished to call on him at once; but his brother [Johann] put it into his head that Clementi should call first. Clementi, although much older, would probably have done this anyway, if some gossip about it had not arisen." As a result:

> We often ate mid-day dinner at the same table at the Swan [tavern]; Clementi with his pupil Klengel, and Beethoven with me. Everyone knew who everyone else was, but neither spoke to the other, or even greeted each other. The two pupils had to follow their masters, probably because each was under the threat of losing his lesson, which for me, at least, would certainly have been irrevocable, since with Beethoven there was never any compromise.[32]

In his stubbornness, his overpowering resentments, his uncontrollable temper, his impatience, his carelessness with money, his simple love of nature, his mercurial volatility, and his intolerance for anything but absolute freedom, Beethoven was an eternal child. No one else who moved in the sophisticated company that Beethoven kept would have admitted to a potential rival, as Beethoven did to the composer Ludwig Spohr, that he was under "house arrest" because he had only one pair of boots, which were so worn out that the soles were full of holes.[33] None with an understanding of society would have exposed himself to ridicule as Beethoven did, after a pretended rival, the pianist Ferdinand Himmel, had tricked him by writing from Berlin

> that the newest thing there was the invention of a lantern for the blind. Beethoven ran about with this piece of news, and of course everyone wanted to know how this was possible. He therefore immediately wrote to Himmel, charging that it was negligent of him not to have sent any further details. The answer he received . . . not only put an end to their correspondence forever, but brought ridicule on Beethoven, since he was rash enough to show it here and there.[34]

Himmel's story of the lantern for the blind may have been payback for a perceived insult he had received from Beethoven sometime before. Ferdinand Ries, who related both stories, wrote:

> Himmel and [Beethoven] fell out in the following manner: when they were together one day Himmel asked Beethoven to improvise and Beethoven did. Afterwards Beethoven insisted that Himmel do the same. Himmel was weak enough to agree. After he had played for quite some time, Beethoven said: "Well, when are you actually going to begin?" Himmel flattered himself that he had been achieving something marvelous already; he therefore left the piano,

and both of them exchanged rude remarks with one another. Beethoven said to me: "I thought Himmel had just been offering a little prelude."[35]

From anyone else, the remark about Himmel's improvisation could fairly be interpreted as malicious; from Beethoven, it seems merely unguarded and impatient, though it is easy to see why Himmel took it as an insult. It was one more instance in which Beethoven's social ineptness resulted in hurt feelings.

On his deathbed, less than two weeks before he died, Beethoven showed to another old rival, the pianist Johann Nepomuk Hummel, a painting of Haydn's birthplace that Beethoven had just received as a present. "'It gave me a childish pleasure,' [Beethoven] said, 'the cradle of so great a man.'"[36]

The author of the most sophisticated music the world had ever heard was not a sophisticated man. This is one reason his character rewards the unending study it has received, and always will receive. He was one of the greatest artists the human race has produced, but as a human being he was often utterly without artifice: he had no recourse to artifice, and often did not know he should have recourse to it. A grown man who acts like a child can be annoying and exasperating, but if he acts without malice he may deserve forgiveness, and Beethoven received forgiveness from his friends—because he was not acting. "Genius is only childhood recovered at will," Baudelaire wrote, "childhood now gifted to express itself with the faculties of manhood." Beethoven had that genius—but only in music.

Beethoven and Schindler

Beethoven often was unaware of his eccentricities, yet painfully aware of his shortcomings in social situations. His personal difficulties and insecurities exacerbated his alienation from others, even from his friends, which aggravated his tendency toward depression, culminating in the profound depression, and extreme eccentricities, of his unproductive years, from 1814 to 1819. But his physical and emotional suffering, depression, social unease, and eccentricities did not constitute the whole of Beethoven's character. He was a fully formed, charismatic and creative person, with an overwhelming personality, and a tremendous store of strength—physical, mental, creative, and emotional. One of his most appealing qualities, his sympathy for the underdog, probably explains his initial attraction to one of the most controversial men in his life—his sometime secretary and factotum, the now disgraced and discredited Anton Felix Schindler.

Schindler, born in Moravia in 1795, went to Vienna to study law in 1813, but eventually abandoned the profession in favor of his first love, music. He was a violinist, and apparently a good one, holding down the job as violin section leader at the Josephstadt Theatre from 1822 to 1825. A music journal in those days reported "that in the violins one heard only the unusually strong tone of the 'vigorous, most attentive, and assiduous orchestra director, Herr Schindler.'"[37] But Schindler is known to history as the author of the first full-length biography of Beethoven. Its first edition was published in 1840. An expanded, second edition appeared in 1845, and a third, extensively revised edition in 1860.

Schindler's credibility was questioned from the beginning, but it took more than 130 years for the extent of his fabrications and forgeries to be fully exposed. They were so great that Maynard Solomon, whose 1977 book *Beethoven* had immediately become the standard modern biography, set to work scouring Schindler's tales from the second edition of the book unless he could confirm them from other sources. "Although Anton Schindler's extensive, deliberate forgeries in the Conversation Books became known in 1977," Solomon wrote, "the extent of his unreliability in every other aspect was not yet fully grasped."[38]

Schindler's memoirs contain some of the most vivid descriptions of Beethoven ever recorded. And because Schindler often was with Beethoven on a regular basis—though not as often as Schindler claimed: only, for certain, in 1822, and from late December 1826 until Beethoven died on March 26, 1827—some of the scenes in Schindler's book probably are true. Clearly, Beethoven existed, things happened to him, and Schindler was an eyewitness to some of them. Solomon wisely accepts only those statements that can be confirmed by documents or by other, independent sources. But Beethoven's relationship with Schindler illuminates some things about the composer beyond the tales Schindler tells of him: for example, what drew Beethoven to Schindler in the first place, what made him tire of the man so quickly, and what made him accept him again at the end. And Schindler's life after Beethoven's death, and the many enemies Schindler acquired, even while Beethoven was still alive, reveal something about the competitive, faction-riddled musical life of Vienna and Europe of those times.

Beethoven's relationship with Schindler is not particularly creditable to either of them. Beethoven showed himself to be irascible, sometimes unjust and unkind, and Schindler revealed himself only after Beethoven was dead. But the relationship does show Beethoven's concern for the persecuted—a concern that he demonstrated, at least this once, by real sympathy for a suffering human being, not just by professing noble ideals, which is so much easier to do, for all of us, and particularly for Beethoven.

As Schindler tells it, he met Beethoven in the winter of 1813-14, when a musical acquaintance asked him to deliver a message to the composer from the violinist Ignaz Schuppanzigh. Beethoven read the message, told Schindler, "Yes," and that was that. Schindler then saw Beethoven intermittently, from afar, at a few concerts in Vienna, and met him again after one of them.

No reason to doubt Schindler so far.

In March 1815, Napoleon escaped from Elba, alarming the crowned heads of Europe and Russia, who were redrawing the map of Europe at the Congress of Vienna. Liberal students in Vienna rioted in support of Napoleon, while to the south, the Carbonari were agitating for a united Italy. Austrian Foreign Minister Klemens von Metternich responded by tightening his already stringent political repression, casting particular suspicion upon students and travelers. Donald W. McArdle, who edited the standard English-language version of Schindler's book, wrote that Schindler "was one of the leaders of the unrest at the University," and "fled to Brünn, where he took a post as a teacher."[39]

Brünn (now Brno) is south of Vienna—toward Italy—and Schindler's flight aroused the suspicion of Metternich's intelligence service. No sooner had he arrived in Brünn, Schindler says, than he was summoned to the police and interrogated about his connections with the Viennese students, and "about certain Italians in Vienna in whose company I had often been observed. To cap it all, my papers were not in order, and the document listing the lectures where I had been in attendance was missing (through no fault of my own), with the result that I was imprisoned." He remained in prison for "a few weeks," until "it was established that I was not a propagandist, and I was released." But he had lost his job and a year of his studies.

Back in Vienna, Schindler wrote, "I received through a close acquaintance of Beethoven's an invitation to present myself at a certain place where the master wanted to hear from my own lips the events that had taken place in Brünn. As I talked, Beethoven revealed such warm sympathy and concern over my unfortunate experience that I could not keep back my tears." The result, Schindler says, was that Beethoven invited him to meet him later at a room in the tavern *Zum Blumenstock*, the composer's haunt in those days, frequented by "a sort of cell of a small number of Josephinists of the truest dye"—liberal supporters, like Beethoven, of the policies of the late Emperor Joseph II—opponents of Metternich's police state.[40]

This is all credible. Beethoven was a political liberal; he haunted the taverns where he could read newspapers and follow European political news, and he had a great enthusiasm throughout his adult life for politically liberal England. But Schindler is certainly lying when he states that by 1816, "I became Beethoven's private secretary—without pay," that "other tasks were soon added to the arrangement," that he served Beethoven regularly "from that time until his death," and that their "association was interrupted only once, briefly, towards the end of his life."[41] No letters survive from Beethoven to Schindler until 1822, and the letters do not become frequent until 1823, when Beethoven soon grew tired of Schindler and rejected him, with insults.

Maynard Solomon says there is no evidence that Schindler "became Beethoven's amanuensis" until late 1822 or early 1823.[42] What's certain is that the composer began a flurry of letters to Schindler in January 1823—seven letters that month, forty-six letters that year. By far the greatest part of the correspondence dealt with business chores—seeking subscribers for the *Missa Solemnis*, writing letters to publishers, arranging short-term loans and the sale of one of Beethoven's bank shares. In January 1823, Beethoven addressed Schindler as "Most Excellent Fellow!" By August, however, Beethoven refused to have anything to do with him, and used his nephew Karl as an intermediary when he required Schindler's services: "I will send you a few lines for Schindler—that contemptible object—chiefly because I do not care to have any direct association with that miserable fellow—". Three days later, Beethoven wrote his brother Johann, "I avoid as far as possible that low-minded, contemptible fellow—" (Perhaps we may give Schindler the benefit of the doubt on this one. In this letter Beethoven calls his housekeeper an "arch swine," his kitchen maid "a beast," and Johann's wife a "former and still active whore, with whom her fellow miscreant slept no less than three times during your illness and who, moreover, has full control of your money, oh, abominable shame, is there no spark of manhood in you?!!!") Three weeks later, Beethoven described Schindler to his friend Ferdinand Ries: "I have never yet met a more wretched fellow on God's earth, an arch scoundrel whom I have sent packing—"[43]

The picture becomes clear. Beethoven sympathized with sufferers. As he aged, he was drawn to young, energetic musicians, such as the violinist Karl Holz, and to creative and politically active men, such as the journalist Johann Friedrich Rochlitz. Schindler's arrest for suspicion of liberalism would have endeared him to the composer, particularly because his imprisonment was unjust—like Florestan's, the hero of Beethoven's *Fidelio*. But "Schindler was altogether the lackey by nature,"[44] and that was something Beethoven could not abide. (An oft-told story relates that Beethoven abandoned a beautiful summer apartment in a baron's villa because of the baron's unctuous manner of bowing to him every time they met.)

Beethoven could not bear to show obeisance to counts and princes, and he despised others who showed such deference to him. In an early letter to Schindler, Beethoven wrote: "When you write to me, just write in exactly the same way as I do to you, that is to say, without giving me a title, without addressing me, without signing your name. Vita brevis, ars longa. And you need not use figures of speech, but just say precisely what is necessary—"[45] But that was not Schindler's way. Walter Nohl, the early Beethoven biographer who called Schindler a natural-born lackey, continued:

> [He was] a worthy, honorable, faithful, and not uncultivated man, but a tool in the hands of the overbearing and headstrong Beethoven, who according to his mood treated him amiably or contemptuously. He never gave him his true confidence and affection; on the other hand, his attitude towards him could be so brutal that it seems almost impossible that a man could bring himself to accept it.[46]

It is difficult to see how anyone other than a besotted admirer or lackey could put up with the treatment Beethoven handed Schindler. Consider the letter from May 1824, after Schindler had worked tirelessly for weeks, and put up with continuous abuse, to help arrange the premiere of the Ninth Symphony. Beethoven wrote:

> I do not accuse you of having done anything wicked in connection with the concert. But stupidity and arbitrary behavior have ruined many an undertaking. Moreover I have on the whole a certain fear of you, a fear lest some day through your action a great misfortune may befall me. . . . In any case I would much rather try to repay frequently with a small gift the services you render me than *have you at my table.* For I confess that your presence irritates me in so many ways. . . . For owing to your vulgar outlook how could you appreciate anything that is not vulgar?! . . . I will certainly invite you occasionally. But it

> is impossible to have you beside me permanently, because such an arrangement would upset my whole existence. . . . I must declare that the purity of my character does not permit me to reward your kindnesses to me with friendship alone, although, of course, I am willing to serve you in any matter connected with your welfare—[47]

The question arises why Schindler would keep a letter like this, unless he was wholly craven, or he figured he could sell it, which he eventually did. To Schindler's credit, he returned to Beethoven's bedside during the composer's final illness and attended him faithfully despite the long string of insults. To Schindler's discredit, and to the misfortune of historians, when Beethoven died, Schindler took an enormous collection of documents, including manuscripts and letters, and all of the composer's private conversation books, many of which Schindler altered or destroyed, some apparently for his own benefit, before selling them to the King of Prussia for 2,000 thalers in cash, plus 400 thalers a year, from 1845 until Schindler departed this life in 1864.[48]

Before selling his trove of documents, Schindler fabricated at least 150 of his own entries in the conversation books. He obliterated others, and destroyed an unknown number of books, ostensibly "because of their weight and bulk" and because "he deemed [them] to be of little or no importance," according to Thayer, who says he got the information directly from Schindler. Thayer believed Schindler lifted more than 400 conversation books from the rooms of the dead composer and destroyed all but 138 of them. Solomon thinks that unlikely, "because of the great monetary value Schindler attributed to these documents." Musicologists Dagmar Beck and Grita Herre, who destroyed Schindler's credibility forever with their reports of his forgeries at the 1977 Beethoven Congress, believe the number 400 may have come from Thayer's mishearing Schindler's "*viel über Hundert*" as "*vier Hundert*."[49]

It is difficult to maintain any sympathy for Schindler, whose much-reproduced photograph, taken two years before his death, presents an image of proud pretension verging upon silliness.[50] It is one more of the many sad things about Beethoven's life that during his final, extended illness, he had to turn for help to a man he did not respect, one of whose defining characteristics was servility.

From 1827 until his own death, Schindler presented himself as the true bearer of Beethoven's flame. In doing so, he became the butt of jokes across Europe. He quarreled with virtually every progressive musician on the continent, including Liszt, Berlioz, Robert and Clara Schumann, Mendelssohn, and Wagner. But apparently there is no truth to the legend that he dined out on the dead composer, with a personal calling card identifying himself as "*Ami de Beethoven*." McArdle attributes the tale to a vicious review of the 1841 musical season in Paris, in which the reviewer, Heinrich Heine, refers to "the friend of Beethoven, '*l'ami de Beethoven*,' as he presents himself everywhere here—even, I believe, on his visiting cards . . . . The French, who have lost all patience with the monotonous chatter of this dreary guest, ask, 'How could the great Master have endured so uninspiring and fatuous a friend?' They forget that Beethoven was deaf."[51]

This is nasty enough, and typical of the venom that characterized the European musical press, and would continue to characterize it in the coming war between enthusiasts of Brahms and Wagner. But McArdle says, "No cards such as Heine described are known, and no one seems to have been prepared to state that he had seen such cards with his own eyes." However, McArdle, perhaps Schindler's most sympathetic chronicler, continues: "The story may probably be dismissed as a virulent piece of writing which, while true in principle, was not true in fact."

Robert Hornstein, a memoirist who knew Schindler, believed the man had "been treated most unjustly."

> It was customary to place him in the position of a servant to his hero, and to deny him any justification for associating with such a man. This was in no wise the case: he was an extremely able man. It was because of his comical appearance and his mannerisms that he was underrated. The tall gaunt man, with his nasal voice and his windmill gestures, made an altogether comical effect.[52]

The two men Beethoven asked to be his biographers—the cellist Karl Holz and the journalist Johann Rochlitz—both declined. Holz apparently did not feel up to the task, and Rochlitz was ill. In the months after Beethoven's death, Rochlitz declined two written requests from Schindler reminding him that Beethoven had selected him for the job, and asking him to do it. Beethoven's friend Stephan von Breuning, who could have written the book, died three months after Beethoven. Franz Wegeler and Ferdinand Ries, whose biographical notes, published in 1838, are among the most valuable, and truthful, memoirs of Beethoven, found they could not work with Schindler.

So Schindler, a vain and difficult man, took nearly two years to write the biography of a man who was even more difficult than he was. In the introduction to his book, Schindler wrote that Beethoven, upon stating his preference that Rochlitz write his biography, said, "it was his sincere wish that whatever might be said about him in the future should in every respect adhere strictly to the truth, even though it might bear hard upon this or that person, or even upon himself."[53] Perhaps Schindler did not destroy the insulting letters Beethoven had written him because he did want to present Beethoven as he was. He actually showed around and seemed to be proud of a letter in which Beethoven called him "Mr. Big-Mouth-Say-Nothing; Mr. Ignoramus-Without-Education."[54] Schindler may have been vain enough to believe that the letter revealed more about Beethoven than it did about him.

Schindler was ill-used by his hero, mocked in his old age, and vilified by later historians. But the intensity of this vilification may be a bit unfair. Given the reactionary, repressive politics of the day, Schindler could have been telling the truth when he said that he obliterated some entries in the conversation books to spare other people political repercussions. Simple vanity probably explains most of the entries in which he falsified his own comments, though some of his lies clearly were meant to bolster the version of history that Schindler recorded in *Beethoven As I Knew Him*, and to slander Schindler's rivals for Beethoven's affection, such as the cellist Karl Holz and Beethoven's nephew Karl, neither of whom Schindler could abide. But Schindler did no worse, and in fact, did not do as much damage as another memoirist of his day, who not only lied about herself, from vanity, but destroyed a valuable historical document completely—or thought she did.

Fanny Burney, a popular novelist and daughter of the music historian Charles Burney, intended to publish her late father's three-volume memoirs. But finding that the famous musical traveler, friend of Europe's greatest musicians, including Handel and Haydn, and familiar of Kings George III and IV, had been, to her taste, too honest in describing the Burneys' undistinguished ancestors, too lavish in praise of his second wife—Fanny's stepmother—and too concerned with his own life rather than the glories of her own, Fanny burned the memoirs, after appropriating, and falsifying, what material she wanted, then publishing it as her own work. Yet history has not heaped upon Fanny Burney anything like the contumely with which it has disgraced Schindler. "That Fanny was consciously dishonest cannot be doubted," says her father's biographer, Roger Lonsdale, whose book incorporated research based on a trove of 1,500 letters found in the 1950s, including fragments of the autobiography that Fanny thought she had destroyed.[55]

Charles Burney was the first professional musician who became known, and accepted in the highest society, as a man of letters. Even Burney's friends were amazed. "[W]e have had *no* experience of such a phenomenon as a professor of Music, & an artist, that was a man of letters, & a good writer.—it is contrary to the uniform course of nature," Burney's lifelong friend, the Rev. Thomas Twining, of the famous family of tea merchants, wrote him in 1766. "The social limitations of the professional musician can be most emphatically illustrated by Lord Chesterfield's definition of 'bad company:' 'such as fiddlers, pipers, and *id genus omne*; most unedifying and unbecoming company for a man of fashion!'"[56] Burney's two books, in four volumes, recording his indefatigable journeys throughout Europe, and his four-volume *General History of Music*, not only elevated the status of the musician but are still read and enjoyed. The fragments of his memoirs that were spared the flames indicate that the autobiography would have been a priceless document.

Fanny not only burned it, she falsified entries—putting praise of herself into the mouth of King George; claiming on one page that her father's memoirs were insipid because he wrote them after becoming senile due to a stroke, then quoting from a letter he wrote years later, to show "the astonishing powers preserved of his Mind, in old age & infirmities"; finally becoming so tangled in her own lies that "Ultimately . . . Fanny was reduced to the demonstrably absurd assertion that Burney wrote the whole of his 'Memoirs' in a few months after his stroke in September 1806."[57]

Lonsdale provides copious evidence of the manner in which Fanny, who married an exiled Frenchman, Alexandre d'Arblay, falsified her father's memoirs. "Fanny's emendation of this sentence is astonishing in its egotism," Lonsdale writes, citing first a sentence as Charles Burney wrote it: "'Their Majesties then both condescended to make some inquiries after my family, though by name only after my daughter d'Arblay.'" (Through her father's influence, Fanny had been employed, unhappily, for five years as Second Keeper of the Robes to Her Majesty. This was after Fanny had gained renown for her first novel, *Evelina,* which was published anonymously.) Here is how the sentence appears in Fanny's version: "'The King then resumed again his old favourite topic of amusement, my daughter d'Arblay's concealed composition of Evelina; inquiring again and again into the various particulars of its contrivance and its discovery." Lonsdale concludes: "Such instance of the falsification of a text offered as direct quotation from her father's 'Memoirs' and of Fanny's senile egotism may be taken as characteristic of her biography as a whole."[58] Fanny Burney was 80 when her *Memoirs of Doctor Burney* were published in 1832.

Historians have criticized Fanny Burney, sometimes severely, for her Bowdlerization, falsification, and destruction of her father's memoirs. Historians also have praised, and continue to praise her, as a novelist whose social satires were precursors to Jane Austen and Thackeray. But all four of Fanny Burney's novels together, plus her false memoirs of her father, are not as valuable or as interesting as Schindler's admittedly imperfect biography of Beethoven.

Let us consider one dramatic scene from Schindler, the public portion of which has been described by other witnesses. In 1822, Beethoven insisted upon conducting the revival of his opera *Fidelio*, against the advice of his friends, who knew he was too deaf to do it. This became evident at the dress rehearsal, which had to be stopped repeatedly because Beethoven could not follow the singers or the orchestra, much less coordinate the entire production.

Schindler wrote:

> The impossibility of continuing under the direction of the creator of the work was obvious. But who was to tell him, and how? Neither the manager, Duport, nor [*Kapellmeister* Ignaz] Umlauf wanted to have to say, "It cannot be done. Go away, you unhappy man!" Beethoven, now growing apprehensive, turned from one side to another, searching the faces to see what was interrupting the rehearsal. All were silent. Then he called me to him. I stepped to his side in the orchestra and he handed me his notebook, motioning me to write down what was wrong. I wrote as fast as I could something like, "Please don't go on. I'll explain at home." He jumped down on to the floor and said only: "Let's get out of here." Without stopping he hastened to his apartment in Pfarrgasse in the suburb of Laimgrube. Once there he threw himself on the sofa, covered his face with his hands, and remained so until we went to dinner. During the meal he did not say a word; his whole demeanor bespoke depression and defeat. After dinner, when I wished to go, he asked me not to leave him until theater time. When I left him, he asked me to go with him the next day to see Dr. Smetana, his physician at the time, a man who had gained a reputation in ailments of the ear.[59]

We may doubt whether Beethoven turned to Schindler for help at the rehearsal. Wilhelmine Schröder-Devrient, who sang the role of Leonore, wrote years later that "*Kapellmeister* Umlauf had to perform the heart-rending task of pointing out to [Beethoven] that the opera could not be given under his direction." But Schröder-Devrient apparently was not on stage during the crucial scene, the opening duet between Marzelline and Jaquino. Her version, which she wrote in 1846, states, "I am told that [Beethoven] resigned himself with a melancholy look upwards."[60]

That Schindler was on good terms with Beethoven in those days is evident from an account by Louis Schlösser, who saw Beethoven leaving the second performance of the *Leonore* revival with Schindler and Stephan von Breuning.[61]

We may doubt whether Beethoven begged Schindler not to leave him alone after dinner on that painful day. We may doubt whether Beethoven asked Schindler to accompany him to the ear doctor. And we may doubt whether Beethoven lay grief-stricken on his couch, hands covering his face, after his public humiliation. But why would Schindler invent such a tale about his hero? There is little reason to doubt this glimpse into the suffering that Beethoven endured, on a daily basis, because of his deafness.

Clearly, both Schindler and Fanny Burney were liars. Both acted from vanity. Historians would be better off today had both aging authors been free of this vice. That Schindler is the more vilified character is probably due to the greater distance, in talent and in historical interest, between Schindler and Beethoven than there is between Fanny Burney and her father.

Fanny Burney could not bear to reveal the truth about her father and the family from which she came, so she presented Charles Burney, inaccurately, as a saintly being. The most charitable interpretation about Schindler must be that he did try to tell the truth about Beethoven—but could not do so about himself.

In the end, Schindler appears a pathetic figure, whom Beethoven, between insults, occasionally felt obligated to protect. "[D]on't indulge in gossip at his expense, for it might injure him," Beethoven instructed his nephew. "Indeed he is sufficiently punished by being *what he is*."[62]

Beethoven was right. Schindler has been exposed, and though it took more than a century to do it, there is nothing to be gained by dancing on his grave. McArdle, too, was correct when he pointed out that despite Schindler's vanity and fabrications, the man saved more authentic material from Beethoven's life than anyone else. Regardless of how many conversation books Schindler altered or destroyed, or why he did it, no one else thought of saving them at all.

Beethoven's Noble Friends

Beethoven's relationships with his noble sponsors were notoriously difficult. He had to be physically restrained from braining Prince Lichnowsky with a chair; he called a count a "swine" and ordered his pupil Carl Ries to stop playing in the count's presence, ruining the evening in an aristocrat's salon; he called his good friend Prince Lobkowitz an "ass;" he refused to play for Countess Thun, though she begged him on her knees; he told his student Carl Czerny that he had refused to play for the King of Prussia because "he did not want to play for his crowd."[63]

Even before he gained continental renown, Beethoven was known as a haughty fellow. In 1799, a review in the *Allgemeine Musikalische Zeitung* compared his piano playing with that of a challenger, Joseph Wolfll. The reviewer preferred Wolfll for polish and execution, but Beethoven for improvisation and imagination, and added: "That Wolffl likewise enjoys an advantage because of his amiable bearing, contrasted with the somewhat haughty pose of Beethoven, is very natural."[64] This was before the great symphonies, before the "heroic" style that conquered the world, and before all the misunderstandings caused by Beethoven's deafness and his withdrawal from society.

Yet as a young man in Bonn, Beethoven was "gentle and lovable," said a woman who lived upstairs in the same house when she was a little girl. A prince's chaplain who spent two days with Beethoven in 1791 called him "the dear, good Bethofen." The chaplain, Carl Ludwig Junker, added:

> The greatness of this amiable, light-hearted man, as a virtuoso, may in my opinion be safely estimated from his almost inexhaustible wealth of ideas, the altogether characteristic style of expression in his playing, and the great execution which he displays. . . . Even the members of this remarkable orchestra are, without exception, his admirers, and all ears when he plays. Yet he is exceedingly modest and free from all pretension.[65]

Beethoven in Bonn—amiable, light-hearted, modest, gentle, and lovable—does not sound like the Beethoven known to history. Could it be that Beethoven's character was changed by associating with the idle and sometimes vicious aristocracy of Vienna? This is not meant to excuse Beethoven's often inexcusable behavior, or to cast him in a soft light by comparing him with men who were worse by nature, inclination, and opportunity. But Beethoven remained naïve, unsophisticated, and idealistic until the end of his life. Exposed to a ruling class for whom adultery was normal, some of whom bought young girls outright from their parents for sexual pleasure, surely some of Beethoven's famous resentment could have sprung from knowledge of the lives of his social betters.

Lewis Lockwood describes Beethoven's sponsors as "a relatively enlightened subset of the larger aristocratic population." Lockwood continues:

> Looking outward from the hollow shells of their lives to their own dreams, the music lovers among them could see in the young Beethoven an artistic commitment they could never emulate. Here was a musician totally bound to the values and necessities of his art who would stand as far apart as he could from their carefully organized lives of social pleasantry while he shamelessly used their wealth and status as springboards to his own career. Inevitably he harbored ill-concealed anger at them, at himself, and at his need to accept their largesse while struggling to free himself from the servitude that had been the lot of musicians from time immemorial.[66]

This goes a long way toward explaining why Beethoven would admit social callers from the revolutionary French army even as France was at war with Austria. Napoleon was destroying the feudal order, and with it the princelings from whom Beethoven earned his living. Beethoven put himself in an equivocal position with his noble Austrian sponsors by associating on friendly terms with the French general Jean Baptiste Bernadotte. That equivocal position was replicated, throughout his life, by Beethoven's relationship with his noble friends and sponsors, the heirs of a feudal order that Beethoven despised, but in whose upper reaches he felt he belonged, and from which he earned his living.

Beethoven's political beliefs have been the subject of endless contention. He bridled at any restraint upon personal freedom, but far from being a democrat by nature, he considered himself an aristocrat by virtue of his talent. Beethoven moved in the highest levels of Viennese society, and his politics—as all politics in the Habsburg empire, or in any feudal society—could not be divorced from personal relations. Despite Beethoven's protestations of the "purity" of his sentiments, there is nothing pure about politics, or about the personal relations of a commoner with a hereditary ruling class.

Many of Beethoven's sponsors were far from honorable men. Princess Lulu Thurheim described Prince Karl Lichnowsky as a whoremonger, "a cynical degenerate and a shameless coward." Lichnowsky's wife supposedly had to disguise herself as a prostitute in a bordello to receive her husband's favors, and she insisted upon raising, educating, and leaving her fortune to a girl whom she was convinced was her husband's bastard. Princess Lichnowsky was faithful to her husband, though Countess Thurheim told Carl Czerny that he "deserved to be cuckolded."[67]

Count Johann Georg von Browne-Camus, to whom Beethoven dedicated four pieces, plus three more to his wife, was, in the words of his tutor, "one of the strangest men, full of excellent talents and beautiful qualities of heart and spirit . . . (but) full of weakness and depravity." Browne blew "the large income from his properties in Livonia" through "squander and dissipation," which may have contributed to his being institutionalized for several months in 1805. Beethoven refused to see his pupil Ferdinand Ries in the summer of 1802 because Ries was associating with Count Browne, who was "indulging himself with pleasures, in which . . . I was taking part," Ries wrote.[68]

The bankruptcies or deaths in poverty of Beethoven's financial supporters Count Ferdinand Waldstein, Count Moritz Fries, and Prince Franz Joseph Lobkowitz cannot be attributed solely to profligacy and dissipation—Austria suffered years of economic crisis during the Napoleonic wars—but profligacy and dissipation were traits of the ruling class. The young Beethoven's first great noble sponsor, Archduke Maximilian Franz, Elector of Cologne, shared a mistress with his finance minister, Kaspar Anton von Belderbusch, who fathered her children, and, says Thayer, "this mistress was the Countess Caroline von Satzenhofen, Abbess of Vilich!"[69]

Haydn's sponsor, Prince Nicolaus II Esterházy—who commissioned a Mass from Beethoven and disparaged it to the composer's face—bought girls from their parents to satisfy his lust. Esterházy kept a hidden, frescoed "temple of debauchery," reached through a revolving fireplace, with a secret escape door, and "two Egyptian pillars which turn out to be, respectively, a gigantic penis and a female sex organ." The most notorious of the noble rakehells was Esterházy's fellow, though lesser prince, Aloys Prince zu Kaunitz-Rieberg. Kaunitz, who bought one of the daughters of Haydn's longtime copyist and servant, Johann Elssler, "seduced numbers of girls in a systematic, business-like fashion by making contracts with the girl's parents," for which he was tried and exiled. Kaunitz's purchase of the Elssler girl was revealed during his trial, during which "Kaunitz plaintively said that there were others who did such seductions on the grand scale, such as Esterházy," who, we may assume, was more circumspect.

Citing a pamphlet on the Kaunitz trial printed for private circulation, H. C. Robbins-Landon says, "Kaunitz used the children's ballet as a rich source, and Haydn must have seen—and at least in one case under his very nose—how the *Hochwohlgeborner Reichsfürst und Herr Herr* bought a child from the Tomasini family." Luigi Tomasini, the girl's father, was Haydn's concertmaster. Robbins-Landon concludes, "If Kaunitz became infamous because his case was brought to trial and he was expelled from the country, Esterházy's was just as well known to the *cognoscenti* and of course to the Eisenstadt musicians, including their old *Capellmeister* Haydn."[70]

It should be no surprise then that Beethoven had, at best, ambivalent feelings about his noble sponsors, and that the impatient and ungovernable composer sometimes treated them with the contempt he felt they deserved. Nor could it have helped that these men mistreated their wives, while Beethoven could not get a wife. Despite his occasional visits to bordellos in his middle age, of which he felt ashamed, Beethoven was a bit of a prude about women. He said he could not have written an opera upon *Don Giovanni* because "art, which is sacred, should never be degraded to serve as a pretext for so scandalous a subject." He "broke off his once familiar intercourse with a distinguished composer and conductor of Vienna, as hardly to return his greetings with common politeness" because the man had gone to bed with another man's wife. He refused to play piano for Magdalena Hofdemel because he believed the rumors that she had been Mozart's mistress, then played for her reluctantly and "only by the urgent solicitations of the Czerny family," with whom she was staying. And when his dining companions one evening secretly encouraged a waitress to flirt with him, Beethoven "received her advances and familiarities with repellent coldness," and when she persisted he "put an end to her importunities with a smart box on the ear."[71]

The list of Beethoven's frustrated loves is a long one: Magdalena Willman and Therese Malfatti—both of whom rejected offers of marriage, Countess Giulietta Guicciardi, Countess Josephine Deym née Brunsvik, Julie von Vering, Countess Marie Erdödy, Antonie Brentano, and others. Beethoven's lifelong friend Franz Wegeler wrote that "in Vienna Beethoven was always involved in a love affair, at least as long as I lived there, and sometimes made conquests which could have been very difficult indeed, if not impossible, for many an Adonis."[72] But Beethoven arranged, consciously or not, to fall in love only with unattainable women. Maynard Solomon has proved beyond reasonable doubt that his famous Immortal Beloved was Antonie Brentano—a married woman.[73] And Beethoven was unable to maintain a friendship with men without quarreling, unless they never saw one another, as with Karl Amenda and his boyhood friend Franz Wegeler.

Beethoven had an idealized conception of women that would inevitably be spoiled by any long-term relationship. "When once I teased him about his conquest of a certain beautiful lady," Ferdinand Ries wrote, "he confessed that she had captivated him more intensely and longer than any other—seven whole months." Beethoven compensated for his frustrations in classic fashion, writing in a conversation book, "And if I had wished to give my vital powers with that life, what would have remained for the nobler, the better?"[74]

Beethoven wanted a spiritual and intellectual companion as well as a lover. "Sensual gratification without a spiritual union is and remains bestial, afterwards one has no trace of noble feeling but rather remorse," he wrote in his private journal, reflecting, no doubt, upon one of his visits to a bordello. After repeated rejections, the aging composer finally abandoned any hope of love. Maynard Solomon points out that of the 870 letters preserved from the last eight years of Beethoven's life, only seven were to women, five of them to women in whom he could have had no romantic interest.[75]

But his friends knew that to appeal to Beethoven's better nature, to persuade him to do what he would rather not, required a woman. When Prince and Princess Lichnowsky and a host of friends, including Gerhard von Breuning, the poet Heinrich von Collin, and cast members from the original version of Beethoven's opera gathered at Lichnowsky's palace to persuade the composer of the necessity of cutting some scenes, Beethoven refused for hours to cut a single note. Not until after midnight did he yield at last, in tears, to the pleas of Princess Lichnowsky, who asked him to do it for her sake, and for the memory of his mother.[76]

Historians have shown unrelenting interest in the question of whether Beethoven contracted a venereal disease. Almost surely he did, but the undying interest in this question reveals more about historians than it does about Beethoven. Thayer is circumspect:

> Spending his whole life in a state of society in which the vow of celibacy was by no means a vow of chastity; in which the parentage of a cardinal's or archbishop's children was neither a secret nor a disgrace; in which the illegitimate offspring of princes and magnates were proud of their descent and formed upon it well-grounded hopes of advancement and success in life; in which the moderate gratification of the sexual was no more discountenanced than the satisfying of any other natural appetite—it is nonsense to suppose, that, under such circumstances, Beethoven could have puritanic scruples on that point. Those who have had occasion and opportunity to ascertain the facts, know that he had not, and are also aware that he did not always escape the common penalties of transgressing the laws of strict purity.[77]

Thayer "had occasion and opportunity to ascertain the facts," and surely would have cleared Beethoven of what the Victorians considered a vice, were it possible. But Beethoven did not have syphilis, or if he did, it mysteriously vanished rather than progressing to the tertiary stage, as it did for the unfortunate Franz Schubert. (The distinction between gonorrhea and syphilis was not made until ten years after Beethoven was dead, by Philippe Ricord, chief surgeon of the Hôpital du Midi for syphilitics in Paris.)[78] Beethoven's contraction of a venereal disease may explain this sad entry in his *Tagebuch*, which Thayer dates to late 1812—after the brief affair with the Immortal Beloved:

> Submission, absolute submission to your fate, only this can give you the sacrifice . . . to the servitude—Oh, hard struggle!—Turn everything which remains to be done to planning the long journey—you must yourself find all that your most blessed wish can offer, you must force it to your will—keep always of the same mind. . . . *Thou mayest no longer be a man*, not for thyself, only for others, *for thee there is no longer happiness except* in thyself, *in thy art*—O God, give me strength to conquer myself, nothing must chain me to life. Thus everything connected with A will go to destruction.[79]

Beethoven's illness reveals much more about the anguish with which he lived than it reveals about his presumed moral state. Living with this disease, one more illness among the many with which he was afflicted, was just another difficulty in a life of forced isolation and often unremitting sadness, from which Beethoven could find relief only by work.[80]

What are we to think of such an unhappy man? Beethoven was a strange and stubborn personality, awkward physically and awkward in society. But the many records left by people who knew him, or visited him, show that Beethoven cared about other people, and thought it was important to be kind to them, even if he often could not do it, and even if they were craven toadies such as Schindler. As early as 1799 he was regarded as haughty, and as his deafness, estrangement from society, and eccentricities increased he was thought to be churlish, unsociable, ill-tempered, and even crazy. Yet time after time, people who were strangers to him sought him out and reported that he treated them with kindness and went out of his way to help them, even when he was old and sick—among them Johann Tomaschek, Cipriani Potter, Maurice Schlesinger, Gioacchino Rossini, Friedrich Rochlitz, Louis Schlosser, Edward Schulz, Carl Maria von Weber, Ludwig Rellstab, and George Smart.[81]

Beethoven was short-tempered and violent. He tried to interfere in the marriages of both of his brothers, called their wives sluts and whores, and got into fistfights with his brothers even in their middle age.[82] Yet he was capable of writing this about a man who had married a woman Beethoven wanted: "He was always my enemy, and that's why I was always as good to him as possible."[83] Five days after writing to his Immortal Beloved that their love was "truly founded in heaven—and, what is more, as strongly cemented as the firmament of Heaven," Beethoven asked his publisher in Leipzig to send some music to Amalie Sebald, "a charming young lady in Berlin . . . we are very fond of her," and he followed that up with nine letters to Sebald that summer, some of them love letters.[84] He hated his sister-in-law Johanna with a violent contempt, yet arranged to send her money secretly when she was ill, so long as she would not know where it came from, and he gallantly added, "I shall make a point of persuading my pigheaded brother also to contribute something to help her."[85]

Very few artists can be compared with Beethoven—Homer and Shakespeare, perhaps Michelangelo. History is full of great artists who were miserable human beings: Brahms, Debussy, Hemingway, Stravinsky, and Picasso were great artists, but as human beings, they ranged from unpleasant to unkind to despicable. Beethoven was not the most pleasant of men. It is not his professed love of mankind that set him apart from the other artists as men—love is easy to profess—but that Beethoven thought that an artist, no matter how great, also had a responsibility to try to be a decent human being. Modest though that claim may be, it unfortunately is necessary to say, and history is full of artists about whom it cannot be truly said.

Beethoven could not live up to his ideals. But with very little formal education, he tried throughout his life to improve himself intellectually, in a time that did not expect it of him and would not reward him for it. "I have not the slightest pretension to what is properly called erudition," he wrote. "Yet from my childhood I have striven to understand *what the better and wiser people* of every age were driving at in their works. Shame on an artist who does not consider it his duty to achieve at least as much."[86]

In his book *The Mozart Myths*, William Stafford warns, "The reader must . . . avoid the mistake of trying to find a perfectly coherent and consistent personality. . . . All too often the author goes imaginatively beyond the evidence, in an attempt to reconstruct an inner core of personal identity unifying the moments of the life. Real people are not like that."[87]

Notes

1. Lewis Lockwood, *Beethoven: The Music and the Life* (New York: Norton, 2003), 6.

2. Commenting upon Beethoven's deafness, the neurologist Oliver Sacks wrote, "Deliberate, conscious, voluntary mental imagery involves not only auditory and motor cortex, but regions of the frontal cortex involved in choosing and planning. Such deliberate mental imagery is clearly crucial to professional musicians—it saved the creative life and sanity of Beethoven after he had gone deaf and could no longer hear any music other than that in his mind. (It is possible, indeed, that his musical imagery was even intensified by deafness, for with the removal of normal auditory input, the auditory cortex may become hypersensitive, with heightened powers of musical imagery.)" Sacks, *Musicophilia* (New York: Knopf, 2007), 33-34. Sacks' parenthetical sentence, if valid, could help explain why Beethoven's late music became increasingly cerebral. If Beethoven was forced to use different brain areas than hearing composers use, or different percentages of brain areas were involved during the creative process, it might have contributed to making his music more intellectual—based more upon "choosing and planning" than upon pure sensuality. Not that that explains the late quartets or the *Grosse Fuge*.

3. F. M. Scherer, *Quarter Notes and Bank Notes* (Princeton, N.J.: Princeton University Press, 2004), 122-126. In Scherer's charts, "Composer births per million population, by 50-year birth-date period," and "Number of composers employed by nation and national groups," Bohemia is represented by modern Czechoslovakia.

4. *Oxford English Dictionary*, Compact Edition, Vol. I (New York: Oxford University Press, 1971), 968 for "Bohemian," 173-174 for "Gipsy." The 1762 edition of the *Dictionnaire de l'Académie française* defines *Bohème, ou Bohémien, Bohémienne*, in part, as *"une sorte de vagabonds que courent le pays . . . On dit familièrement d'une maison où il n'y a ni ordre ni règle, que 'C'est une maison de Bohème.'"*

5. O. E. Deutsch, *The Schubert Reader: A Life of Franz Schubert in Letters and Documents* (New York: Norton, 1947), 300.

6. Emily Anderson, *The Letters of Mozart and His Family* (London: Macmillan, 1989), 764.

7. Franz Wegeler and Ferdinand Ries, *Beethoven Remembered* (Arlington, Va.: Great Ocean Publishers, 1987), 99-100.

8. In his biography of music historian Charles Burney, Roger Lonsdale described Burney's lapse of manners with King George III in 1786: "[I]n his excitement and ignorance of the correct ritual, Burney replied in a very informal manner, taking it upon himself to direct much of the conversation—'that was always thought high treason,' according to Walpole—and eagerly following the King around the room instead of keeping his distance and speaking only when addressed." Roger Lonsdale, *Dr. Charles Burney* (Oxford: Oxford University Press, 1965), 331.

9. Oscar Sonneck, *Beethoven: Impressions by His Contemporaries* (New York: Dover, 1967), 20-21.

10. H. C. Robbins-Landon, *Haydn: Chronicle and Works, Vol. I: Haydn at Esterháza 1766-1790* (Bloomington: Indiana University Press, 1978), 270.

11. Alessandra Comini, *The Changing Image of Beethoven: A Study in Mythmaking* (New York: Rizzoli, 1987), 17, 51, 186.

12. Sonneck, *Beethoven: Impressions by His Contemporaries*, 145-146.

13. H. C. Robbins-Landon, *Beethoven: A Documentary Study* (New York: Macmillan, 1970), 325-326; and Alexander W. Thayer, *Thayer's Life Of Beethoven*, ed. Elliot Forbes (Princeton, N.J.: Princeton University Press, 1973), 851.

14. Emily Anderson, ed., *The Letters of Beethoven* (New York: Macmillan, 1961), 266-267, 274, 276.

15. Anderson, *Letters of Beethoven*, 268-269.

16. Anderson, *Letters of Beethoven*, 269.

17. Thayer-Forbes, *Thayer's Life Of Beethoven*, 232, 244; and Wegeler-Ries, *Beethoven Remembered*, 107.

18. Agatha Fassett, *The Naked Face of Genius: Béla Bartók's American Years* (New York: Riverside Press, 1958), 117.

19. Thayer-Forbes, *Thayer's Life Of Beethoven*, 620.

20. Sonneck, *Beethoven: Impressions by His Contemporaries*, 158.

21. Sonneck, *Beethoven: Impressions by His Contemporaries*, 20-21.

22. Anderson, *Letters of Beethoven*, 227.

23. Robbins-Landon, *Beethoven: A Documentary Study*, 324.

24. Thayer-Forbes, *Thayer's Life Of Beethoven*, 413.

25. Anderson, *Letters of Beethoven*, 1,321.

26. Thayer-Forbes, *Thayer's Life Of Beethoven*, 413.

27. Anderson, *Letters of Beethoven*, 161. A portrait of Marie Bigot appears in George R. Marek, *Beethoven: Biography of a Genius* (New York: Funk & Wagnall's, 1969), 448.

28. Anderson, *Letters of Beethoven*, 162.

29. Anderson, *Letters of Beethoven*, 162-163.

30. Anderson, *Letters of Beethoven*, 163-164.

31. Anderson, *Letters of Beethoven*, 380-381. Anderson believes "H." is Hamburg.

32. Wegeler-Ries, *Beethoven Remembered*, 88-89.

33. Thayer-Forbes, *Thayer's Life Of Beethoven*, 547.

34. Wegeler-Ries, *Beethoven Remembered*, 98.

35. Wegeler-Ries, *Beethoven Remembered*, 97-98.

36. Thayer-Forbes, *Thayer's Life Of Beethoven*, 1,046.

37. Donald W. McArdle, "Anton Felix Schindler, Friend of Beethoven," *Music Review* 24 (1963), 59.

38. Maynard Solomon, *Beethoven* (New York: Schirmer, 1998), xviii.

39. Anton Felix Schindler, *Beethoven As I Knew Him*, ed. Donald W. McArdle, trans. Constance Jolly (New York: Norton, 1972), 21 (hereafter Schindler-McArdle); McArdle, "Anton Felix Schindler, Friend of Beethoven," 50.

40. Schindler-McArdle, *Beethoven As I Knew Him*, 203-204.

41. Schindler-McArdle, *Beethoven As I Knew Him*, 204.

42. Maynard Solomon, *Beethoven Essays* (Cambridge, Mass.: Harvard University Press, 1988), 137.

43. Anderson, *Letters of Beethoven*, 992, 1,080, 1,081, 1,086.

44. McArdle, "Friend of Beethoven," 58.

45. Anderson, *Letters of Beethoven*, 1,041-42.

46. McArdle, "Friend of Beethoven," 58, citing Walter Nohl's article in *Die Musik* 17 (1925).

47. Anderson, *Letters of Beethoven*, 1,124-125.

48. Schindler-McArdle, *Beethoven As I Knew Him*, 23.

49. Thayer-Forbes, *Thayer's Life Of Beethoven*, 730; Solomon, *Beethoven*, xii, 431.

50. Schindler's photograph is reproduced in Comini, *The Changing Image of Beethoven*, 50; Anderson, *Letters of Beethoven*, opposite 1,169; Marek, *Beethoven: Biography of a Genius*, 551; and Editha and Richard Sterba, *Beethoven and His Nephew* (New York: Schocken Books, 1971), opposite 129.

51. McArdle, "Friend of Beethoven," 66-68, citing Heine's review in the *Augsburg Zeitung* of April 29, 1841. Thayer makes, or repeats, the accusation that Schindler "informed the world for many years afterward on his visiting card [that he was] '*L'Ami de Beethoven*,'" in *Thayer's Life Of Beethoven*, 821-822.

52. Memoirs of Robert Hornstein (1833-1890) cited in McArdle, "Friend of Beethoven," 69.

53. Schindler-McArdle, *Beethoven As I Knew Him*, 31.

54. McArdle, "Friend of Beethoven," 58.

55. Lonsdale, *Dr. Charles Burney*, vii, 438-455.

56. Lonsdale, *Dr. Charles Burney*, 131-133.

57. Lonsdale, *Dr. Charles Burney*, 441.

58. Lonsdale, *Dr. Charles Burney*, 440, 451.

59. Schindler-McArdle, *Beethoven As I Knew Him*, 237.

60. Thayer-Forbes, *Thayer's Life Of Beethoven*, 811-812.

61. Sonneck, *Beethoven: Impressions by His Contemporaries*, 134-135; Thayer-Forbes, *Thayer's Life Of Beethoven*, 812.

62. Anderson, *Letters of Beethoven*, 1,083.

63. Thayer-Forbes, *Thayer's Life Of Beethoven*, 135, 307-308, 384, 403; Robbins-Landon, *Beethoven: A Documentary Study*, 64.

64. Thayer-Forbes, *Thayer's Life Of Beethoven*, 205.

65. Thayer-Forbes, *Thayer's Life Of Beethoven*, 63, 105, 315. Thayer interviewed "the widow Karth," who had lived upstairs from the young Beethoven, in 1861.

66. Lockwood, *Beethoven*, 77.

67. Robbins-Landon, *Beethoven: A Documentary Study*, 67.

68. Wegeler-Ries, *Beethoven Remembered*, 104; Thayer-Forbes, *Thayer's Life Of Beethoven*, 76, 212, 296.

69. Thayer-Forbes, *Thayer's Life Of Beethoven*, 17.

70. Robbins-Landon, *Haydn: Chronicle and Works, Vol. IV*, 46-47.

71. Sonneck, *Beethoven: Impressions by His Contemporaries*, 44; Thayer-Forbes, *Thayer's Life Of Beethoven*, 244-245; H. C. Robbins-Landon, *1791: Mozart's Last Year* (New York: Schirmer, 1988), 180.

72. Wegeler-Ries, *Beethoven Remembered*, 43.

73. Solomon, "Antonie Brentano and Beethoven," Chapter 12 in *Beethoven Essays*, 166-189.

74. Wegeler-Ries, *Beethoven Remembered*, 104-105; Thayer-Forbes, *Thayer's Life Of Beethoven*, 290.

75. Maynard Solomon, "Beethoven's *Tagebuch* of 1812-1818," in *Beethoven Studies 3*, ed. Alan Tyson (New York: Norton, 1973), 268; and Solomon, *Beethoven*, 338-339.

76. Sonneck, *Beethoven: Impressions by His Contemporaries*, 260-268.

77. Thayer-Forbes, *Thayer's Life Of Beethoven*, 244-245.

78. Otto Erich Deutsch, *The Schubert Reader: A Life of Franz Schubert in Letters and Documents* (New York: Norton, 1947), 286-287.

79. Thayer-Forbes, *Thayer's Life Of Beethoven*, 549.

80. Francois Martin Mai, in the latest book-length study of Beethoven's health problems, is the first medical authority to state unequivocally that he thinks Beethoven was an alcoholic, and that his years of heavy drinking caused, or precipitated, his death. Mai, *Diagnosing Genius: The Life and Death of Beethoven* (Montreal, McGill-Queen's University Press, 2007), 146-150.

81. Sonneck, *Beethoven: Impressions by His Contemporaries*.

82. Anderson, *Letters of Beethoven*, 1,081. In an Aug. 19, 1823, letter to his brother Johann, Beethoven calls Johann's wife "that former and still active whore," and refers to her and her child as "that loutish fat woman and her bastard." See too Wegeler-Ries, *Beethoven Remembered*, 76, and Thayer-Forbes, *Thayer's Life Of Beethoven*, 551.

83. Thayer-Forbes, *Thayer's Life Of Beethoven*, 290.

84. Anderson, *Letters of Beethoven*, 380, 382, 384-390.

85. Anderson, *Letters of Beethoven*, 1,101, 1,103.

86. Anderson, *Letters of Beethoven*, 246.

87. William Stafford, *The Mozart Myths: A Critical Reassessment* (Stanford, Calif.: Stanford University Press, 1991), 269.

Chapter 4

Music and Meaning

"If you are looking for really profound mysteries, essential aspects of our existence for which neither the sciences nor the humanities provide any sort of explanation, I suggest starting with music," the physician Lewis Thomas wrote in *Late Night Thoughts on Listening to Mahler's Ninth Symphony.*

> The professional musicologists, tremendous scholars all, for whom I have the greatest respect, haven't the ghost of an idea about what music is, or why we make it and cannot be human without it, or even—and this is the telling point—how the human mind makes music on its own, before it is written down and played. The biologists are no help here, nor the psychologists, nor the physicists, nor the philosophers, wherever they are these days. Nobody can explain it. It is a mystery . . . The Brandenburgs and the late quartets . . . carry the news that there are deep centers in our minds that we know nothing about except that they are there.[1]

It is fortunate for humans that music can console us, and that it consoles us for problems that only humans seem to have. Music is so consoling and fascinating and so peculiarly human that people have been trying to explain it for thousands of years. But twenty-five centuries after Pythagoras invested the subject with philosophical seriousness, and essentially invented the discipline of music theory, the experts still do not agree on such basic questions as whether absolute music has meaning; and if so, what it means to say it has meaning; and if not, what *that* means. Here are fifteen other elementary things we don't know about music:

1. Why are such a high percentage of Classical themes eight measures long?
2. Why does virtually every performer end virtually every opening and closing movement of a Baroque, Classical, or Romantic composition with at least a slight *ritard*?
3. Why does ascending through the cycle of fifths create tension, and why does descending through the cycle relax it?
4. Why do we feel tension or relaxation or emotions in response to harmonic progressions at all?
5. Why does it seem necessary to repeat sections of a composition?
6. Why can we comprehend, or follow, only about four musical lines at a time?

7. Why do we call tones high and low, and why do we all agree on which are high and which are low?

8. Why does the combination of high and low tones create the illusion of space? (And if it's true that music stimulates our brains to create the illusion of height and depth because the labyrinth of the inner ear contains the vestibular organ, which orients us to gravity—in other words, gives us a sense of up and down—what, if anything, does that tell us about music?)

9. Why do we generally prefer some vibrato to no vibrato at all, and why and at what point does too much vibrato become annoying?

10. Why do people feel such intense emotional relationships with some pieces of music, and why or how do they derive consolation from it?

11. Why do we call music sad or happy, and why do we nearly all agree on which is sad and which is happy?

12. How does music exist outside of time in our minds?

13. Why do we believe some tunes are beautiful and others are not?

14. Why do we feel that a tempo is right, or effective, and another, nearly identical tempo is not?

15. Why do people make music at all, and why has every human culture ever discovered made music?

It would not be difficult to come up with fifteen more basic things we don't know about music. Fortunately, musicians do not have to know the answer to any of these questions to give an effective performance, nor does the audience need to know the answers. Something is irretrievably lost in translation from music to speech; the translation can never be perfect, and so the subject becomes: What is it that was lost? And the fact that this is not a strictly musical question does not make it any less interesting or important.

When we hear a piece of music that we would like to hear again, it almost surely has appealed to us on at least two levels: our intellect and our emotions. These components of human apprehension—intellectual and emotional—are not "opposites." They coexist and influence one another and are to some extent inextricable, in music and in other human endeavors, try though we may at times to separate them. Many composers in the past century, including Igor Stravinsky, argued that music need not—perhaps does not—have an emotional component. We need not tackle that question now. The distinction between intellect and emotion is to some extent artificial. Yet two books—both excellent, both influential—approached the problem of musical meaning as though these two modes of apprehension were indeed opposite. Leonard Meyer attempted intellectual rigor in *Emotion and Meaning in Music*, whereas Deryck Cooke insisted, in *The Language of Music*, that music "can only express feelings."[2]

"Composers and performers of all cultures, theorists of diverse schools and styles, aestheticians and critics of many different persuasions are all agreed that music has meaning and that this meaning is somehow communicated to both participants and listeners. This much, at least, we may take for granted,"[3] Meyer wrote in the opening sentences of *Emotion and Meaning in Music*, a fine book, which is learned, intelligent, and wrong.

It's not cricket to begin by assuming what one hopes to prove—that music has meaning. And whether Meyer is correct about this or not, he is wrong to say that composers, performers, theorists, aestheticians, and critics "are all agreed." There is no agreement at all on whether music has meaning, beyond the purely musical, or what it would mean for absolute music (music without words) to have meaning. Meyer's book, whose first edition came out in 1956, was written under the baleful influence of behaviorism and information theory, which offered new and apparently scientific ways to be wrong.

To reduce human behavior to measurable phenomena because one wishes to study phenomena that can be measured, and to allow as subjects of scientific inquiry only those terms and behaviors that one can measure and define, will surely produce clean results, but whether the results are meaningful we may be permitted to doubt.

Meyer claims that the listeners' lack of physical response to Western concert music is a major reason for the strong emotional responses it arouses: that because of social norms we do not relate to the music physically, and this "inhibition of a tendency to respond"—which he calls the root of all musical meaning—creates or amplifies the emotional experience.

> [T]he inhibition of a tendency to respond or, on the conscious level, the frustration of expectation was found to be the basis of the affective and the intellectual aesthetic response to music. If this hypothesis is correct, then an analysis of the process of expectation is clearly a prerequisite for the understanding of how musical meaning, whether affective or aesthetic, arises in any particular instance.[4]

This sounds wonderfully, or horribly, scientific, and is provably wrong. If one cranks up the volume and dances like a heathen to the fourth movement of Beethoven's Seventh Symphony, the music does not become less meaningful because one is physically responding to it. We should not be seduced by the terms of science just because they are so unseductive.

Meyer states, correctly, that we derive pleasure from music's arousal of expectations, and from the suspension and eventual fulfillment of those expectations, but he goes too far in claiming that this is the entire reason for the aesthetic pleasure we get from music. As a behaviorist, Meyer was far too ready to accept an "answer" in the terms he invented, or adopted. Information theory allowed him to discuss music in terms such as the ratio of signal to noise, but this brings us no closer to the answer of the difficult question of what it means to say that music has meaning, and what, if anything, this meaning or lack of meaning has to do with our emotional response to music.

"[O]n the whole," Meyer laments, "musical theorists have concerned themselves with the grammar and syntax of music rather than with its meaning or the affective experiences to which it gives rise."[5] But once musical analysis goes beyond the "grammar and syntax of music," it is dealing with realms far beyond music, including psychology, neurology, and all the things and processes that create a culture. Beethoven regarded science and art as the highest forms of human endeavor—"only art and science give us intimations and hopes of a higher life"[6]—but beyond a certain point, it may be as fruitless to expect science to explain music as it would be to expect music to illuminate science. Quasi-scientific explications of music appear to give some people intellectual and perhaps emotional satisfaction, but no one has yet explained satisfactorily why it is that we get a different sort of intellectual and emotional satisfaction from music.

When he was 89 years old, Artur Rubinstein gave a master class at the Manhattan School of Music. After beaming for an hour upon a succession of talented young pianists, Rubinstein arose and said these few words to the packed hall: "You must keep playing music. When people get old, sometimes they get sad, and music is the only thing that can console them. So you must keep playing music."[7]

Surely Rubinstein was right, and surely it is worthwhile exploring how it is that music can console us. But behaviorism and information theory cannot provide the answer. Here Meyer explains how or why we respond to a fugue:

> We have, let us say, a concept of what a fugue is. The concept is not of this or that particular fugue but is based upon our experience of a multitude of fugues. As we listen to a particular fugue we compare its special progress with the progress expected on the basis of our normalized concept of a fugue. Those progressions which seem irregular and unexpected relative to the generalized fugue of our imagination are then the deviants (the delays and resistances) which arouse the affective aesthetic response.[8]

This too is provably wrong. Many years ago, I brought a three-year-old Salvadoran refugee to the United States. Carlos had been separated from his mother for more than a year, and had been subjected to horrible scenes of violence. When we brought him to his new home he was a nervous wreck, even after being reunited with his mother. He had never heard Western Classical music. Yet when I put Glenn Gould playing J. S. Bach on the stereo, Carlos walked up to the speaker, lay down in front of it, and contentedly fell asleep. This worked without fail. It was better than toys, better than food, better than words or kisses. Meyer might say that the first notes that Carlos ever heard of the *Well-Tempered Clavier* were sufficient to give him a normalized concept of a fugue, and to arouse in him expectations that the succeeding notes would occur in certain melodic and harmonic patterns, and that he enjoyed the suspension and eventual fulfillment of his expectations, but I think that's exceedingly doubtful.

In response to the behaviorist mania that then dominated U.S. psychology, Deryck Cooke wrote *The Language of Music* in 1959, three years after Meyer's book was published. Cooke insisted that "music can only express feelings" because "music is the expression of emotion."

> [T]he most articulate language of the unconscious is music. But we musicians, instead of trying to understand this language, preach the virtues of refusing to consider it a language at all; when we should be attempting, as literary critics do, to expound and interpret the great masterpieces of our art for the benefit of

> humanity at large, we concern ourselves more and more with parochial affairs—technical analyses and musicological *minutiae*—and pride ourselves on our detached, de-humanized approach.[9]

The Language of Music was a healthy reaction to the cerebral, sometimes sterile, serialism and a tradition of academic writing that dominated "serious" Western music in the mid-twentieth century. The book is all the more admirable for contradicting the dominant trends of the day's "advanced" musical composers, and the academicians who controlled the appointments in Cooke's field, dominated by theorists far drier than Meyer. Surely it is true that if music did not move human emotions, humans would be far less interested in music. But in insisting that music can be understood only through the emotions, Cooke tried to prove too much, and simultaneously too little, and to do this he employed false dichotomies, exaggerations, and unsupported and unsupportable statements.

It may be true, as Cooke insists, that "the fact that the new music shuns the basic acoustical consonances of the octave, fifth, fourth, and triad, suggests that it does not express the simple fundamental sense of being at one with nature and life."[10] Cooke may be overreaching, or he may be illuminating the obvious, as he "tries to pinpoint the inherent emotional characters of the various notes of the major, minor, and chromatic scales, and of certain basic melodic patterns which have been used persistently throughout our musical history."[11] He reports that "a phrase of two notes (the minor sixth of the scale falling to the fifth) is to be found expressing anguish in music by Josquin [in the 1400s] . . . [through] Bach . . . Mozart . . . Schoenberg . . . [and] Stravinksy."[12] In support of this, Cooke cites works by eleven composers over more than 500 years—Josquin, Morley, J. S. Bach, Mozart, Schubert, Mussorgsky, Verdi, Wagner, Schoenberg, Stravinsky, and Britten. But surely he is overreaching to say that "whereas the minor sixth is an expression of anguish in a context of flux, the minor second is an expression of anguish in a context of finality; in other words, the minor sixth expresses an active anguish, the minor second a hopeless anguish."[13]

Cooke culls the music of six centuries to illustrate similar claims about major and minor seconds, thirds, and sevenths, and the augmented fourth or diminished fifth. He makes an even broader, and far more interesting, claim in discussing the Catholic Church's centuries-long attempt to keep the interval of the third out of sacred music.

> The major triad (and the major scale) belonged to the popular, secular life founded on the desire for pleasure; and this always threatened to undermine the religious ideal of a humble, God-centered existence, in which the emphasis was on the acceptance of one's lot in "this vale of tears," and to replace it by the concept of a proud, man-centered existence, in which the emphasis was on personal happiness.[14]

Cooke claims that due to Western man's tendency toward secularism,

> the center of musical life moved from the church to the opera-house (seventeenth-century) and concert-hall (eighteenth-century), and an increasingly secular society expressed its sense of human pleasure and pain by means of the ma-

> jor and minor systems, regular rhythms, and four-bar periods—until the tide turned. Ever since about 1850—since doubts have been cast, in intellectual circles, on the possibility, or even the desirability, of basing one's life on the concept of personal happiness—chromaticism has brought more and more painful tensions into our art-music, and finally eroded the major system and with it the whole system of tonality.[15]

Cooke goes even further: "Since the new language is unrelievedly chromatic by nature, it must be restricted to expressing what chromaticism always was restricted to expressing—what indeed we feel even the very earliest chromaticism of the sixteenth-century Italians still to this day expresses—emotions of the most painful type."[16] This alienation from "natural" intervals and rhythms was intensified by mid-twentieth century composers' preference for "irregular rhythm . . . meticulously measured down to the last fraction of a beat, so as to assure the maximum irregularity, expressing that modern affliction, a high state of nervous tension."[17]

Cooke's conclusions may be persuasive, but they are limited, needlessly, by his insistence that music is a purely emotional language. No matter how many examples he provides of the "anguish" of a minor sixth resolving to the dominant, this says nothing, and can say nothing, about Beethoven's propensity to modulate to that degree of the scale, and what that means, emotionally or in any other way. Nor is chromatic music necessarily painful, unless the pain includes the prospect of judging a contest of young violinists attempting the *Flight of the Bumblebee*.

Often, Cooke simply substitutes emotional terms for musical ones, and the analysis does not thereby benefit. In analyzing the emotional effects of the fourth degree of the scale, in C major, he writes:

> [I]t is "easy" and indeed "defeatist" to fall into the subdominant; quite possible to stay in the tonic, by "optimistically" insisting on the major seventh (note 15 [in the overtone series]); and extremely "difficult" to rise into the dominant, insisting on the "optimistic" version of note 11 (F sharp) against the "pessimistic" version of it (F natural) and the "defeatist" note 7 (B flat). . . . Functioning in this way, the sharp fourth obviously expresses the same violent longing (upward emotional tension in a major context) as the major seventh, but not in a context of finality; rather in a context of pushing outward and upward, aspiring towards something higher.[18]

In other words, in C major, an F-sharp nudges the music toward the dominant and B-flat pushes it toward the subdominant. Perfectly true. But it is doubtful whether music can be taught, learned, or understood more successfully through Cooke's terms than through the traditional ones. And his purely emotional language is a far from adequate tool to illuminate the large-scale structures that make, for example, Beethoven's late quartets such staggering works of art and intellect.

In his final chapter, "Large Scale Functioning of Musical Language," Cooke insists that large-scale musical form "is nothing more mysterious than the presentation of some general but clearly defined attitude toward existence by the disposition of various terms of emotional expression in a significant order."[19] Even for Beethoven, who rewrote the most basic elements of his compositions more intensely and more often than any other composer in history, Cooke insists,

> [T]his conscious effort was not different in aim from the unconscious one: it merely continued its work and eventually fulfilled its intention—the building up of the right musical form of the composer's emotion. . . . However complex and allusive the form of an expressive musical work may be, it is still simply the means whereby the composer has expressed an emotional attitude towards existence by imposing a meaningful order on expressive terms; and it is the continual failure to recognize this fact that is responsible for our generally ambiguous and fruitless approach to music—which can be summed up as "form is form, and expression is expression, and never the twain shall meet."[20]

Yet that's a self-defeating argument if Cooke insists, as he does, that music can be understood only in emotional terms.

Occasionally, Cooke is simply wrong. For example, he claims "there is no connection between the intellectual-emotional organization of words into coherent statements by means of the logic of verbal syntax, and the intellectual-emotional organization of notes into coherent statements by means of the logic of musical syntax."[21] In fact, Cooke and the behaviorists would agree that it's the human brain that constructs meaning—whatever meaning may be—and the manner in which the brain does this, and, probably, the areas of the brain that do it, are similar for language and for music. And it is ludicrous for Cooke to say that "a theme of the type used in polyphonic music acts very much like a brick or a block of stone (as something of no importance in itself, only useful as raw material to be built into a structure), [but] the thematic material of other types of music—opera, song, symphony—*is* important in itself, being emotionally expressive."[22] This is nonsense, and a cursory glance through *The Well-Tempered Clavier* will prove it. A few pages later, moreover, Cooke spends an entire paragraph demonstrating that a single note "can make an immediate artistic-emotional effect, before other notes or words follow."[23] He claims that the note "A," played by a solo trumpet to begin the Overture to Wagner's *Rienzi*, "is at once beautiful, mysterious, and thrilling," and that it "awakens the emotions of awe and wonder, and a subdued expectancy of heroic events to come."[24] Presumably, it can be all these things because it does not become a fugue subject.

Still, *The Language of Music* is an important and often persuasive book, written in a time that direly needed a defense of the emotional interpretation of music, to combat what Cooke called Igor Stravinsky's "harmful" and "extremist theory" that music is "powerless to express anything at all."[25]

"Try singing the word 'Crucifixus' to the music of Handel's Hallelujah Chorus, or the word 'Hallelujah' to the music of the Crucifixus in Bach's B Minor Mass!" Cooke wrote, and there is no counterargument to this.[26] The problem with Cooke's approach is not that he is utterly wrong—he is not; neither is Meyer—it is that both theorists straitjacket themselves in a doctrine.

Meyer's doctrine, based upon stimulus and response, physical inhibition, logical predictions, and the denial of expectation, raises the question why we can still enjoy music after repeated hearings, even after committing it to memory. Meyer's response is far from persuasive: "We can forget."[27] But this is an escape hatch, not the completion of a theory.

Cooke asks whether we can fairly say that listeners understand, or fail to understand, the Allegretto of Beethoven's Seventh Symphony, because of their emotional reactions to it. "I have found [the Allegretto] leads some people into a pseudo feeling of profound melancholy, while another group takes it for a kind of scurrilous scherzo, and a third for a subdued kind of pastorale. Each group is justified in judging as it does."[28] Yet Cooke concludes, three pages later, that "anyone who conceives a quasi-funeral-march movement [the Allegretto] to be a 'kind of scurrilous scherzo' must be considered emotionally abnormal, (or simply unmusical) to a degree."[29]

Whether Cooke's conclusion is true or not, the nature of his question limits the interest of his answer. Beethoven's music *is* highly emotional; it also is an astounding intellectual creation. It is not a case of "neither the twain shall meet," but that neither of the twain satisfactorily illuminates the nature of the other. A much better question to ask about the Allegretto of Beethoven's Seventh Symphony is whether anyone can distinguish between the melody of the main theme and its harmony. In fact, it is impossible to do this, and that's a far more interesting point, and problem, at any level of musical understanding, than mulling over how the music makes us feel.

Questions involving music and meaning are so wide-ranging that the most fruitful approach must be a multi-disciplinary one.

In another essay in *Late Night Thoughts*, Lewis Thomas wrote:

> Surely, music, along with ordinary language, is as profound a problem for human biology as can be thought of. A few years ago the German government set a large advisory committee to work on the question of what the next Max Planck Institute should be taking on as its scientific mission. The committee worked for a very long time and emerged with the recommendation that the new Max Planck Institute should be dedicated to the problem of music—what music is, why it is indispensable for human existence, what music really means—hard questions like that. The government, in its wisdom, turned down the idea, muttering something in administrative language about relevance, and there the matter rests.[30]

Perhaps we should not blame the German government for questioning why it should spend millions of dollars on nuclear magnetic resonators and neural imaging machines to map brain waves of people listening to Mahler and Mozart when we cannot answer the simplest sort of questions about music. "It all depends, of course, on what we mean by musical thought," Hans Keller wrote in his splendidly cantankerous book *The Great Haydn Quartets*.

> You can think *about* music, which is what musicologists and critics and, alas, most teachers do, or you can *think music* . . . . It is thought *about* music which

> is the real foe of musical thought; at the present stage in the history of interpretation, it has, to a mortally dangerous extent, replaced transitive musical thinking—the capacity to think music in the same natural, spontaneous way the "normal," unmusical human being thinks pictures, words, concepts, terms: the laws of musical logic are best followed without the intervention of the very different laws of conceptual thought.[31]

Thus in a single, accurate blast, Keller dismisses most of "our overflowing, largely superfluous literature on music and its history."[32]

Perhaps the most that a writer of words about music may hope for is to create a really good crutch. Suppose we say that Beethoven expanded the language of tonality by his use of mediant key relations as substitute dominants. And suppose we point out that his Opus 95 String Quartet in F Minor, the *Quartetto Serioso*, requires all of six measures to modulate to the remote key of G-flat—though it doesn't modulate, actually, in the sense of using a retrospectively ambiguous pivot chord to move away from one tonal center toward another; it simply moves up a half step, from F minor to G-flat. Then suppose we say that Beethoven's expansion of tonal architecture helped begin the process of breaking down the system of Classical tonality (though Charles Rosen insists that "the breakdown of tonality" is "a fiction"—that adding resources to a language, be it spoken or musical, does not break the system. "Between Mozart and Schoenberg, what disappeared was the possibility of using large blocks of prefabricated material in music."[33] We have used the phrase "breakdown of tonality" for want of a better one, and because most musicians understand what is meant by it). Musicians may find this discussion interesting, the general reader less so. But what, if anything, does it mean, and can it mean anything beyond the technical language of music?

Most modern theorists would say that's an illegitimate question. They could cite Stravinsky's famous statement:

> [M]usic, by its very nature, is essentially powerless to express anything at all, whether a feeling, an attitude of mind, a psychological mood, [or] a phenomenon of nature . . . . Expression has never been an inherent property of music. That is by no means the purpose of its existence. If, as is nearly always the case, music appears to express something, that is only an illusion and not a reality. It is simply an additional attribute which, by tacit and inveterate agreement, we have lent it, thrust upon it, as a label, a convention—in short, an aspect which, unconsciously or by force of habit, we have often come to confuse with its essential being.[34]

Still, we would have liked to ask Stravinsky why it "is nearly always the case [that] music appears to express something." We also may ask whether Stravinsky, a contrarian bomb-thrower, actually believed what he said. Aaron Copland thought he may not have believed it, that the "intransigent attitude of Stravinsky's may be due to the fact that so many people have tried to read different meanings into so many pieces."[35] Stravinsky's pronouncement, like Cooke's and Meyer's books, are results of carrying one tendency of writing about music—the analytical—to its purely logical, but actually illogical, extreme. However, as the composer Roger Sessions said, "If a musical expression is something unique and untranslatable it does not therefore follow that it is without human significance."[36]

Copland summed it up: "This whole problem can be stated quite simply by asking, 'Is there a meaning to music?' My answer to that would be, 'Yes.' And 'Can you state in so many words what the meaning is?' My answer to that would be, 'No.' Therein lies the difficulty."[37]

Broadly speaking, there are four ways of writing about music. The project of trying to extract some philosophical lessons from music—to determine the meaning of musical meaning—is a fifth category, which is barely about music at all, and which Keller presumably would call a "foe of musical thought."

Composers must, and performers should, learn the grammar and syntax of music, the technical language of how to "speak music." This involves learning a specialized, though small, vocabulary, such as contrary motion, modulation, chord inversions, suspension, appoggiaturas and tone rows, and learning how to hear all this. Learning the metalanguage—the language about musical language—can clarify what it is we are doing when we speak music, when we listen to music or interpret it. Keller would not call this style of writing a foe of musical thought, but a prologue or necessary adjunct to being able to think music.

Keller's foes of musical thought are, first, traditional music history, which includes biography and the traditional histories of styles and influence, such as, for instance, Donald J. Grout's *A History of Western Music*. This category includes thousands of books that study small and smaller portions of the subject, be it the composers of a certain century, or of a particular nation, individual composers or individual works—perhaps a book like this one.

The second foe, even more execrable, we will call the Romantic tradition, in which the historian or critic tries to recreate in the reader the sensations and emotions that the music created in the writer, and to invest the music with philosophical meaning, or to interpret the extra-musical meaning that the critic assures us is in there somewhere. Even highly intelligent writers, such as Sir George Grove and Nobel laureate Romain Rolland, have succumbed to this virus, for which there appears to be no cure. Here is a sample from Grove's book, *Beethoven's Nine Symphonies*, in which the eminent scholar discusses the second movement of Beethoven's Third Symphony:

> Then occurs a passage as of stout resistance, the trumpets and horns appealing against Fate in their loudest tones, and the basses adding a substratum of stern resolution. But it cannot last; the old grief is too strong, the original wail returns, even more hopeless than before, the basses again walk in darkness, the violins and flutes echo their vague tones so as to aggravate them tenfold, and the whole forms a long and terrible picture of gloomy distress.[38]

This is closer to emotional pornography than to musical analysis. This style may be counted on to produce wretched writing of less than no value, even from a musician and critic so eminent as Grove, editor of the indispensable dictionary that bears his name. The finest exponent of this style, E. T. A. Hoffmann, the writer of macabre tales, was one of the most perceptive and earliest literary champions of Beethoven. His review of Beethoven's Fifth Symphony, which appeared in the *Allgemeine Musikalische Zeitung* of July 1810, is justly famous. But the Romantic style of music criticism probably reached its high point in this article, which is to say it's been going downhill since it began.

Hoffmann's articles, however, generally contain a great deal of technical description. Here is an excerpt from his famous article on the Fifth Symphony:

> The first Allegro—2/4 meter in C minor—begins with a principal idea only two measures long, which reappears in many different guises in the course of the movement. In the second measure there is a fermata, followed by a repetition of the principal idea a tone lower, and by another fermata; both times only strings and clarinets . . . . Not even the tonality is yet established; the listener expects E-flat major. The second violin begins again with the principal idea, and in the following measure C, the fundamental note, is played by the cellos and bassoons, while the viola and the first violin, entering in imitation, establish C minor. Finally, these same instruments build the opening idea into a two-measure cell which, repeated three times (the last time with full orchestra) imparts a foreboding of the unknown and the mysterious to the listener's spirit.[39]

This blow-by-blow description of who played what when, a traditional and perhaps necessary element of musical instruction, is of limited value. Virtually everything is lost in the translation of music into words. But Hoffmann felt, correctly, that he needed to present a long, pedestrian exegesis to justify the indulgence in his real purpose, which was to show that the Fifth Symphony "more than any other work of Beethoven, reveals his romanticism in a climactic unfolding which mounts until the end, and draws the listener irresistibly into the wonderful, infinite spirit-kingdom."[40] These forays into the empyrean depend upon Hoffmann's dry analysis to give to his purple prose whatever credibility it may have. It is this sort of dry analysis, combined with the parsing of musical grammar, that forms what Keller would call the third superfluous tendency of writing about music.

This foe of musical thought holds the field today. The analytical style was championed by the nineteenth century's most influential music critic, Eduard Hanslick, who believed that the role of a writer-about-music is to analyze the formal construction of compositions, free of extra-musical associations, though informing them with stylistic or historical comments. This, mixed with comments drawn from traditional history, is the style that has triumphed in modern criticism. It takes many forms, from Charles Rosen's *The Classical Style: Haydn, Mozart, Beethoven*, the finest book written on the subject, enormously learned and thoroughly convincing from beginning to end, to the theories of Heinrich Schenker, whose influential book, *Der freie Satz*, Roger Sessions described, wonderfully, as "difficult . . . repulsive and sterile," full of "obvious self-adulation" and "pseudo-philosophical assumptions which . . . are in the most self-revealing manner the outcome of his personal frustrations and fantasies. His megalomania alienates even the patient and open-minded reader by its constant effort, a tendency all too frequent in contemporary German writing, not to convince or illuminate, but to intimidate."[41] Both Rosen, whose book was first published in 1971, and Sessions, who reviewed Schenker's book in 1938, used musical analysis to illuminate subjects far afield from music, though Rosen confined himself more closely to purely musical matters.

There is a fifth, and recent, tendency in writing about music, the scientific. This approach uses neurology, experimental science, and advances in brain-imaging technology in a grand attempt to decipher how the mind works as it listens to music. The objects of study are the mental processes of the listening brain—what sort of music the brain listens to is of secondary importance. Earlier attempts at constructing a psychology of music produced some practical results with praiseworthy goals—teaching or therapy—but the science underlying the practical results was beset with problems—including whether it was truly science at all.[42] However, in the past two decades, scientists using sophisticated brain-scanning devices have been able to identify specific areas of the brain that "process" music, and that presumably decode or create or assign to music whatever meanings or emotions we associate with it. Dr. Daniel Levitin, a recording engineer turned neuroscientist, reports that when researchers asked people to remember a piece of music, the act of remembering—whatever that is—activated the same brain areas, though not quite as intensely, as were activated by the act of listening to the music. Levitin reports that "trying to follow along with music that you know" involves our "memory center" in the hippocampus, and the inferior frontal cortex; that keeping rhythm in one's mind involves "the cerebellum's timing circuits"; that performing music requires the motor cortex in the parietal lobe and the sensory cortex; that reading music involves the visual cortex in the occipital lobe; and that listening to or recalling lyrics recruits Broca's and Wernicke's areas "as well as other language centers in the temporal and frontal lobes."[43]

Oliver Sacks' book, *Musicophilia: Tales of Music and the Brain*, is full of the wondrous, bewildering, and illuminating case histories for which Sacks is justly famous, including the tale of a 68-year-old man with no musical training who suddenly began composing Classical music while suffering from the early stages of frontotemporal dementia. "He continued composing even when his loss of language and other cognitive skills became severe."[44] The biology of music is a worthwhile and exciting topic, but it remains to be seen whether, and to what extent, neuroscience can inform us about music and musical questions, including the question of what it means to say that music does or does not have meaning.

The specialization required for the scientific study of the listening, or creating, musical brain must necessarily restrict the inquirer from the broader, farther fields that inspired the specialized neurological studies. The question "Does music have meaning?" may not be a properly scientific question. The answer, if there is an answer, almost surely lies beyond, or apart from, the realm of neurology. An interesting approach is offered by evolutionary linguistics.

Music Is an Evolved Trait

Consider the dog—any dog—whose sense of smell is superior to any human's, by several levels of magnitude. When the subject is aromas, the greatest flavor chemist or perfume manufacturer on Earth is an idiot compared to the average dog. A dog's sense of smell so far exceeds our own that when humans speak of aromas we have no concept whatsoever of the level of intelligence the average dog brings to the subject. A dog's sense of hearing, too, is more acute than any human's, covering a greater range of sounds and with greater sensitivity. But the dog is a musical idiot. Dogs show no interest in music, and so long as it is neither too loud nor too high, seem neither attracted nor repelled by it. The human sense of music exceeds a dog's as greatly as a dog's sense of aroma exceeds ours.

This is because a dog's sense of smell helps it survive. Music has no survival value for a dog, so the species never evolved an ability to interpret it, beyond simple learned associations such as drums or horns might mean a hunt. Humans' sense of hearing does have survival value, in itself and because it involves our ability to use logic and language, to calculate, to remember, and to predict. Music stimulates all these brain functions, and probably developed along with them. It is the human brain that not only makes music, but that makes it fascinating. Music recruits complex areas of the human brain—and logic and language have great survival value for humans.

Though humans' musical abilities almost certainly evolved along with our senses of language and logic, there is no physical record that can be unearthed to prove this. Humans are fascinated by music not because we hear better than other animals, but because music recruits more areas of the human brain—particularly areas that handle language and logic—than it does of other animals' brains. Because there is no physical record of this evolution, the arguments for it must of necessity be logical or analogical ones. The proposition can be proved fairly conclusively, but the approach must be multidisciplinary.

Logic and language have far greater survival value for humans than these talents do for other animals. And it is because music stimulates these areas in the human brain—areas that are not as well developed in other animals—that humans' musical abilities have evolved so far beyond those of other species. In other words, it is the human brain that not only makes music, but that makes it fascinating.

But the scientific study of music—including the psychology of music—has lagged far behind allied disciplines for a number of reasons. Most research in the psychology of music, as we have said, has been devoted toward the practical aims of teaching or therapy. But music involves so many areas of the brain and of human activity that any attempt to confine its study within a narrow discipline is bound to fail. And once an academic discipline expands to include—as the study of music must—cultural anthropology, mathematics, acoustics, biology, physics, linguistics, neurology, and art history—the academician gets nervous, and with good reason. But music is a deep subject, and, at the risk of offending a few professors, we must insist that the results obtained thus far from the psychology of music have been mostly of academic interest. There is no way other than a multidisciplinary one to study the concept of musical meaning in its wider sense—in the sense beyond musical grammar and purely musical form.

Fortunately, evolutionary linguists have prepared the way for this. Evolutionary linguistics itself began evolving as a discipline only in the late 1980s, after Noam Chomsky had dominated the field for a generation, with his theory that grammar is an innate ability of the human brain, a biological and neurological process or processes that give us the ability to transform a limited number of sounds into infinite meaningful sentences. We believe that most of the conclusions of evolutionary linguistics can be applied fruitfully to music.

In 1990, Steven Pinker and Paul Bloom, both of the Department of Brain and Cognitive Sciences at the Massachusetts Institute of Technology, proposed that humans' language ability evolved through natural selection, just as other animals' senses evolved, including animal talents such as "echolocation in bats or stereopsis in monkeys." In their influential paper, "Natural Language and Natural Selection," Pinker and Bloom wrote: "All human societies have language. As far as we know they always did; language was not invented by some groups and spread to others like agriculture or the alphabet."[45] This also is true of music. So too is virtually every aspect of human language, as Pinker and Bloom describe it.

> All languages are complex computational systems employing the same basic kinds of rules and representations, with no notable correlation with technological progress: the grammars of industrial societies are no more complex than the grammars of hunter-gatherers; Modern English is not an advance over Old English. Within societies, individual humans are proficient language users regardless of intelligence, social status, or level of education. Children are fluent speakers of complex grammatical sentences by the age of three, without benefit of formal instruction. They are capable of inventing languages that are more systematic than those they hear, showing resemblances to languages that they have never heard, and they obey subtle grammatical principles for which there is no evidence in their environments. Disease or injury can make people linguistic savants while severely retarded, or linguistically impaired with normal intelligence. Some language disorders are genetically transmitted. Aspects of language skill can be linked to characteristic regions of the human brain. The human vocal tract is tailored to the demands of speech, compromising other functions such as breathing and swallowing. Human auditory perception shows complementary specializations toward the demands of decoding speech sounds into linguistic segments.[46]

Pinker rather notoriously believes that music is only "auditory cheesecake," an "evolutionary accident piggybacking on language," but with only a few word substitutions, his description of language accurately describes music. Children in all societies rapidly become fluent "speakers" of music, regardless of their ability to read or write music. They acquire this talent at an early age, without formal instruction. They invent melodies that they have never heard, and they obey musical principles of which they are unaware, such as beginning or ending on the tonic, and following a melodic leap by contrary stepwise motion. Disease or injury have impaired people's musical abilities, and have made some people musical savants.[47] Musical talent appears to be heritable. Aspects of musical skill can be linked to specific areas of the human brain. (The weakest musical parallel to Pinker's and Bloom's eleven aspects of language is the first one. Beethoven's music surely is more "complex" and "advanced" than the music of Classical Greece. Yet it evolved from the scales and the unequal divisions of the octave that the Greeks discovered. But even if we discard this parallel, that leaves ten of eleven defining, fundamental aspects that music shares with language. And this parallel cannot be wholly discarded, for even though Beethoven's music is more complex harmonically and structurally than ethnic music, the bar line and tempered intonation impose rhythmic and melodic restrictions on Western Classical music that are not imposed upon ethnic music, as the field work of, among others, Béla Bartók and Zoltan Kodály showed, and as any student of the microtonal music of American Indians will assert.)

These are not the only parallels between music and language.

Descriptive linguistics traditionally broke down language into syntax, phonetics, and semantics. A descriptive science of absolute music could do the same. Absolute music has richer phonetics than spoken language, and probably a richer syntax, but it has no semantic dimension—though Richard Wagner tried to give it a sort of semantics with his use of the leitmotif, which actually constricts the language of music rather than expands it (as Roger Sessions explains, below).

Pinker's and Bloom's proposal for a science of evolutionary linguistics brought a feeling of liberation to many linguists. Chomsky, the most influential linguist of his generation, had always championed the idea that language has not evolved, but is innate. Faced with the warm reception of Pinker's and Bloom's paper, Chomsky refined his definition of human language, calling it a presumably unique system that includes "recursion"—the ability to embed phrases inside one another, and to understand such constructions: for example, "The professor the students like hit the boy dunking the book in the fountain inside the library." Music, however, particularly Western Classical music, also has a wonderful ability to embed phrases inside one another. One need only think of the fugues of J. S. Bach, or Beethoven's use of a fugue theme in diminution over the same fugue in augmentation in the bass, as in the fugal finale of the Opus 110 Piano Sonata in A-Flat.[48]

The point is not that language and musical are identical, but that music possesses virtually all the elements of language—except semantics.

After they described the elements of language, Pinker and Bloom continued:

> It would be natural, then, to expect everyone to agree that human language is the product of Darwinian natural selection. The only successful account of the origin of complex biological structure is the theory of natural selection, the view that the differential reproductive success associated with heritable variation is the primary organizing force in the evolution of organisms. But surpris-

> ingly, this conclusion is contentious. Noam Chomsky, the world's best-known linguist, and Stephen Jay Gould, the world's best-known evolutionary theorist, have repeatedly suggested that language may not be the product of natural selection, but a side effect of other evolutionary forces such as an increase in overall brain size and constraints of as-yet unknown laws of structure and growth. . . .
>
> In this paper we will examine this position in detail, and will come to a very different conclusion. We will argue that there is every reason to believe that language has been shaped by natural selection as it is understood within the orthodox "synthetic" or "neo-Darwinian" theory of evolution. In one sense our goal is incredibly boring. All we argue is that language is no different from other complex abilities such as echolocation or stereopsis, and that the only way to explain the origin of such abilities is through the theory of natural selection. . . .
>
> In the final section, we refute the arguments that have claimed that an innate specialization for grammar is incompatible with the tenets of a Darwinian account and thus that the two are incompatible.[49]

Music may stimulate the human brain, at times, even more powerfully than language, not only because of its rhythmic element, and its appeal to the body, but precisely *because* music has no semantic dimension. (Though how this could be tested, we acknowledge, is beyond us.) The human brain is determined to make sense of the world—that is what the human brain does—and with all the elements of language operating in music, save semantics, the brain may be stimulated more strongly, and more continuously, because there is no "short circuit" that ends with an assigned, semantic meaning.

Music Is a Natural Language

Music is a natural language. A natural language is one that is spoken before its grammar and syntax—its "rules"—are codified. In contrast, an artificial language, such as computer programmers use, is created from rules that are made up before the language is used. Artificial languages are more precise by their nature, but they "mean" things in a different way than natural languages do. In a computer language, 00101101 means what the programmer says it means, and that's it. It has no power to evoke in the human mind things beyond its assigned meaning, and it's not supposed to.

Every language spoken on Earth, except Esperanto, is a natural language. Esperanto was, or is, an artificial language cobbled together from elements of selected natural languages. It never has acquired either the precision of an artificial language or the power and evocativeness of a natural one.

Some of the power and evocativeness of natural languages derive from their imprecision—from their ability to call up allied meanings that point beyond the literal, and to create a web with the literal meanings. As we have said, music has a richer syntax and richer phonetics than spoken languages, but it has no semantic dimension. So when we speak of musical meaning, if we can speak of it at all, it must be a meaning without semantics—if such a thing is possible. (This illustrates one of the shortcomings of Deryck Cooke's emotional theory. More than two-thirds of Cooke's hundreds of musical examples are of music with words. This makes it easy to show that music can evoke the same emotional reactions as the words express. It is far more difficult to make this argument with absolute music.)

Philosopher Susanne K. Langer insisted it is not possible to speak of music as a language, or to speak of meaning without semantics. In her oft-cited chapter, "On Significance in Music," from *Philosophy in a New Key*, Langer wrote:

> If music has any significance, it is semantic, not symptomatic. Its "meaning" is evidently not that of a stimulus to evoke emotions, nor that of a signal to announce them; if it has an emotional content, it "has" it in the same sense that language "has" its conceptual content—*symbolically*. . . . Music is not the cause or cure of feelings, but their *logical expression*; though even in this capacity it has its special ways of functioning, that make it incommensurable with language, and even with presentational symbols like images, gestures, and rites.[50]

Music, Langer says, "is not, logically speaking, a language, for it has no vocabulary." To insist otherwise, she insists, "is a useless allegory, for tones lack the very thing that distinguishes a word from a mere vocable: fixed connotation, or 'dictionary meaning.'" Langer concludes that "music has all the earmarks of a true symbolism, except one: the existence of an *assigned connotation. . . . (M)usic at its highest, though clearly a symbolic form, is an unconsummated symbol.*"[51]

We have argued that music's lack of a semantic dimension may enhance its emotional power. Despite Langer's warning, we will continue to speak of music as a language, not because the corollary is perfect, but because it is useful and illuminating. We cannot agree with Langer's contention that because music lacks a semantics, then to study music as a language is a "useless allegory." Parallels need not be perfect to be illuminating. Consider the case of Richard Wagner, who attempted to create a musical semantics through the leitmotif, "more often than not extremely short and characterized by a single harmonic or rhythmic trait." But, Roger Sessions continues, this reversed the practice of centuries of Western music, and actually interferes with the process of musical development.

> Its introduction is often motivated by dramatic, not musical necessities and once introduced it intentionally dominates the scene, to the obliteration of what surrounds it. The musical coherence is there, to be sure—but in a passive sense; the detail is more significant than the line, and the "theme" more important than its development. It is all too seldom noted to what an overwhelming extent the reverse is the case in earlier music.[52]

Musicians spoke the language of tonality before its "rules" were deciphered, or invented, by theoreticians. Composers had been using chord inversions for hundreds of years, for their sonorous properties, and to avoid parallel fifths, before Jean Philippe Rameau "discovered" the concept of the chord inversion, and defined it in his 1722 *Treatise on Harmony*. The "rules" for writing a fugue were deduced primarily from the music of Johann Sebastian Bach. (Though in his last, unfinished book, *Beethoven*, Sir Donald Francis Tovey wrote: "[T]he so-called Classical rules of fugue are the most entirely fictitious rules in the whole history of academic bluff, and . . . I shall take no notice of them whatever in dealing with Beethoven's fugues."[53]) The "rules" of sonata form were not defined until long after its greatest exponents—Haydn, Mozart, and Beethoven—were dead. Beethoven's pupil Carl Czerny first explicated the essentials of sonata form in 1840.

This does not mean that sonata form, fugue, and chordal inversions do not exist, or that a musician need not understand them. But the grammar, or rules, of a natural language never can cover the entire subject for the same reason that laws, no matter how reasonable, never can cover the complete range of human activities—because the prescriptive grammars and the laws come after the activities, and are derived from the activities, not vice-versa.

Chomsky believes that humans are born with the ability to sense the "rules" of language, a few elemental "transformations" by which we use the rules to convert a large though finite number of sounds and words into infinite meaningful, or meaningless, sentences. That process also applies to tonal music. Musicians have been transforming the twelve chromatic tones into infinite musical sentences for centuries. And it may be the case—I believe it is the case—that one reason many people do not care for serial music is that serialism is not a natural language. It's an Esperanto. If a composer devises a tone row, and chooses the rules by which he will transform it, and then writes the composition, the result may be interesting, depending upon the musicality of the composer, but the process and the resulting composition are not products of a natural language. An English speaker could decide to speak only in sentences that each contain two nouns, one verb, an adjective, no adverbs, one article, and an optional preposition phrase—and he could do it, and it would sound like English—but that's not the way people use natural languages. Then again, a speaker of English could decide to speak, or write, in iambic pentameter, or in rhythms that approximate it. This decision, less strictly rule-bound than counting the parts of speech, would be much closer to the sort of decisions that Classical composers made in writing music.

Let us call the statement, "Music is a natural language" an axiom, in our quest to determine whether absolute music can have meaning. A second axiom is that there is a relationship between music and the human body. Sessions makes this claim when he writes that music is not "simply a matter of tones and rhythmic patterns," but "the organization of time in terms of human gesture and movement":

> The final question regarding all music that is mechanically reproduced seems to be bound up with the fact that our active sense of time is dependent in large degree on our sense of movement, and that mechanical repetition mitigates and finally destroys the sense of movement in any given instance; it destroys also

> our sense of expression through movement, which plays so large and obvious a part in our musical experience.[54]

Sessions comes very close to the origin of meaning in music when he adds that "if the expression of movement is to become effective, we require not only the evidence of movement from one point to the next, but a sense of the motivating energy behind it."[55]

A corollary to the axiom that there is a relationship between music and the human body is that there is a relationship between music and breath—even if the music is not produced by breath, but, for example, by a violin or a piano. This was dramatically illustrated in a master class given by Yehudi Menuhin. A young violinist who was unhappy with her vibrato asked the maestro for some exercises to improve it. "Let me hear you play," Menuhin said. She played a few measures, beautifully, and Menuhin interrupted and suggested she inhale on the up-bow and exhale on the down-bow. She started over, and the improvement was remarkable, though Menuhin had not made any mechanical changes to the way she produced vibrato. He had showed her how to create music from a more intimate relationship with her body.[56] Pianists too speak of a breathing melodic line, though the piano is even farther removed from the human breath than the violin.

Music's source in the human body may help explain the flowering of Western music in the Baroque and Viennese Classical periods. Musical training in the eighteenth century began with the human voice and the violin. Students had to learn how to produce music from their body—there are no frets or markings on the neck of a violin. Only in the late Classic and early Romantic period did the keyboard become the basis of musical training. And the keyboard, for all its glories, does not require an intimate production of sound from the human body, nor so intimate an involvement and adjustment of tone production to the ear. This transition accelerated in the early nineteenth century, and was lamented by music critic Eduard Hanslick in the 1860s, who noted that "today the teaching of music has been entirely absorbed by piano instruction."

Leon Botstein cited Hanslick's comment in his essay "The Patrons and Publics of the Quartets: Music, Culture, and Society in Beethoven's Vienna." Botstein wrote:

> Amateurs in Beethoven's time were required to anticipate pitch from a printed score or reproduce notes learned by rote (particularly from one's voice). The huge Viennese oratorio performances included, among the over 1,000 participants, many members of the second society, high aristocrats, and professionals, who performed with little rehearsal. This was possible because so many amateurs and professionals could read music and accurately reproduce pitches vocally and on string instruments. By the 1820s, the decade of Beethoven's late quartets, the explosion in the piano's availability . . . had begun to diminish the popularity of the quartet form . . . a shift from strings and pitch competence to mechanical facility on the keyboard had taken place.[57]

Without being reductionist about it, there is no doubt that the eighteenth-century system, based on sight singing and string instruments, produces musicians who have a far surer grasp of the subject than those who learn music from a box in which intonation and the fine gradations of the scale are handled by a piano tuner, rather than the musician's own body. The technological development of the piano changed music, and musicians, and the manner in which and ends toward which musicians develop, as surely and as irrevocably as the development of electronic technologies in the twentieth century changed them. (Most serial music springs from a less intimate relationship to the human body than did Classical, tonal music, particularly if serial technique is applied to rhythm. This may be another reason why so many fans of Western concert music prefer Haydn to serialism.)

Music, then, appears to be related in some way to the human body, and if it has meaning, it is a meaning without a semantic dimension—whatever that may mean. It may be the case—in fact, it is the case—that some absolute music has meaning, but most of it does not. Every musical composition is an experiment, and just as in the other sciences, some experiments are more meaningful than others—and some experiments have no meaning at all. Many of Beethoven's compositions stimulate in us these feelings of meaning more intensely than other music is able to do. And the fact that the meaning comes from us does not negate the statement that some absolute music can have meaning.

The psychiatrist Victor Frankl wrote in his influential book that *Man's Search for Meaning* is a basic human need, as elemental as the search for food, water, sex, and warmth. Frankl survived the Auschwitz death camp, and later worked as a therapist with victims of Auschwitz and other concentration camps. He saw people die quickly in Auschwitz, sometimes without an obvious physical cause, because, Frankl said, they simply gave up on living—their life no longer had meaning. The people who survived, Frankl said, seemed determined to extract some meaning from what was happening to them—whether that meaning could be "proved," or demonstrated in any way at all. In working with concentration camp survivors after the war, Frankl found that his patients had to construct some sort of meaning for what had happened to them, even though the meaning they devised may have been wholly at odds with the indications of history. Those who could not create or discover a personal meaning in a catastrophe that was, on a very deep level, irrational, had a much harder time living the rest of their life. We all know that lack of food, water, or warmth can kill us, and lack of sex can kill a species. In the extreme conditions to which he was subjected, Frankl said, he saw that lack of meaning can be fatal too.[58]

Many people feel intensely that some music communicates something significant to them. They may agree with others about what the music appears to be expressing, though none of them may be able to express quite what it is. This is because people create the meaning, and ascribe it to the music. And it seems to be the case that more people do this with Beethoven's music, and do it more intensely, than with the music of any other composer of absolute music. One reason for this may be that if a musical theme has contrasts and variety within it—as a typical Haydn or Mozart theme does—then we hear it simply as music. In a few cases, particularly with some of Beethoven's compositions, or with a well-written fugue, the themes are so basic and simple, with so few elements, and the architecture of the movement is so clearly derived from those few elements, that our brain searches it for meaning, insists that it has meaning—and the elements are so few that no matter what meaning we assign the theme and its transformations, the piece appears to make philosophical sense.

The themes are Langer's "unconsummated symbols," to which our brains impose a meaning. What's more, we may impose a different meaning upon a composition on successive rehearings—even upon an unchanged recording of it —and each of our new interpretations "makes sense." The simplicity of some of Beethoven's themes—the axioms of his compositions—lends the music, to our brains, nearly a semantic dimension. The clearest example of this may be the first movement of the Fifth Symphony, which contains less melodic variation in its 626 measures than are contained in many eight-bar Italian opera tunes. No matter what meaning we ascribe to the Fifth Symphony's four-note theme, it dominates those minutes of our lives. It overwhelms everything, particularly the solo oboe. It is inescapable. It is wholly convincing, no matter what it "means," and we are satisfied, and grateful, when the movement ends and we are released from it.

One reason that some movements of Beethoven's Late Quartets, including the *Grosse Fuge*, appear to be products of philosophical thought is the simplicity of their themes. To put it another way, the pieces have fewer axioms, and simpler axioms, than most musical compositions, and the axioms are developed at great, sometimes astonishing length, without losing their essential nature. Just as mathematicians derive or create mathematical systems from as few axioms as possible, and believe that the simplest and most self-evident axioms create the most powerful systems, so are Beethoven's themes simple axioms from which he created the most powerful music the world had yet heard.

Obviously, this is far from a complete explanation. The musical themes of many modern, "minimalist" American composers are simple, yet their compositions often seem not only meaningless, but pointless. The manner in which musical themes are handled, developed, and varied, or not, contributes far more to any meaningful aspect a musical composition may have, or seem to have, than the relatively few notes that constitute the theme itself. Beethoven's genius, as virtually all commentators have noted, is revealed in the large-scale tonal architecture of his works, what Joseph Kerman, in the best of all the books written on Beethoven's quartets, calls "melodic details projected into structural harmonic features."[59] Analysts and critics are still debating whether Beethoven consciously manipulated by retrograde inversion the four-note motto he used in the three fugal movements of the Late Quartets—the *Grosse Fuge*, the A Minor and the C-Sharp Minor Quartets. But even if we could determine whether he did this consciously or not, and what, if anything, Beethoven meant by it, we would be little closer to determining whether the fugues have extra-musical meaning, or what that might be, or whether they mean what, if anything, Beethoven thought they did.

Musical Perception Is a Form of Synesthesia

There is another reason that people find music powerful, pleasurable, and evocative. Musical perception is a form of synesthesia. This statement surely will provoke more resistance than our previous two axioms, but the proof is self-evident. Everyone understands the concepts of high and low tones in music. The convergence or divergence of high and low tones give a spatial quality to sound: Musical sound can appear to create volumes in space. And we perceive musical sound as directional. Artfully constructed sound unfolding in time appears to create height, depth, direction, and volume (in the sense of space, and perhaps even mass, not in the sense of loudness). That's a collapse of sensory categories —a synesthesia—and it is a form of synesthesia that most human beings possess. The percentage of people who wholly lack this form of synesthesia is probably somewhat greater, but not enormously so, than the percentage of people who have other forms of synesthesia—people who have colored hearing, or who taste shapes, or for whom numbers and letters come in colors. Dr. Richard Cytowic, an authority on synesthesia, estimates its prevalence in the general population as one in 2,000 or less.[60] The number of wholly unmusical people is surely somewhat larger, but not by an enormous order of magnitude.

We may use Samuel Johnson's description of himself as an example of a "wholly unmusical" person. Dr. Johnson told music historian John Hawkins that music "excites in my mind no ideas, and hinders me from contemplating my own." Johnson told James Boswell that music "was a method of employing the mind without the labor of thinking at all," and added that "no man of talent, or whose mind was capable of better things, ever would or could devote his time and attention to so idle and frivolous a pursuit."[61]

Oliver Sacks estimates that as many as 5 percent of people are tone-deaf—or have an "amusia"—but this may be too high, as Sacks describes several types of amusia, some partial, some total. Some people cannot identify rhythms, some cannot tell if one tone is higher than another, some cannot identify melodies, and some apparently have "an impairment of the ability to perceive dissonance."[62] Sacks believes different types of amusia stem from different areas of the brain. However, the same estimate of 5 percent of the population being tone-deaf occurred in studies from 1948 and 1968, which tried to determine whether tone deafness was inherited. In these studies, "Twenty-five popular tunes were each presented with its pair, either the same or differing by one or two wrong notes so that the incorrect version is readily selected by 95 percent of people, with a clear segregation of scores from the 5 percent tone-deaf. Segregation was also found within families, but no clear-cut mode of inheritance could be discerned."[63]

Accepting, for sake of argument, that these estimates are correct, or reasonably so, then tone deafness occurs roughly one hundred times more frequently than synesthesia. Its extraordinary nature and rarity make synesthesia an abstruse and baffling concept, yet the synesthetic nature of musical perception has been in plain sight, though unnoticed, for decades, if not centuries. In *Phi-*

losophy in a New Key, Langer cites a "remarkable and careful work" from 1923 that studied

> the successive emergence of expressive factors in the apprehension of the simplest possible tonal patterns—bare pitch patterns of two and three tones, stripped of all contextual elements of timbre, rhythm, volume, etc., by their uniform production on an electrical instrument, in timed succession and equal strength. The subjects were instructed to describe their experiences in any terms they chose: by their qualities, relations, meanings, emotional characters, somatic effects, associations, suggestions, or what-not. They were asked to report any images or memories evoked, or, failing such experiences, simply to convey their impressions as best they could.[64]

The author of the study, Kurt Huber, found:

> The most primitive factor in the perception of tonal movement is a sense of its *direction*. . . . The apprehension of a *width of tonal intervals* is independent of this sense of direction; and "all spatial symbolism in the interpretation of motives has its roots in this impression of inter-tonal distance." . . . The idea of a *musical step* requires a joint perception of tonal distance and direction.[65]

The objection surely will be raised that this is just a culturally acquired, metaphoric way of speaking about music. Huber, after all, was not investigating whether musical perception is a form of synesthesia—though that could be used to buttress both sides of this argument. But most people, even children, grasp the concept of musical direction, movement, and musical space far more readily than they acquire other, simpler concepts, including the culturally assigned relations of specific sounds with specific letters.

Synesthesia is a mode of perception, not a manner of speaking. The science behind most of our arguments—including the statement that synesthesia exists—is drawn from the second edition of Dr. Richard Cytowic's book, *Synesthesia: A Union of the Senses*. Cytowic, a neurologist, is one of the world's foremost authorities on synesthesia; his book summarizes most of the work that had been done on the condition up until its publication, in 2002.

Perhaps the most famous statement from a synesthete is the description of "a crumbly yellow voice," made by a man with multiple synesthesias, and identified only as S, in A. R. Luria's 1968 book, *The Mind of a Mnemonist*.[66] Cytowic calls synesthesia a "collapse of categories" or a "cross-modal transference,"[67] with "mode" understood as one of the five modes of perception—sight, smell, taste, touch, and hearing. A synesthete "recognize(s) something in one modality first encountered in another."

> Those who know the term synesthesia through the literary symbolism of Yeats, Swinburne, Baudelaire, Hart Crane, Edgar Allan Poe, or Dame Edith Sitwell will not find any explication here. We are not talking about sound symbolism or metaphor, but a perception, a literal joining of the senses.[68]

Synesthesia can be induced by drugs, such as hashish, peyote, or LSD, but a synesthete does not experience the condition because he is on drugs, nor is the experience optional. Cytowic calls it an "unelaborated percept" or a "binding."[69]

That is, a synesthete can describe the shape in which tastes arrive to him, or the color of sounds, but the sensations do not arrive as discrete, separated forms or modalities. The separate modes of perception are bound together in a synesthetic experience. "Synesthesia is 'abnormal' only in being statistically rare," Cytowic says. "In fact, I will develop the argument that synesthesia is possibly a normal brain process that is prematurely displayed to consciousness in a minority of individuals."[70]

Some neurologists believe that most or all newborns are synesthetic, but lose those perceptions as their brain develops. Two specialists in synesthesia, Simon Baron-Cohen and John Harrison, theorize that "we might all be colored-hearing synesthetes until we lose connections between these two areas somewhere about three months of age."

> In normal development, according to this theory, a synesthetic "confusion" gives way in a few months, with cortical maturation, to a clearer distinction and segregation of the senses . . . . In those individuals with synesthesia, it is supposed, a genetic abnormality prevents complete deletion of this early hyperconnectivity [of neurons in the brain], so that a larger or smaller remnant of this persists in adult life.[71]

Cytowic does not believe that synesthesia is universal in babies, nor does he support this theory of "hyperconnectivity." He believes the synesthetic brain somehow brings to consciousness connections between the basic, "reptilian" brain in the brainstem and limbic system, and the higher brain systems that produce consciousness. Cytowic agrees, however, that synesthesia is more common in children, and cites ten scientific studies that support this. He estimates that synesthesia is three times more prevalent in children than in adults.[72]

Synesthesia also has been explained as a "release" phenomenon—a mode of perception released, or recovered, when other senses are lost. Oliver Sacks, and others, believe that this might explain why "the only significant cause of permanent acquired synesthesia is blindness."

> The loss of vision, especially early in life, may lead, paradoxically, to heightened visual imagery and all sorts of intrasensory connections and synesthesias. The rapidity with which synesthesia can follow blindness would scarcely allow the formation of new anatomical connections in the brain and suggests instead a release phenomenon, the removal of an inhibition normally imposed by a fully functioning visual system.[73]

The scientific literature on synesthesia links it repeatedly to blindness, and comments repeatedly upon the apparent link between early onset blindness and musical talent.[74]

The novelist Vladimir Nabokov discovered that he was synesthetic "one day in my seventh year, as I was using a heap of old alphabet blocks to build a tower. I casually remarked to [my mother] that their colors were wrong. We discovered then that some of her letters had the same tint as mine and that, besides, she was optically affected by musical notes." Nabokov elaborated on his synesthesia in his autobiography, *Speak, Memory*:

> The long *a* of the English alphabet (and it is this alphabet I have in mind farther on unless otherwise stated) has for me the tint of weathered wood, but a French *a* evokes polished ebony. Oatmeal *n*, noodle-limp *l*, and the ivory-backed hand mirror of *o* take care of the whites. . . . Passing on to the blue group, there is steely *x*, thundercloud *z*, and huckleberry *k*. Since a subtle interaction exists between sound and shape, I see *q* as browner than *k*, while *s* is not the light blue of *c*, but a curious mixture of azure and mother-of-pearl. . . . The yellows comprise various *e*'s and *i*'s, creamy *d*, bright-golden *y*, and *u*, whose alphabetical value I can express only by "brassy with an olive sheen."[75]

Nabokov had two forms of synesthesia. He saw "colored graphemes," which is the most common form, occurring in two-thirds of a group of 365 synesthetes; and he heard "colored phonemes," which was reported by 9.6 percent of the sample group. Other relatively common forms of synesthesia include colored musical sounds (reported by 14.5% of the sample group of 365), colored general sounds (12.1%), colored tastes (6.3%), colored odors (5.8%), colored pain (4.4%), and colored personalities (4.4%).[76]

John Locke may have been the first person to describe synesthesia in *An Essay on Human Understanding* (1689). Locke tells of a blind man who "bragged one day, that he now understood what scarlet signified. Upon which, his friend demanding what scarlet was? The blind man answered, it was like the sound of a trumpet." The first medical reference to synesthesia dates from 1710, when the English ophthalmologist Thomas Woolhouse described a blind man who saw sound-induced colored visions. Perhaps the earliest scientific description from a synesthete came from an albino physician named Sachs, who described his own perception of colored vowels in his 1812 Ph.D. dissertation at Erlangen, Germany.

Synesthesia came to the attention of the general public through statements of artists, particularly the French Symbolist poets. Arthur Rimbaud, who may have been synesthetic, drew attention to the concept with his famous 1871 sonnet on *Vowels*: "A black, E white, I red, U green, O blue: vowels / I shall tell one day of your mysterious origins . . ." Other well-known artists who were synesthetes include the composers Alexander Scriabin and Olivier Messiaen and the artist David Hockney.[77]

Cytowic provides copious statements from synesthetes who describe their conditions. (To maintain their privacy, he identifies them only by initials.) For DSc, "The word butter is blue."[78] In his book, *The Man Who Tasted Shapes*, Cytowic describes one man's synesthesia in detail.

> MW, the gustatory synesthete, perceives shape, texture, weight, and temperature whenever he tastes or smells foods. He describes the taste of spearmint as "cool glass columns." Such a description can easily lead to the assumption that he is using metaphoric speech or that such a description is a product of imagery. It is not. It is a verbal interpretation of a sensory experience.[79]

When another synesthete, JM, found that her pregnant niece planned to name her baby Paul if it was a boy, JM became "distraught" because "the name Paul is such an ugly color. It's gray and ugly. I told her, 'Anything but Paul.' And she couldn't understand why and I said, 'It is such an ugly color, that name Paul.' She thought I was out of my mind." JM also reported, "Somebody says to me, 'How is your dog?' First I see the word DOG in color, then I think of my dog. That's how it goes. The color always comes first before I can think of the thing."[80]

The synesthete RP reported, "The synesthetic sense is definitely not 'in my mind.' It is just sort of there. It is sort of a translucent overlay that I can see through. It is kind of like a heat shimmer, only without the distortion."[81]

Cytowic's informant SO reported, "I recently mistakenly called a new acquaintance 'Diane' instead of 'Elaine' because she was dark-haired, and 'D' is black whereas 'E' is red-orange. If a person has a dark, warm coloring then I can easily recall their name if it is a dark, warm name. Trying to recall a dark name belonging to a light-haired person is hopeless."[82]

Here is how the synesthete MLL, who sees music, described a figure-skating competition:

> A young woman named Zayas skated to a piece of music that was green and full of squares. Her costume was totally black; her routine started out with curving motions. It became uncomfortable to me to watch such a mismatch, so I just looked at my hands in my lap. She placed last in her category at the end of the evening's judging.[83]

Clearly, synesthesia is a strange phenomenon. Cytowic draws parallels—incorrectly, I believe—between synesthesia and the musical phenomenon of perfect pitch. "Perfect pitch is similar to synesthesia in four aspects," Cytowic says. "1. It is either all or nothing. The talent is either present or it is not. 2. The skill appears naturally without necessity to develop it through the practice that characterizes acquisition of other musical skills." Cytowic compares the experiences described by many synesthetes with the results from a 1988 study in the *Journal of Medical Genetics* by J. Profita and H. Bidder, who reported, "3. 'Most of our subjects with perfect pitch recalled their astonishment on learning that *everyone* did not have this capacity.'" And "4. It manifests itself at an early age: 5 (26%) of Profita & Bidder's 19 subjects recognized the capacity by age 5, 89% (17/19) by age 10. Pedigrees are compatible with autosomal recessive inheritance; that 80% of those affected [with perfect pitch] are female suggests that the trait is sex-related."[84]

Synesthesia too appears more frequently in women, by a factor of at least 2.5 to 1. It appears to have an autosomal dominant genetic component linked to the X chromosome: Cytowic has never found a case of male-to-male transmission, though synesthesia tends to run in families.[85] But Cytowic's parallel with perfect pitch is less than perfect, for perfect pitch can be learned; synesthesia cannot. This may come as a surprise to Cytowic and to non-musicians, but perfect pitch can be acquired through assiduous practice, or one may develop the skill until it is indistinguishable from perfect pitch.[86] But there is no way to acquire synesthesia.

Many people, including some neurologists, do not believe synesthesia exists. Its acceptance as a valid subject of scientific study has waxed and waned over the years. More than seventy scientific papers were written about it from 1881 to 1931. Its acceptance, and interest in it in these years, was probably due in part to the influence of the Symbolist poets. But from 1932 until 1974 only sixteen papers appeared. "There can be no doubt that the advent of B. F. Skinner's behaviorism, which precluded reference to mental states, contributed to this decline," Cytowic says. "Only in the last two decades have mental states again become acceptable topics of scientific inquiry."[87]

We must accept the existence of mental states in a quest for musical meaning, for sound, like the tree that falls in the forest, cannot be music unless someone hears it—even if, like Beethoven, he hears it only in his mind. The existence of synesthesia, however, unlike the existence of musical meaning, can be demonstrated through experiments. Tests have shown that synesthetes' perception of colored numbers and letters is consistent over the years, even when they do not know they will be retested, and even after as many as 46 years have passed between tests.[88] Once a synesthete sees 2 as lavender, for example, it remains lavender throughout her life, and she will identify it that way if asked. Cytowic and others have tested synesthetes against control subjects by flashing colored letters on a screen, asking the subjects to call out the color of the letters as quickly as possible, and timing their response. Synesthetes consistently take longer to respond when the letters are in the "wrong" color for them. In another test, synesthetes and control subjects were asked to call out the number of numbers, as opposed to letters, in a box that looks something like this (in the actual experiment, many of the letters are printed at odd angles):

S S S S S
S S S 5 S S S
S S S S S S S S
S S S S S S S
S S S 5 S S S 5 S
S S S S S S S S S
S S S S S S S S S S

Synesthetes consistently count the three 5s more quickly than do the control subjects, because the colored numbers jump out of the jumble for them and form a colored triangle. (Of course, this works only if the synesthete sees 5 and S in different colors.)[89]

Also important is the synesthetes' absolute conviction of the reality of their experience, and the fact that they have nothing to gain by claiming to have the condition. In fact, many synesthetes are stigmatized as insane, and have been sent to mental health specialists as presumed schizophrenics or psychotics after revealing their perceptions.

In response to newspaper and magazine articles about his work, Cytowic has received numerous unsolicited letters from synesthetes, many of whom had no idea what synesthesia is, but who were mocked and called crazy, even by their spouse, so that they finally just stopped talking about it. Cytowic presents excerpts from six unsolicited letters, including these typical responses: "I nearly fell over when I saw the article about you . . . I ran to my husband, shouting, 'See! This is me! I'm not nuts!'" Another woman wrote:

> I read the article . . . concerning your work with synesthesia. It's an affirmation that I am not nuts and whatever my other problems may have been, being crazy was not one of them. . . . You have no idea (or maybe you do at that!) how exciting it is to read someone else's description—and from a total stranger—of an experience that I have never been quite sure wasn't the result of my imagination, or being insane. I have never met anyone else who saw sound. When enough people tell you that you are imagining things it's easy to doubt yourself. I've never been quite sure that I'm not crazy.[90]

The assistant principal of a high school recommended that a synesthetic girl get psychological counseling after she told him that "when I kissed my boyfriend I saw orange sherbet foam."[91] Another of Cytowic's synesthetic subjects—he has more than 100 of them—reported:

> As a child I once mentioned my colors to a teacher, who promptly told my parents I was schizophrenic. That ended my telling anyone about it for quite a while. . . . I know that it was very much a part of my life as a child, a sort of test of friendship, to see how others reacted when I told them. If they didn't believe me, I didn't want to be their friend.[92]

Cytowic himself had to overcome prejudice against synesthesia because he chose to specialize in it. "When I first mentioned the geometrically shaped taste of my proband, MW, to my neurology colleagues over two decades ago, their reflexive response was, 'Stay away from it, it's too weird, too New Age. It will ruin your career.' They thought I was out of my mind."[93]

After more than twenty years of study, Cytowic has found five criteria that define idiopathic synesthesia—synesthesia that is not drug induced, and is not a result of epilepsy or brain lesions. I believe that all five criteria apply to musical perception—that is, the perception of sound creating direction through volumes of space.

"1. *Synesthesia is involuntary but elicited.*" Synesthesia cannot be turned off, nor can it be conjured up. "It happens to someone, automatically, in response to a discrete stimulus." And, like the musical creation of space, "If subjects are deeply engaged (in something else), the synesthesia may be attenuated, whereas focused attention on it in a relaxed state may make it seem more vivid."

"2. *Synesthesia is spatially extended.*" The synesthetic percept seems to exist "out there," not in the brain.

"3. *Synesthetic percepts are consistent and discrete.*" Cytowic says, "If a sound is blue, it will always be blue." (In listening to music, divergence of voices creates a sense of greater volume in space; convergence of voices shrinks the space. Divergence of voices will never appear to condense the space, and convergence of voices will never appear to expand it.)

"4. *Synesthesia is memorable.*"

"5. *Synesthesia is emotional.*"[94]

Additional evidence that musical perception is a form of synesthesia comes from Levitin and Sacks, though neither of them suggests—and probably would not agree—that musical perception is a form of synesthesia. Sacks cites two recent studies that indicate that musicians' brains have "increased volumes of gray matter in motor, auditory, and visuospatial areas of the cortex, as well as in the cerebellum" compared to non-musicians.[95] The increased volume of the "visuospatial area" is an interesting result. Levitin cites "spatial location" as one of the nine perceptual "dimensions" of music that our brains organize into "higher-level concepts." The others are tone, pitch, timbre, loudness, tempo, rhythm, contour, and reverberation—(another spatial dimension). Sacks cites Levitin's nine dimensions in discussing the forms of amusia.[96]

Synesthesia is an essential element of "normal" musical perception, and its nearly universal prevalence as a mode of perception, among all but the tone-deaf, suffices to explain why no one has remarked upon it before. Though it is "only" a mental process, the synesthetic nature of musical perception is real. Synesthetes, too, "have an unshakable conviction and sense of validity that what they perceive is real," Cytowic says.[97] His subjects say they "love" their colors and would miss them if they were taken away. MM, who hears shapes and colors, wrote, "I find it a wonderful addition to life and would hate to lose it." A woman who sent Cytowic an unsolicited letter wrote, "I love my colors, can't imagine being without them." RB, who feels shapes in pain and hears shapes in music, "thought everyone felt this way. When people tell me they don't, it's as if they were saying they don't know how to walk or run or breathe." And JM, who described her synesthesia when she was 61, wrote that she "never talked about it, not out of shyness but because I believed that all people were like that. Only after reading Nabokov's description of his synesthesia did I realize that this was rather unusual. . . . I enjoy it very much and would be hard put if these colors would suddenly vanish."[98]

The mental response to Western Baroque and Classical music, in which sound appears to create volumes of space, and directed movement through that space, meets all five of Cytowic's criteria for synesthesia—it is involuntarily elicited, spatially extended, consistent and discrete, memorable, and emotional. Medieval and Renaissance polyphony also can elicit this synesthesia.

Music need not be polyphonic to elicit a synesthetic response, though polyphony does have a wonderful power to intensify the feeling of musical space. But a homophonic section of an orchestral work by Mozart also creates the synesthetic perception of sound moving through volumes of space, and most well-crafted melodies will create sense of direction. It is interesting, and significant, that Renaissance composers such as Giovanni Gabrieli and his contemporary Venetians, through the Romantic Hector Berlioz, to the high-fidelity stereo fans in the twentieth and twenty-first centuries, have been obsessed with positioning choirs, orchestras, or sound systems to create, or recreate, the synesthetic properties of music.

Not all music can elicit the spatial synesthetic response. Bebop jazz, for example, as exemplified by the music of Charlie Parker—which demonstrates a very high level of musical intelligence indeed—does not create the sensation of volumes of space because of its concentration upon the single musical line, though it does create an intense synesthetic feeling of two-dimensional direction.

Objections surely will be raised to the statement that a normal person's response to music involves a form of synesthesia. One could object: "You are saying that some forms of music, or some compositions, elicit responses in the brain that other pieces are unable to." That's correct. One could object: "You are saying that some pieces of music evoke entirely different and more complex neurological and biological responses than others." That's also correct. One could object: "This theory is nothing but repugnant cultural chauvinism." That is not the case. A concert by the sarod player Ali Akbar Khan and the tabla master Alla Rakha elicited synesthetic responses from this hearer that were as powerful or more powerful than those elicited by many a Bach fugue. And the traditional, microtonal music of the Tohono O'odham tribe in Arizona also induced synesthesia.[99]

We are not claiming that Western concert music is superior to other forms of music because of its power to evoke spatial synesthesia. We are simply claiming that it can evoke spatial synesthesia. It is undeniable that some human activities involve many more systems in the brain and body than others, whether we participate in the activities or observe them. This helps to explain why most of us prefer making love to playing croquet, and why, after one reaches a certain age, watching or playing a game of chess is more satisfying, and satisfying in a different way, than a game of tiddlywinks, and it is not cultural chauvinism to say this.

Some musical compositions can elicit more intense synesthetic responses than others, just as some pieces of absolute music more strongly elicit from us the conviction that they have meaning, even if we cannot "translate" the meaning into words. A great deal of the world's well-crafted music involves synesthesia at some level, but it is more evident in some compositions than others. Many people get a feeling of spaciousness from a Bach fugue, or from the tremendous expansion of the melodic G that concludes the cavatina in Beethoven's Opus 130 into the four-octave G that begins the *Grosse Fuge*. This spatial synesthesia is far less noticeable in, for example, rock and roll, but it may explain why rock fans and sound engineers enjoy reverberation effects—it's a cheap and easy way to elicit the synesthetic response.

Music partakes of other synesthetic qualities that are not so closely bound to it as its ability to create space. An orchestral trumpet player would know how to respond if his conductor asked for a brighter tone, or a darker one. Most people understand what is meant when a critic says a soprano has a thin voice, or a round one, and one saxophonist understands what another one means if he speaks of a fat tone or a thin one, or a rough or smooth tone. If experimental subjects were played a tape of a flute being played in its high register, and a tuba being played in the low register, and were told to assign shapes and colors to each sound, and the only choices available were thin and silver and fat and dark brown, I believe the responses would be nearly unanimous. These are metaphorical constructs, though we all understand them. But the perception that music creates space, and the apparent movement in space of well-constructed polyphony, are inherent qualities of the mind as it listens to music.

No one knows what creates synesthesia, or why some people have it and some do not. Possible explanations include "undifferentiated neuronal activity": some people, including Simon Baron-Cohen and John Harrison, suggest that babies are born synesthetic, but lose the cross-modal perceptions as they develop.[100] "Linkage theories" assume some sort of "cross-wiring" in the brain. Cytowic believes none of these theories is correct. Nor does he agree with the psychological theory of association, that "if A suggests B, then A and B have been experienced simultaneously at some previous time." Nor does he believe that synesthesia is created by linguistic associations. His theory of "microgenesis" involves complex issues of brain anatomy and the relationship between the very basic "reptilian" brain in the brainstem and limbic system, and the "higher brain" areas involved in human thought, so that the "synesthetic object" is perceived in addition to the "normal" perceptions evoked by the stimulus.[101] Cytowic believes that the synesthetic brain somehow intercepts, or brings to consciousness, the processing of perceptions that for most people are hidden. He credits German neurologist and psychiatrist Kurt Goldstein with being the first to explain synesthesia as "the premature display of a normal cognitive process."[102] Cytowic adds: "Synesthesia is 'abnormal' only in being statistically rare. In fact . . . synesthesia is possibly a normal brain process that is prematurely displayed to consciousness in a minority of individuals."[103]

Synesthesia can be, and probably is, displayed to consciousness in a majority of individuals through music, but we are so inured to our reactions to music, and most of us are so unfamiliar with the strange concept of synesthesia, that we do not recognize our response to music as synesthesia. Of more interest to us is Cytowic's question, "What is synesthesia good for?" He responds in words that apply just as well to music, and that recall Artur Rubinstein's words about the power of musical consolation: "Synesthesia is a rich way of feeling, highly enjoyable for those who possess it. To lose it would be a catastrophe . . . akin to going blind or not being alive at all."[104]

Notes

1. Lewis Thomas, "On Matters of Doubt," in *Late Night Thoughts on Listening to Mahler's Ninth Symphony* (New York: Bantam, 1983), 162-163.

2. Leonard B. Meyer, *Emotion and Meaning in Music* (Chicago: University of Chicago Press, 1956), citations in text are to the 1968 edition; and Deryck Cooke, *The Lan-*

guage of Music (Oxford: Oxford University Press, 1959), citations are to the 2001 edition. Cooke quotations used with permission of Oxford University Press.

3. Meyer, *Emotion and Meaning in Music*, 1.

4. Meyer, *Emotion and Meaning in Music*, 43. Meyer's overreliance upon behaviorist psychology, which dominates and distorts the book, are particularly evident on 7-13.

5. Meyer, *Emotion and Meaning in Music*, 6.

6. Emily Anderson, ed., *The Letters of Beethoven* (London: Macmillan, 1961), 1,141.

7. The author attended the March 6, 1976, master class by Artur Rubinstein at the Manhattan School of Music.

8. Meyer, *Emotion and Meaning in Music*, 57-58. Parentheses in original.

9. Cooke, *The Language of Music*, xii, ix, x.

10. Cooke, *The Language of Music*, xiii.

11. Cooke, *The Language of Music*, xii.

12. Cooke, *The Language of Music*, 14.

13. Cooke, *The Language of Music*, 78.

14. Cooke, *The Language of Music*, 54. Parentheses in original.

15. Cooke, *The Language of Music*, 54. Parentheses in original.

16. Cooke, *The Language of Music*, xiii.

17. Cooke, *The Language of Music*, 37.

18. Cooke, *The Language of Music*, 81. Parentheses in original.

19. Cooke, *The Language of Music*, 212.

20. Cooke, *The Language of Music*, 213, 216.

21. Cooke, *The Language of Music*, 28.

22. Cooke, *The Language of Music*, 8. Parentheses in original.

23. Cooke, *The Language of Music*, 27.

24. Cooke, *The Language of Music*, 27.

25. Cooke, *The Language of Music*, 11, citing Igor Stravinsky, *Chronicle of My Life* (London: Victor Gollancz, 1936), 91.

26. Cooke, *The Language of Music*, 14.

27. Leonard Meyer, *Music, the Arts, and Ideas* (Chicago: University of Chicago Press, 1969), 53.

28. Cooke, *The Language of Music*, 21.

29. Cooke, *The Language of Music*, 24. Parentheses in original.

30. Thomas, "Things Unflattened by Science," in *Late Night Thoughts on Listening to Mahler's Ninth Symphony*, 79.

31. Hans Keller, *The Great Haydn Quartets* (New York: George Braziller, 1986), 15.

32. Keller, *The Great Haydn Quartets*, 19.

33. Charles Rosen, *Arnold Schoenberg* (New York: Viking Press, 1975), 20.

34. Stravinsky, *Chronicle of My Life*, 91.

35. Aaron Copland, *What to Listen for in Music* (New York: New American Library, 1957), 19.

36. Roger Sessions, "The New Musical Horizon," in *Roger Sessions on Music: Collected Essays* (Princeton, N.J.: Princeton University Press, 1979), 49.

37. Copland, *What to Listen for in Music*, 19.

38. Sir George Grove, *Beethoven's Nine Symphonies* (Boston: George Ellis, 1888), 74-75.

39. Robin Wallace, *Beethoven's Critics: Aesthetic Dilemmas and Resolutions During the Composer's Lifetime* (Cambridge: Cambridge University Press, 1989), 22. Parentheses in original. E. T. A. Hoffmann's entire review from the July 4 and July 11, 1810,

Allgemeine Musikalische Zeitung appears in Wayne M. Senner, Robin Wallace, and William Meredith, eds., *The Critical Reception of Beethoven's Compositions by His German Contemporaries, Vol. 2* (Lincoln: University of Nebraska Press, 2001), 95-114.

40. Wallace, *Beethoven's Critics*, 22-23.

41. Charles Rosen, *The Classical Style: Haydn, Mozart, Beethoven* [1971], *Expanded Edition* (New York: W.W. Norton, 1998). Sessions, "Escape by Theory," in *Roger Sessions on Music*, 256. Sessions' essay first appeared in *Modern Music*, Vol. 15, No. 3 (1938), 192-197. Our endorsement of Sessions' criticism of Schenker should not be interpreted as a rejection of Schenker's theories, which have been enormously influential, and rightfully so. But Sessions' criticism is nonetheless valid.

42. The first academic program in music therapy was established in 1944 at Michigan State University, after it was found that music therapy could help the physical and psychological pain of veterans wounded in World War II. Dorothy M. Schullian and Max Schoen, eds., *Music and Medicine* (New York: Henry Schuman, 1948). The National Association for Music Therapy was formed in 1950. "But music therapy remained, for the next quarter of a century, scarcely recognized." Oliver Sacks, *Musicophilia: Tales of Music and the Brain* (New York: Alfred A. Knopf, 2007), 251. Steven Mithen presents later developments in music therapy in chapter 7 of *The Singing Neanderthals*: *The Origins of Music, Language, Mind, and Body* (Cambridge, Mass.: Harvard University Press, 2006), 85-101.

43. Daniel Levitin, *This Is Your Brain on Music: The Science of a Human Obsession* (New York: Dutton, 2006), 82-84.

44. Oliver Sacks, *Musicophilia* (New York, Alfred A. Knopf, 2007), 313.

45. Steven Pinker and Paul Bloom, "Natural Language and Natural Selection," in *Behavioral and Brain Sciences*, Vol. 13, No. 4 (1990), 707-784, www.bbsonline.org/documents/a/00/00/04/99/bbs00000499OO/bbs.pinker.html (Sept. 1, 2008). Pages in the online version are not numbered.

46. Pinker and Bloom, "Natural Language and Natural Selection."

47. For example, Hikari Oe, the son of Japanese novelist and Nobel laureate Kenzuburo Oe, was born with a severely deformed brain that made him developmentally disabled, but he has a gift for musical composition. *Music of Hikari Oe*, compact disc recording (Japan: Nippon Columbia Records, 1994); and David Remnick, "Reading Japan," *The New Yorker*, Feb. 6, 1995. Sacks, *Musicophilia*, contains a chapter on musical savants, 151-159.

48. Charles Rosen's analysis of the fugal finale of Beethoven's Piano Sonata in A-Flat, Opus 110, is a brilliant example of musical analysis. Charles Rosen, *The Classical Style: Haydn, Mozart, Beethoven, Expanded Edition* (New York: W.W. Norton, 1998), 501-507.

49. Pinker and Bloom, "Natural Language and Natural Selection" (citations omitted).

50. Susanne K. Langer, *Philosophy in a New Key: A Study in the Symbolism of Reason, Rite, and Art* (New York: New American Library, 1951), 185.

51. Langer, *Philosophy in a New Key*, 194, 203-204.

52. Sessions, "The New Musical Horizon," in *Roger Sessions on Music*, 47.

53. Donald Francis Tovey, *Beethoven* (New York: Oxford University Press, 1945), 125.

54. Sessions, "Problems and Issues Facing the Composer Today," in *Roger Sessions on Music*, 85. First printed in *Musical Quarterly*, Vol. 46, No. 2 (April 1960), 159-171.

55. Sessions, "Song and Pattern in Music Today," in *Roger Sessions on Music*, 85-86. First printed in *Score*, No. 17 (September 1956), 73-84.

56. The author attended the master class by Yehudi Menuhin at the Manhattan School of Music, in 1975 or 1976.

57. Leon Botstein, "The Patrons and Publics of the Quartets: Music, Culture, and Society in Beethoven's Vienna," in Robert Winter and Robert Martin, eds., *The Beethoven Quartet Companion* (Berkeley: University of California Press, 1994), 90. Parentheses in original.

58. Victor Frankl, *Man's Search for Meaning* (New York: Pocket Books, 1984).

59. Joseph Kerman, *The Beethoven Quartets* (New York: W.W. Norton, 1966), 328.

60. Dr. Richard E. Cytowic, *Synesthesia: A Union of the Senses* (Cambridge, Mass.: MIT Press, 2002), 54-55. Quotations used with permission of the author. Copyright 2002 by Richard E. Cytowic, M.D. Published by Springer Verlag. All Rights Reserved.

61. Roger Lonsdale, *Dr. Charles Burney* (Oxford: Oxford University Press, 1965), 64.

62. Sacks, *Musicophilia*, 100-101, 109.

63. R. T. C. Pratt, "The Inheritance of Musicality," in Macdonald Critchley and R. A. Henson, eds., *Music and the Brain: Studies in the Neurology of Music* (London: William Heinemann, 1978), 29.

64. Langer, *Philosophy in a New Key*, 194.

65. Langer, *Philosophy in a New Key*, 195.

66. Alexandr R. Luria, *The Mind of a Mnemonist* (New York: Avon, 1969), 24. Oliver Sacks says S's name was Shereshevsky. Sacks, *Musicophilia*, 178.

67. Cytowic, *Synesthesia*, 110.

68. Cytowic, *Synesthesia*, xxiii-xxiv.

69. Cytowic, *Synesthesia*, 33-34.

70. Cytowic, *Synesthesia*, 2.

71. Sacks, *Musicophilia*, 181, citing Simon Baron-Cohen and John Harrison, *Synaesthesia: Classic and Contemporary Readings* (Oxford: Oxford University Press, 1997).

72. Cytowic, *Synesthesia*, 276, 285, 338-349.

73. Sacks, *Musicophilia*, 181-182.

74. Cytowic, *Synesthesia*, 27-28, 40, 261-262; Macdonald Critchley, "Ecstatic and Synaesthetic Experiences During Musical Perception," in Critchley-Henson, eds., *Music and the Brain*, 225-226; Daphne Maurer and Catherine J. Mondloch, "Neonatal Synesthesia: A Reevaluation," in Lynn C. Robertson and Noam Sagiv, eds., *Synesthesia: Perspectives from Cognitive Neuroscience* (New York: Oxford University Press, 2005), 198-200.

75. Vladimir Nabokov, *Speak, Memory* (New York: Vintage, 1989), 34-35.

76. Cytowic, *Synesthesia*, 17. Cytowic's chart summarizes data compiled by him and other researchers.

77. Cytowic, *Synesthesia*, 306-320, includes excerpts from Cytowic's interview and correspondence with David Hockney.

78. Cytowic, *Synesthesia*, 40.

79. Cytowic, *Synesthesia*, 33.

80. Cytowic, *Synesthesia*, 35, 45.

81. Cytowic, *Synesthesia*, 34.

82. Cytowic, *Synesthesia*, 38.

83. Cytowic, *Synesthesia*, 38.

84. Cytowic, *Synesthesia*, 59. Oliver Sacks estimates that fewer than one in 10,000 people have absolute, or perfect, pitch. Sacks, *Musicophilia*, 124. Sacks devotes chapter 9 to the subject of perfect pitch.

85. Cytowic, *Synesthesia*, 52-59.

86. When the author attended the Manhattan School of Music in the mid-1970s, freshmen were instructed to buy a tuning fork and memorize middle C. With assiduous repetition, this can be done rather quickly. With relative pitch—the ability to hear and

identify intervals—it is then possible to identify any tone. This, of course, is not the same thing as perfect pitch. But the author observed, and the literature bears it out, that many people are not certain, even upon reflection, whether they have absolute, i.e., "perfect," or relative pitch. Like synesthetes, some people with perfect pitch are surprised to learn that everyone does not have it (Sacks, *Musicophilia*, 125-126). We do not wish to press the point, and concede that people born with absolute pitch—if such a thing happens—may have talents and abilities beyond those of people who acquire it. But this distinction—between perfect pitch and relative pitch developed so highly that it is indistinguishable from perfect pitch—seems far less absolute than the distinction between people who have synesthesia and those who do not.

87. Cytowic, *Synesthesia*, 71.

88. Cytowic, *Synesthesia*, 68.

89. Charts and examples of this and other tests for synesthesia are printed between pages 148 and 149 in Robertson and Sagiv, eds., *Synesthesia: Perspectives from Cognitive Neuroscience*.

90. Cytowic, *Synesthesia*, 18, 19.

91. Cytowic, *Synesthesia*, 43-44.

92. Cytowic, *Synesthesia*, 44.

93. Cytowic, *Synesthesia*, xxii.

94. Cytowic, *Synesthesia*, 67-69.

95. Sacks, *Musicophilia*, 94.

96. Levitin, *This Is Your Brain on Music*, 14-16. Sacks cites Levitin's nine dimensions in discussing the forms of amusia, *Musicophilia*, 144.

97. Cytowic, *Synesthesia*, 69.

98. Cytowic, *Synesthesia*, 18, 28, 30.

99. Ali Akbar Khan and Alla Rakha, at a concert at Reed College, Portland, Ore., 1970; Tohono O'odham traditional music, at Nolic village on the Tohono O'odham reservation, 1981. The possibility exists that this author is synesthetic, but I don't think so. I have never had a synesthetic experience aside from the spatial perception induced by music. Conversations and long experience with other musicians, and with music lovers who are not musicians, persuade me that my experiences are not unusual.

100. Sacks, *Musicophilia*, 181.

101. Cytowic, *Synesthesia*, 338-349.

102. Cytowic, *Synesthesia*, 349.

103. Cytowic, *Synesthesia*, 2.

104. Cytowic, *Synesthesia*, 46.

Chapter 5

The *Grosse Fuge*

The *Grosse Fuge* was so far ahead of its time, and was played so infrequently, that it had no influence upon the next century of music. This is remarkable, as Beethoven's music dominated the nineteenth century, and still dominates the concert platform. More than one hundred years after Beethoven's death, Igor Stravinsky said that he had been "alienated . . . from Beethoven for many years" because Beethoven so completely dominated the musical world.[1]

To understand what a radical break with tradition the *Grosse Fuge* represented, consider this excerpt from a letter Wolfgang Mozart wrote to his father in 1781—one of the most famous of Mozart's statements about music. He is describing how he composed an aria in his new opera, *Die Entführung aus dem Serail*:

> [A]s Osmin's rage gradually increases, there comes (just when the aria seems to be at an end) the *allegro assai*, which is in a totally different meter and in a different key; this is bound to be very effective. For just as a man in such a towering rage oversteps all the bounds of order, so must the music too forget itself. But since passions, whether violent or not, must never be expressed to the point of exciting disgust, and as music, even in the most terrible situations, must never offend the ear, but must please the listener, or in other words must never cease to be *music*, so I have not chosen a key foreign to F (in which the aria is written) but one related to it—not the nearest, D minor, but the more remote A minor.[2]

For Mozart, "music, even in the most terrible situations, must never offend the ear, but must please the listener, or in other words must never cease to be *music*." Haydn expressed similar sentiments when he chastised himself for attempting too remote a modulation in his Symphony No. 42 in D. In the second movement of that piece, written in 1771, Haydn sketched a continuation of the first violin part which began on B-sharp, then abandoned it, writing himself a note: "*Dieses war vor gar zu gelehrte Ohren*" ('That was for much too learned ears')."[3]

In writing the *Grosse Fuge*, Beethoven was no longer operating within the limits that Haydn and Mozart had set for themselves, or that their sponsors and audience had set for them. He was not concerned with pleasing the listeners or calibrating his music against their musical intelligence. He abandoned Classical ideals of symmetry and balance, and the Baroque and Rococo ideas of decoration that had carried over into the Classical period. The *Grosse Fuge* is Beethoven's equivalent, one hundred years before Pablo Picasso did it, of driving a nail through the canvas. The *Grosse Fuge* is not about surface, not about creating a pretty object, it is not about moderation and grace, not even about taste: it is the inexorable working out of a musical idea. More: it is allowing a musical idea to work itself out. Richard Kramer compares the "reminiscence" of the slow G-flat fugue in measures 493-510 in the *Grosse Fuge*, and the halting fragmentation of the theme in measures 511-532, with the string bass "recitative" interspersed with reminiscences of earlier movements that precede the *Freude* theme in the finale of the Ninth Symphony (mm. 9-90), to observe: "The work is shown enacting its own composition."[4]

"No composer before Beethoven ever disregarded the capacities of both his performers and his audience with such ruthlessness," Charles Rosen wrote.[5] The *Grosse Fuge* was the first piece—and would be the only one—that went beyond the tremendously difficult technical and aesthetic challenges of the great fugue, also in B-flat, with which Beethoven concluded his Opus 106 *Hammerklavier* Sonata. In Opus 106, Rosen says, "the emancipation of piano music from the demands of the amateur musician was made official, with a consequent loss of responsibility [to the performers, and purchasers, of the piece] and a greater freedom for the imagination."[6] In the *Grosse Fuge*, Beethoven cut the listeners loose as well.

This was a generation before poets and critics dreamed up the phrase, "Art for Art's Sake," and five generations before the serial composer Milton Babbitt wrote an article that *High Fidelity* magazine published under the insulting title, "Who Cares If You Listen?" (Babbitt said that *High Fidelity*'s title made him "very distressed." He had titled the article "The Composer as Specialist.") In that 1958 article, Babbitt attributes the isolation of the modern, "serious" composer to "a half-century of revolution in musical thought."[7] Babbitt's "revolution in musical thought," however, began long before 1908—it began with Beethoven, though Beethoven did not share Babbitt's aesthetic ideals. The differences are worth noting.

Babbitt claimed that composers of "'serious,' 'advanced,' contemporary music" had developed their trade (or art, or science) beyond the point that audiences could be expected to understand it. He claimed that the fact that this music, "for, of, and by specialists" is in a "condition of musical and societal 'isolation' . . . is not only inevitable, but potentially advantageous for the composer and his music." The layman no longer expects to be able to understand the most advanced work in mathematics, philosophy, or physics, and there is no reason for laymen to expect to understand the most "specialized music," Babbitt says. He imagines a man, who is not a mathematician, who attends a lecture on "Pointwise Periodic Homeomorphisms," and declares afterward, "I didn't like it." Babbitt says this layman's judgment would be "irrelevant," because he is not qualified to judge the subject. He makes the same claim for modern music. Babbitt says the public has "its own music, its ubiquitous music: music to eat by, to read by, to dance by, and to be impressed by. Why refuse to recognize the possibility that contemporary music has reached a stage long since attained by other forms of activity?"

Beethoven famously declared that he did not "write for the galleries,"[8] and he obviously did not feel obligated to write for laymen. But unlike Babbitt, Beethoven felt that one of the purposes of music was—if we may be permitted to state this in archaic and unscientific terms—to move the human soul. The *Grosse Fuge* is as difficult and advanced an intellectual creation as any music written by Babbitt's serial school, but despite its intellectual rigor—which remains beyond the grasp of the layman—the *Grosse Fuge* remained rooted in human gesture and human declamation. Beethoven wanted to communicate with others through music, and we venture to say he wanted to communicate even with musical laymen. He did not view his music as a purely experimental science. When Gerhard von Breuning told Beethoven, on his deathbed, that his *Grosse Fuge* "didn't go over very well," Beethoven did not respond, "Who cares if they understand it?" He responded, "It will please them some day. . . . I know; I am an artist."[9]

Beethoven's late period style was not willfully eccentric or capricious; he did not indulge in virtuosic writing for the sake of virtuosity, and he did not deliberately try to alienate himself from the musically literate public, though he was accused of all those things. Charles Rosen wrote:

> The aspect of many of these late works is not ingratiating; to many, the *Great Fugue* is disagreeably harsh. But when it is played, as it should be, as the finale of the B flat Quartet op. 130, there is nothing eccentric in this harshness, or in the broken sobs (marked "strangled") of the *Cavatina* that precedes it. What makes some of these works appear willful is that they are uncompromising.[10]

Some analysts—including Stravinsky—see foreshadowings of twelve-tone music in the *Grosse Fuge*. (As a young man, Stravinsky was less than enthusiastic about the *Grosse Fuge,* though he eventually came around, and said it was "pure interval music, and I love it.")[11] The nature of the fugue's primary theme lends itself particularly well to description as a "pitch set," though, as we have said, Beethoven's artistic and aesthetic intentions should not be confused with those of the serialists.[12]

Here it might be useful to discuss just what is the point of musical analysis—a task we have put off as long as possible, for we feel that the *Grosse Fuge* raises questions that will be of interest even to readers who are unprepared or unwilling to submit themselves to formal musical analysis.

Musical analysis is done for two primary reasons: to understand how a piece is put together—how it "works"—and this is done to help elucidate how one should perform it, or listen to it. There are, of course, other reasons to which musical analysis can be put, such as elucidating general, and generally fictitious, "rules" by which composers operated, or by which music operates; for purposes of broad stylistic analysis; to compare the music of different eras or of different composers, and so on. Musical analysis operates at the very limits of its usefulness when it points out subtleties that, with the best will in the world, the performer or listener is not able to hear. This distinguishes musical analysis from musical theory; the distinction is worth a brief digression.

In the years after World War II, serialism, mathematical and aleatory (chance, or random) techniques, and electronic works dominated the world of "serious" Western concert music. Like the visual artists who dominated the New York art world for an even longer period, this music gave great importance to the "concept" from which the art, presumably, sprang. Two pieces by John Cage, his famous *4'33"*—4 minutes and 33 seconds of silence at a piano—and *As Slow As Possible*—a piece for church organ, a performance of which has begun in Germany and will take 639 years to complete—are perhaps the purest examples of conceptual music.

There is no doubt that the music of this era had many salutary effects. It expanded the listening capacities of well-intentioned listeners; it expanded the performing capacities of musicians; it brought into music a tremendous range of sounds previously thought "unmusical," which can be used powerfully and effectively in music; it enlarged the language of musical notation; it began the project, which surely will continue for centuries, of using electronics for purposes other than merely recording sounds played on traditional instruments; and most usefully, perhaps, it fundamentally altered the nature, and purposes, of musical rhythm. (We have pointed out that the music of this school divorced music's rhythm and pulse from its previous intimate relationship with the human body. This is a fundamental change in the nature of Western concert music; it is an expansion of the language; therefore our criticism, or observation, should not be taken, necessarily, as pejorative.)

What distinguishes musical analysis from theory, in this case, is that musical analysis is retrospective; musical theory need not be. Also worth noting is that, to the undying frustration of theorists and analysts, neither theory nor analysis can wholly determine whether a piece of music is successful. Analysis can point out errors or weaknesses—parallel fifths, weak bass progressions, vapid harmonies—but an opera by Meyerbeer is not less successful than an opera by Mozart because Meyerbeer's music is riddled with errors. It is less successful because the music isn't as good. Nor are so many pieces of the serial school unsuccessful because the theory is uninteresting.

Any musical analysis of a great work, such as the *Grosse Fuge*, will necessarily fall short. It cannot fully explain why the music "works," nor why the music is great. And to a certain extent, the lengthier the analysis, the more frustrating it is. It is bound to fall short; it is operating in a realm other than the realm of music; it is propaedeutic. Musical analysis, to be useful, must be done by each musician, or each listener, with the score. A teacher's assistance is helpful, and sometimes necessary, but anything other than direct study of the score is cheating. Musical analysis of a great composition is never complete, for it informs and is informed by the piece on each rehearing. But for the general listener, any analysis that continues at exhausting length but does not help the reader hear the work with greater comprehension, is somewhat beside the point. We will confine our analysis of the *Grosse Fuge* to its broad outlines.

This author hears the *Grosse Fuge* as a compressed, four-movement symphony. Its slow introduction, or *Overtura*, is followed by an opening fugue, *allegro*, in B-flat (measures 30-158); a slow movement in G-flat (mm. 159-232); a scherzo transition that begins in B-flat (mm. 233-272) and continues as a fugue in A-flat (mm. 273-492); then a reminiscence of the slow movement and another transition (mm. 493-532) lead to a scherzo-like finale. This concluding section can be heard as a fourth movement; or as a development and tremendous coda to the third movement; or as a recapitulation, with added development, and coda to the entire piece. In a piece of such complexity, there is no "correct" solution to the nature of its finale[13]—the entire *Grosse Fuge* is a finale.

Alternatively, and less persuasively, one can interpret the *Grosse Fuge* as a giant sonata. In this analysis, the G-flat section would be the second, contrasting subject in the exposition; the B-flat transition and A-flat fugue would be the development section; measures 533 to 662 would be the recapitulation, and the coda begins at measure 663.

We do not believe anyone hears it that way. The length of the first fugue, and the clear break at measure 159, preclude such an interpretation, for this listener. Technical analysis of the *Grosse Fuge* misses the point, however, unless it constantly remarks upon the piece's challenge to all previous notions of musical aesthetics, and the remarkable manner in which the piece seems to develop from itself, from its smallest detail to its sectional divisions and its entire form.

The fugue is built from replications of small fragments of itself.
It is an eight-note theme
built from a four-note theme,
that is built from a two-note motif.

The theme is constructed from half-step intervals, inverted, then inverted again, and each time separated by leaps.

The *Grosse Fuge* moves within a restricted range of keys; it is not harmonically daring, but is formally bewildering. The A theme appears in four guises in the *Overtura*. They will be developed in reverse order. We hear the theme first as finale,

then as scherzo,

then as accompaniment to a slow movement,

and finally as it will appear, "in disguise," in the opening fugue.

"This sequence proceeds from the clearest thematic statement to the most obscure," William Kinderman says. "Conversely, the main sections of the fugue unfold with a sense of progress from the obscure to the coherent; the most basic form of the fugue is withheld until the final passages."[14] (More than a century later, this broadly mirrorlike form would become beloved of atonal composers.)

The first six notes express a strong urge to modulate up a whole tone—from G to A. Beethoven will, as Joseph Kerman says, inflect the nature of the theme into the structure of the entire composition, after he modulates abruptly to G-flat at the conclusion of the first section. The smoothest way to return from G-flat to the tonic, B-flat, would be to slip down a half-step to the dominant, F. Instead, Beethoven creates a sense of titanic effort by modulating up a whole tone to A-flat for another fugal section, then up another whole tone to the tonic. This is one of many examples in which Beethoven's musical decision reveals itself over time as intellectually deep and emotionally powerful.

There is a tremendous amount of tension in both themes. In the leaping B theme, the tension is melodic, in the A theme, harmonic. Each leap, and each chromatic fragment, creates a tension that needs to be resolved. Such unremitting tension is unusual for a Classical theme, which usually expresses a clear tonality, and generally conveys some degree of repose along the way, as it alights upon various scale steps. But there are only three possible points of repose in this theme, and all are unsettling: the F-to-E half-step implies the resolution of a dominant chord, but not on the tonic; the G-sharp-to-A half-step implies a modulation away from the tonic; and though the final two notes are the traditional leading tone and tonic, Beethoven places the resolution in the weakest possible rhythmic position, at the tail end of two grace notes. The rhythmic weakness of the theme's final notes makes the entire theme feel unresolved, throwing greater importance onto its development.

The A theme itself, constructed from parts of itself in half-steps and leaps, encapsulates the contrast between the A theme and the B theme, the contrasting, leaping subject of the opening fugue. Amid all the dissonance to come, the A theme's chromatic steps and leaps are so recognizable that they lend any chromatic step, or leap, and any section built upon those elements, an added intelligibility, and added tension. Thus the thematic transformation of the E-flat episode that begins in measure 416 is heard as another fragmentation and distortion of the A theme.

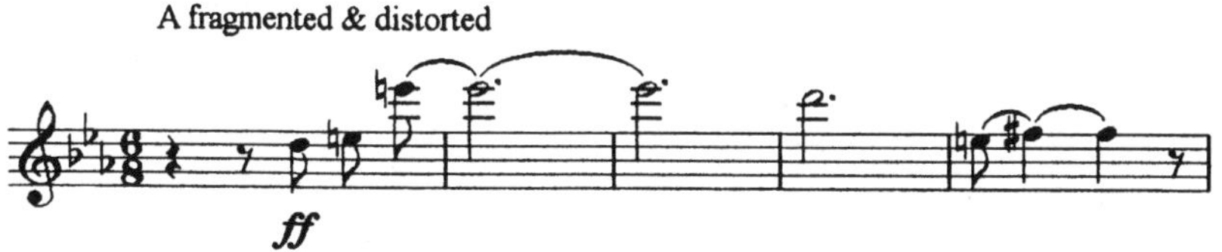

The continuous trills in the 45-bar section from measure 377 to 412 are derived from the single, theme-ending trill of the Overture's measure 10. And though the closing theme-fragment that begins at m. 565 introduces a notable relaxation of tension, the tension remains because the chromatic fragment implies a leap to come.

The most violently contrasting thematic transformations, or fragmentations, are all related to, and generated from, the germinal A theme.

The half-step is the most powerful melodic interval in tonal music. Its most common and most powerful functions are as a leading tone resolving upward to a tonic; or as the dissonant seventh of a dominant chord resolving downward to a consonance; or, non-functionally, as a chromatic passing tone, often, as in Mozart, with emotional content. In the *Grosse Fuge*, the final half-step lands the A theme back on the tonic, an octave higher than it began. The A theme implies an enormous amount of tonal movement in a very brief space—in its second, scherzo version, it occupies only two bars. Violent as the contrasts ahead will be, and unusual as the form is, the fugue, like its primary subject, fulfills the traditional, Classical ideal of dramatic movement, away from and back to a tonal center.

The B theme is surely the only theme in Classical, Baroque, or Romantic music that prominently features, and insistently repeats, a leap of a diminished twelfth—a tritone plus an octave—*fortissimo*. It dominates the A theme in the opening B-flat section, which is a double fugue—a fugue upon two subjects—in which the A theme appears in its "disguised" version. From the beginning, Beethoven turns the Classical ideal of form and beauty on its head. In a traditional, "beautiful" melody, the *da capo* aria, a theme is presented in its simple form, then repeated with ornamentation. The ornaments, presumably, make the theme even more beautiful. Beethoven develops his theme first in its most deformed version, distorted and syncopated so as to be almost unrecognizable.

Not surprisingly, the experts disagree about the form, or forms, of the *Grosse Fuge*. Philip Radcliffe says it is "best understood if regarded, not as a highly eccentric fugue, but as a kind of symphonic poem consisting of several contrasted but thematically related sections and containing a certain amount of fugal writing."[15]

Joseph Marliave, who despised the fugue, divided it into six sections, though he did not even bother to analyze the piece in his 379-page book, but merely gave a student's notes on it from a lecture by Vincent D'Indy.[16]

A. E. F. Dickinson said the fugue consisted of an introduction followed by "four distinct movements": i) a double fugue in B-flat on themes A and B; ii) a double fugue in G-flat on themes A and C—theme C being the second subject to our A theme in its slow-movement form, first presented in mm. 21-25; iii) a prelude and double fugue on themes A and a presumed theme D in A-flat—theme D being the fragmentation and inversion of the first three notes of theme A—with a reminiscence of (ii) "in order to deliver with full pressure—iv) Prelude (*da capo*) and recovery of the initial combination, in a less strict rhythm, in B-flat."[17]

Warren Kirkendale considers the *Grosse Fuge* an eight-part work—six parts plus the Overture and a coda: the A section being the double fugue in B-flat (mm. 31-158); the B section a "double fugato" in G-flat (mm. 159-232); the C section a "march-like episode . . . scarcely fugal" (mm. 233-272); the D section a fugue followed by a "free fantasy" on both themes (mm. 273-492). The fifth section, B(1), is a reprise of the B section (mm. 493-510) followed by a transition (mm. 511-532); leading to section C(1), a reprise of the C section (mm. 533-564); and the coda (mm. 565-741), a "free homophonic section followed by the coda proper," which begins at m. 657, "with reminiscences of everything which has preceded."[18]

Joseph Kerman, after presenting a lengthy technical analysis, concludes, "In the B-flat Fugue, the main 'device' after the double counterpoint of the exposition is—thematic transformation . . . [and] the thematic transformations . . . range stylistically beyond the bounds of fugue and even beyond the bounds of counterpoint."[19]

Lewis Lockwood offers the most concise analysis, in a blissfully brief page and one-quarter. Lockwood offers three choices: a ten-part series of fugues, fugatos, and fantasies, with two codas; and/or a grand sonata form laid over, or under, those ten sections; and/or "the equivalent of a multi-movement work," with a first movement Overture and Allegro, a slow movement, an interlude followed by "the equivalent of a scherzo," and then "more or less a composite finale."[20]

Charles Rosen agrees with this multi-form analysis and compares the *Grosse Fuge* to two other great, late compositions, the Ninth Symphony and the fugal finale of the *Hammerklavier* Sonata.

> The two fugal finales—the *Great Fugue* op. 133 (the last movement of the String Quartet op. 130) and the fugue of the *Hammerklavier*—are both conceived as a series of variations, each new treatment of the theme being given a new character. Like the last movement of the Ninth Symphony, they both have the harmonic tensions characteristic of sonata-allegro form, along with its sense of a return and extensive resolution. They both, too, impose upon this another structural idea of several movements: this is particularly evident in the *Great Fugue*, which has an introduction, Allegro, slow movement (in a new key), and Scherzo finale as almost completely separate divisions.[21]

Some analysts do not hesitate to draw psychological conclusions from the *Grosse Fuge*. After a lengthy and detailed analysis, Martin Cooper concludes:

> It is clear that the ability to conceive such a work argues certain psychological traits—a huge fund of aggression, in the first place, and an instinctive resentment of restriction in any form—and a "philosophy of life" (something quite different from the intellectual systems of professional philosophers, for which Beethoven had little or no understanding) based on the struggle for self-development on the one hand and self-mastery on the other.[22]

We have already presented, in our opening pages, some comments from critics who seem to have regarded the *Grosse Fuge* as an insult, or a joke in poor taste.

Clearly, analysis of the *Grosse Fuge* can lead far afield rather quickly. The unprecedented nature of its form; the violence of its "melody" and of its contrasts; its demand to be heard as an intellectual creation as much as a musical one; the tremendous sense of struggle, unremitting except in the G-flat section, where the silken return of the primary theme reminds us of the elements from which the work was constructed, all lend themselves to dramatic or philosophic interpretations. This led the quartet expert Hans Keller into a rare misjudgment—not in his argument, but in his conclusion.

> As for Beethoven, possibly humanity's greatest mind altogether, his quartets are a special case. . . . [W]hile his evolution as a quartet composer eventually carried him into spheres of unheard-of—in fact, unheard—expression where nobody, with the possible exception of Schoenberg, has been able to follow, let alone join him, it was inevitable that on the way, he had to sacrifice classical perfection to the extent of discovering the beauty of ugliness in general, and of an ugly quartet sound in particular. . . . [A] certain—very certain, very acutely imagined—kind of imperfection, of both instrumental and sheer acoustic strain, became part and parcel of the creative act. This is not, of course, a criticism; the obverse, rather. It does mean, however, that at his sublimest, Beethoven is sometimes at his most problematic: in the case of one famous, discarded finale—Op. 130's first—he burst the bounds of the string quartet altogether, and can only be heard without aural frustration in Furtwangler's self-conducted, string-orchestral arrangement.[23]

Keller's conclusion is unfortunate. In fact, it is wrong. A performance of the *Grosse Fuge* that can be "heard without aural frustration" is impossible. If it were possible, it would be pointless. Frustration is an essential element of the work. Concluding the piece with its second, leaping theme, rather than the A theme, was the only way out of this frustration. That its emotionally satisfying conclusion is made possible only by violating the technical perfection of the work—which would require concluding it with the theme with which it began—is essential to the work too. The *Grosse Fuge* is an imperfect work. It was not written with perfection in mind. It was written by a human, to be played by humans, for other humans. To perform the *Grosse Fuge* by minimizing its sense of strain—its aural frustrations—would betray the piece altogether.[24]

Because the *Grosse Fuge* concludes with the B theme—the "antithesis" to its primary theme—it invites a Hegelian interpretation. And in fact, Lewis Lockwood points out that Vincent D'Indy, in an article for *Cobbett's Cyclopedia*, did interpret the work

> along Hegelian lines as revealing a mighty dialectic in which there is an opposition of two antagonistic views of nature, represented by the primary themes that form the opening double fugue: "one gently melancholy" (the "A" theme), the other "exuberant in its gaiety" (the "B" theme). As D'Indy sees it, "after the presentation of the two subjects, open war begins between careless merriment and serious thought," the latter gradually winning over its thoughtless and frivolous opponent.[25]

But D'Indy's argument is imperfect, not just for its very nature, but because the *Grosse Fuge* ends with what he calls the "thoughtless and frivolous" theme. Still, Lockwood concludes, "As superficial as this viewpoint may be, it has the advantage over formal taxonomies of stressing the dynamic, outsized, Armageddon-like character of much of the work."[26]

The *Grosse Fuge* does seem at times to be a philosophical argument, and a far more abstruse one than, for instance, the recitative section in the finale of the Ninth Symphony, in which the basses ask the orchestra for a fitting theme with which to conclude.

Is it possible for absolute music to raise philosophical questions? Even if a critic disapproves, or pretends to disapprove, of such a proposition, still, he may indulge himself by the simple expedient of citing others who raise the question. In the case of the *Grosse Fuge*, it is the piece in its entirety—not any details of it—that is revolutionary. And it was revolutionary that once Beethoven conceived of the work, he went ahead and wrote it. Though technical analysis can clarify the apparent chaos of the *Grosse Fuge*, and reveal it as an astonishing intellectual creation, some critics feel its intellectual power overwhelms any beauty it contains, making it difficult or impossible to derive pleasure from listening to it.

Warren Kirkendale claims the *Grosse Fuge* was Beethoven's somewhat academic response to J. S. Bach's final, uncompleted piece, *The Art of Fugue*. Kirkendale claims that "the whole conception of the work" was derived from a page in a textbook by Beethoven's old teacher Johann Georg Albrechtsberger, who cited the fugal techniques of augmentation, diminution, abbreviation, syncopation, and stretto, and concluded: "*Doch kann mann selten alle zugleich in einer einzigen Fuge anbringen*." (One can rarely use all the techniques in a single fugue.) Kirkendale continues: "In the last sentence Beethoven obviously found a challenge: 'to employ all of them at once in a single fugue.' He made this his principle of composition, his means to build up a large-scale fugue."[27]

Kirkendale claims Beethoven also used Johann Joseph Fux's celebrated counterpoint textbook, *Gradus ad Parnassum*, which still is used to teach species counterpoint, to seek a countersubject:

> In search of a countersubject for the main theme . . . of Op. 133 he tried out every conceivable species, with 2, 3, 4, 6 and 8 notes respectively against one note of the theme. . . . The style of the fugal sections in the finished composition is still determined by the species principle: the juxtaposition of various uniform ostinato rhythms, for example with one (b[ar] 194, 493), three (b. 86, 139), four (b. 31, 167, 493), and six (b. 58) notes against one, as well as the fourth species (syncopation, b. 111, 139).[28]

Kirkendale clinches his argument by citing Albrechtsberger's reference to the technique of "Interruption," which Albrechtsberger demonstrates with a theme in half notes, rewritten in an interrupted, and syncopated, version as alternating quarter-note rests and quarter notes. "Here we discover the source of the peculiar rhythmisation of Beethoven's (A) theme, one of the most puzzling aspects of the *Great Fugue*: *(See musical example: A theme disguised and as accompaniment to B theme.)* This '*Zierlichkeit*' [device] is mentioned in no other book on counterpoint."[29]

Kirkendale calls this "the final, incontestable proof that Albrechtsberger's treatise was the point of departure for the *Great Fugue*."[30]

> Without the suggestion of a great theoretical compendium the "giant movement," the *Great Fugue* would never have been written. As a practical composition it has its roots in the tradition of the Baroque *Kunstbuch* (skill-book). Here its direct prototype is J. S. Bach's *Art of Fugue*. We know that Beethoven was familiar with this work. (He copied a few bars from contrapunctus 4 in a sketchbook for op. 106 and the Ninth Symphony. . . .) The *Great Fugue* was his *Art of Fugue*, his summary of the various fugal techniques—hence the subsequent dedication to his pupil in counterpoint Archduke Rudolph, for whom he had originally copied the passage from Albrechtsberger, the clue to our interpretation.[31]

Kirkendale concludes that the *Grosse Fuge* is "an extraordinary and highly original work," which Beethoven wrote "at the height of his powers." But he says, mysteriously, that "the 'restoration'" of the *Grosse Fuge* as the finale to the Opus 130 B-Flat Quartet, "is by no means justified."[32]

It is difficult to disagree with the author of such a tour de force, but we find Kirkendale's conclusion inexplicable. The *Grosse Fuge* belongs as finale of Opus 130 for purely musical reasons related to the entire B-Flat Quartet, and for broader stylistic reasons.

Beethoven ended the fifth movement, the cavatina, with an imperfect cadence: a melodic G in the first violin rather than the tonic E-flat, which a perfect cadence requires. The reason, as numerous commentators have remarked, was to set up the tremendous expansion of that melodic G into the four-octave G that begins the *Grosse Fuge*. It is a simple and beautiful link to the rapid chain of descending fifths that brings the Overture in 29 bars from G to C to F to the home key, B-flat.

Were the fugue broken off from the rest of the quartet, this rapid harmonic descent would make no sense. It is barely possible, by Beethoven's expanded standards, to begin a single-movement work in G and then write the work in B-flat. But it has no musical meaning, divorced from the rest of the B-Flat Quartet. It turns a beautiful link into an eccentricity. In the substitute finale, there is no link to the cavatina, whose final G remains suspended forever.

To recapitulate other arguments from our first chapter: the outer movements of the Quartet in B-Flat are thematically related, but only with the *Grosse Fuge* as finale; the first theme of the Opus 130's first movement is derived from the *Grosse Fuge* theme, with the initial chromatic step in descent rather than ascent, and the upward leap of a sixth delayed; the modulation to G-flat in the first movement anticipates the *Grosse Fuge*'s modulation to that key; the chromatic accompaniment figure in measures 101 to 130 of the first movement are transpositions of the first two notes of the fugue's A theme; and the thematic reminiscences in the first movement anticipate the reminiscence that will occur in the *Grosse Fuge*.

The broader stylistic argument is just as strong. The *Grosse Fuge* is certainly, as its critics have said, an overwhelming finale. If the *Grosse Fuge* is a great error in taste, it is one of immoderation. But the alternate finale errs in the other direction. It is frivolous, unbearably light, wholly lacking in substance and weight, particularly as the finale to a six-movement quartet. It degrades the work from philosophy to slapstick.

Critics through the years have been nearly united in criticizing Mozart for the unsatisfactory final movement of his great G Minor String Quintet, K. 516. The nearly unanimous opinion is that the finale is too lightweight to conclude such a great and serious work. Not that Mozart's finale is poorly written, only that it is disappointing, insufficient in weight and seriousness for that great quintet.

The *Grosse Fuge*, on the other hand, is criticized for overwhelming Beethoven's Opus 130.

It is difficult to see how both criticisms can be correct. Mozart's fourth movement does lack the grandeur and tragedy of the three movements that preceded it. So does the alternate finale Beethoven wrote—at the request of his publisher, for extra payment—for his Opus 130. Beethoven's light, alternate concluding movement, often called Haydnesque, is even less adequate as a finale, coming after five movements of equal or greater weight than Mozart's three.

The purely musical arguments—formal, melodic, and harmonic—for keeping the *Grosse Fuge* as finale to the Opus 130 Quartet are sufficient. The broader stylistic argument is just as strong. There is also the argument by analogy. Tolstoy ended *War and Peace* with a 50-page meditation upon men and war. These 50 pages may be the philosophical key to Tolstoy's entire work, or they may show that Tolstoy was a better novelist than philosopher. With the best will in the world, it is difficult to resist the conclusion that these unconvincing and unfortunate pages form a boring end to that great work. But as a conclusion to a 1,400-page novel, Tolstoy's 50 pages of head-scratching are far more successful than it would have been to end the novel with a few pages of slapstick. Even if Tolstoy's conclusion is insufferably long and unsuccessful—and it is—it is artistically appropriate where it is. The *Grosse Fuge* too may be long, discordant, taxing, and overwhelming. But it is far more artistically appropriate as a finale to a great, six-movement work, than the alternate version which Beethoven wrote, for 15 gold ducats, to satisfy his publisher.

It is interesting that Beethoven may have derived the idea for the *Grosse Fuge* from a textbook, and may have written it to measure himself against J. S. Bach. But that is not a sufficient argument to claim that the work is unsuccessful, or academic, or inappropriate, or that it does or does not belong as the finale of the B-Flat Quartet. We cite Kirkendale's opinion at the conclusion of our book in a spirit of rueful honesty. We believe that musical analysis proves conclusively that the *Grosse Fuge* belongs as the finale of the Opus 130 Quartet. Kirkendale believes it does not. Beyond that relatively simple question is the larger problem that musical, not philosophical, analysis is the only tool that can explain, or illustrate, how music "works"—but it always falls short. It is incapable of explaining why Beethoven is more emotionally exhausting to listen to than Haydn or Mozart. It is incapable of explaining what it is that so often is present in the works of Mozart, Beethoven, and J. S. Bach that so seldom is present in the works of other composers—even the greatest of them. And it surely is incapable of proving the statement with which we will end our book.

Even if our final statement is rejected out of hand, it should not affect the judgment of any of our other arguments, however good or bad they may be. They can stand or fall without relying upon this final observation.

We have said that the *Grosse Fuge* is built from replications of small fragments of itself. These fragments are fragmented again, inverted, augmented, diminished, abbreviated, syncopated, interpolated, interrupted—manipulated in every way possible. Yet each form of manipulation is a simple, basic operation. The large-scale form of the fugue is derived from the fugue's simplest elements. The half-step pair leaps to another pair of half-steps, which are inverted; then comes the inversion of the leap, and the repetition of the basic paired notes, separated or joined by the final leap to the final base pair, which are not inverted this time. The structure of the *Grosse Fuge*, from the smallest detail to the largest, has an elegance that does not sound elegant at all; it sounds, and it is, crude and powerful. It has not escaped our notice that this four-note motif might have an analogue in nature.[33] In fact, if one wanted to compose a musical analogue of a double helix, it would be difficult to find a better approximation than the theme of the *Grosse Fuge*.

Notes

1. "In our early youth we were surfeited by his works, his famous *Weltschmerz* being forced upon us at the same time, together with the 'tragedy' and all the commonplaces voiced for more than a century about this composer who must be recognized as one of the world's great musical geniuses. Like many others I was disgusted by this intellectual and sentimental attitude, which has little to do with serious musical appreciation. This deplorable pedagogy did not fail in its result. It alienated me from Beethoven for many years." Igor Stravinksy, *Chronicle of My Life* (London: Victor Gollancz, 1936), 189.

2. Emily Anderson, *Letters of Mozart and His Family* (London: Macmillan, 1989), 769. Parentheses in original.

3. H. C. Robbins-Landon, *Haydn: Chronicle and Works, Vol. II* (Bloomington: Indiana University Press, 1978), 279.

4. Richard Kramer, "Between Cavatina and *Ouverture*: Opus 130 and the Voices of Narrative," in *Beethoven Forum, Vol. 1*, ed. Lewis Lockwood and James Webster (Lincoln: University of Nebraska Press, 1992), 169. Kramer feels the *Grosse Fuge* belongs where Beethoven originally put it, as the finale to Opus 130. He concludes: "It is a finale in concept. The permutations of its thematic material echo, and its tonal proportions ground, the music of earlier movements. Did Beethoven, capitulating under the pressure to compose a new finale and agreeing to publish the fugue separately, think that we might not notice?" Kramer, "Between Cavatina and *Ouverture*," 189.

5. Charles Rosen, *The Classical Style: Haydn, Mozart, Beethoven* (New York: W.W. Norton, 1998), 385.

6. Rosen, *The Classical Style*, 404.

7. Milton Babbitt, "Who Cares If You Listen?" *High Fidelity*, February 1958. All the Babbitt quotations are from this article. Pages are not numbered in the online version:

www.palestrant.com/babbitt.html (Nov. 8, 2008). Babbitt said in a 1975 interview, reprinted in Josiah Fisk, ed., *Composers on Music: Eight Centuries of Writings. A New and Expanded Revision of [Sam] Morgenstern's Classic Anthology* (Boston: Northeastern University Press / University Press of New England, 1997), 393:

> The title of the article as submitted to *High Fidelity* was "The Composer as Specialist." There was no imputation whatsoever of "who cares if you listen," which as far as I am concerned conveys very little of the letter of the article, and nothing of the spirit. Obviously the point was that I cared a great deal who listened, but above all *how* they listened. I was concerned about the fact that people were not listening. But their, of course, was a much more provocative title, and journalists are concerned to provoke, and do.
>
> I'm very distressed by this, because inevitably the article is what I'm known by, and I don't really care to be known at all if I have to be known by that. The piece was reprinted twice in anthologies, and I asked in both cases that my original title be restored, along with some of the sentences. Some of the sentences had been changed in *High Fidelity*, not because of my alleged obscurity, but because at the last moment some new advertisements came in, so they just cut a few phrases and sentences to make room. That is the story of "Who Cares If You Listen?," my most celebrated achievement.

8. Beethoven, feeling he had been cheated on receipts for his opera in 1806, complained to the manager of the *Theater an der Wien*, Baron Peter von Braun, who responded that he, Braun, stood to lose more money on the opera than Beethoven did. Braun unfortunately added, "My dear Sir, even Mozart did not disdain to write for the galleries." Beethoven, furious, demanded his score back. Alexander W. Thayer, *Thayer's Life Of Beethoven*, ed. Elliot Forbes (Princeton, N.J.: Princeton University Press, 1973), 397-398.

9. Gerhard von Breuning, *Memories of Beethoven: From the House of the Black-Robed Spaniards* (Cambridge: Cambridge University Press, 1995), 96.

10. Rosen, *The Classical Style*, 445. Parentheses in original.

11. Igor Stravinksy, "Dialogues and a Diary," in *Contemporary Composers on Contemporary Music*, ed. Elliott Schwartz and Barney Childs (New York: Da Capo Press, 1998), 50. The nature of a twelve-tone row is determined by the intervals between the notes. Though the row can be transposed to any pitch, and presented in inversion, retrograde or cancrizans (retrograde inversion), the intervals remain the same. Charles Rosen offers a typically lucid explanation, with examples from tone rows used by Arnold Schoenberg and Alban Berg, in chapter four of *Arnold Schoenberg* (New York: Viking Press, 1975), 88-103.

12. The A theme of the *Grosse Fuge* is not a pitch set because two notes are repeated—G-sharp and G—before all twelve notes are sounded. But the nature of the theme, the way Beethoven manipulates and transforms it, and that it is heard and remembered as a succession of intervals as much as a declamatory or melodic statement in a clear key, all suggest techniques of twelve-tone composition.

13. For instance, Martin Cooper and Lewis Lockwood place the beginning of the coda 100 measures apart. Cooper hears it begin at measure 657, with the first reminiscence; Lockwood places it at measure 565, with what we hear as a closing theme. Martin Cooper, *Beethoven: The Last Decade, 1817-1827* (Oxford: Oxford University Press, 1986), 387; Lewis Lockwood, *Beethoven: The Music and the Life*, (New York: W.W. Norton, 2003), 464.

14. William Kinderman, *Beethoven* (Oxford: Oxford University Press, 1997), 306-307. Kinderman credits Lawrence Kramer for the observation, citing his article, "Primi-

tive Encounters: Beethoven's 'Tempest' Sonata, Musical Meaning, and Enlightenment Anthropology," in *Beethoven Forum, Vol. 1*, 31-66.

15. Philip Radcliffe, *Beethoven's String Quartets* (London: Hutchinson & Co., 1965), 138.

16. Joseph de Marliave, *Beethoven's Quartets* (New York: Dover, 1961), 293-295.

17. A. E. F. Dickinson, *Bach's Fugal Works* (New York: Pitman Publishing Co., 1956), 233-235.

18. Warren Kirkendale, "The 'Great Fugue' Op. 133: Beethoven's 'Art of Fugue,'" *Acta Musicologica*, Vol. 35, Fasc. 1 (January-March 1963), 15.

19. Joseph Kerman, *The Beethoven Quartets* (New York: W.W. Norton, 1966), 279.

20. Lockwood, *Beethoven*, 464-465.

21. Rosen, *The Classical Style*, 440. Parentheses in original.

22. Martin Cooper, *Beethoven: The Last Decade*, 388.

23. Hans Keller, *The Great Haydn Quartets* (New York: George Braziller, 1986), 17.

24. The author studied the Late Quartets with the pianist Phillip Evans. One day I walked into class ten minutes early and Mr. Evans was practicing Beethoven's Opus 111 Piano Sonata in C Minor. Mr. Evans was knocking the stuffing out of that piano. I sat in stunned delight for several minutes, until Mr. Evans paused to crush out one of his ever-present Kool cigarettes and light another. "Isn't that great?" he said. "Did you hear all those mistakes?" He launched back into it and after a few more minutes stopped again to crush out the cigarette. "To play Mr. Beethoven, you've got to make mistakes," Mr. Evans said. "You can play it the other way, but who wants to listen to that?"

25. Lockwood, *Beethoven*, 465. Parentheses in original.

26. Lockwood, *Beethoven*, 465.

27. Kirkendale, "The 'Great Fugue,'" 17, citing Johann Georg Albrechtsberger's *Gründliche Anweisung zur Composition* (Leipzig: 1790), 189.

28. Kirkendale, "The 'Great Fugue,'" 16. Parentheses in original.

29. Kirkendale, "The 'Great Fugue,'" 18.

30. Kirkendale, "The 'Great Fugue,'" 17.

31. Kirkendale, "The 'Great Fugue,'" 24. The sentence in parentheses is from Kirkendale's footnote.

32. Kirkendale, "The 'Great Fugue,'" 15.

33. The phrase, "it has not escaped our notice," comes, shamelessly, from the conclusion of James Watson's and Francis Crick's paper, "A Structure for Deoxyribose Nucleic Acid," in *Nature*, April 25, 1953: "It has not escaped our notice that the specific pairing we have postulated immediately suggests a possible copying mechanism for the genetic material." We also have shamelessly borrowed the phrase "base pair" from Watson and Crick, who wrote, "only specific pairs of bases can bond together. These pairs are: adenine (purine) with thymine (pyrimidine), and guanine (purine) with cytosine (pyrimidine)." The base pairs of the *Grosse Fuge* are the chromatic steps, which are organized around the chain of leaps.

Bibliography

Abert, Hermann. *W. A. Mozart*, translated by Stewart Spencer, edited by Cliff Eisen. New Haven, Conn.: Yale University Press, 2007.

Adorno, Theodor W. *Beethoven: The Philosophy of Music*, translated by Edmund Jephcott. Stanford, Calif.: Stanford University Press, 1998.

———. *Philosophy of Modern Music*, translated by Anne G. Mitchell and Wesley V. Blomster. New York: Seabury Press, 1973.

Albrecht, Theodore, trans. and ed. *Letters to Beethoven and Other Correspondence*. Lincoln: University of Nebraska Press, 1996.

Anderson, Emily, ed. *The Letters of Beethoven*. London: Macmillan, 1961.

———. *The Letters of Mozart and His Family*. London: Macmillan, 1989.

Babbitt, Milton. "Who Cares If You Listen?" *High Fidelity* (February 1958).

Barnes, James J. *Authors, Publishers and Politicians: The Quest for an Anglo-American Copyright Agreement*. London: Routledge & Kegan Paul, 1974.

Baumol, William, and Hilda Baumol. "On the Economics of Musical Composition in Mozart's Vienna." New York: C.V. Starr Center for Applied Economics, New York University, Department of Economics, September 1992.

Beethoven, Ludwig van. *Complete String Quartets*. New York: Dover, 1970.

———. *The Nine Symphonies of Beethoven in Score*. New York: Bonanza, 1935.

———. *Piano Sonatas*. Munich: G. Henle Verlag, 1980.

Bekker, Paul J. *Beethoven*, translated by M. M. Bozman. London: J. M. Dent & Sons, 1939.

Bran, Werner. "The 'Hautboist': An Outline of Evolving Careers and Functions," 123-158 in *The Social Status of the Professional Musician from the Middle Ages to the 19th Century*, edited by Walter Salmen, translated by Herbert Kaufman and Barbara Reisman. Hillsdale, N.Y.: Pendragon Press, 1983.

Braunbehrens, Volkmar. *Mozart in Vienna: 1781-1791*, translated by Timothy Bell. New York: Grove Weidenfeld, 1990.

Breuning, Gerhard von. *Memories of Beethoven: From the House of the Black-Robed Spaniards*, edited and translated by Maynard Solomon, translated with Henry Mins. Cambridge: Cambridge University Press, 1995.

Bruford, W. H. *Germany in the Eighteenth Century: The Social Background of the Literary Revival*. London: Cambridge University Press, 1965.

Burk, John N. *The Life and Works of Beethoven*. New York: Modern Library, 1946.

Burney, Charles. *The Present State of Music in Germany, the Netherlands and United Provinces, or, the Journal of a Tour through Those Countries, Undertaken to Collect Materials for a General History of Music*. London: Travis & Emery, 2003. A facsimile of the 1773 London edition.

Burnham, Scott. *Beethoven Hero*. Princeton, N.J.: Princeton University Press, 2005.

Comini, Alessandra. *The Changing Image of Beethoven: A Study in Mythmaking*. New York: Rizzoli, 1987.

Cooke, Deryck. *The Language of Music*. Oxford: Oxford University Press, 2001.

———. "The Unity of Beethoven's Late Quartets." *The Music Review* (February 1953): 30-49.

Cooper, Barry. *Beethoven*. Oxford: Oxford University Press, 2000.

———. *Beethoven and the Creative Process*. Oxford: Clarendon Press, 1990.

Cooper, Barry, ed. *The Beethoven Compendium*. London: Thames & Hudson, 1991.

Cooper, Martin. *Beethoven: The Last Decade, 1817-1827*. Oxford: Oxford University Press, 1986.

Copland, Aaron. *What to Listen for in Music*. New York: New American Library, 1957.

Critchley, Macdonald, and R. A. Henson, eds. *Music and the Brain: Studies in the Neurology of Music*. London: William Heinemann, 1978.

Cytowic, Richard E. *Synesthesia: A Union of the Senses*. Cambridge, Mass.: MIT Press, 2002.

Czerny, Carl. "Recollections from My Life," translated by Ernest Sanders. *The Musical Quarterly* Vol. 42, No. 3 (July 1956): 302-317.

Dahlhaus, Carl. *Ludwig van Beethoven: Approaches to His Music*, translated by Mary Whittall. Oxford: Clarendon Press, 1993.

Dean, Winton, with Anthony Hicks. *The New Grove Handel*. New York: W.W. Norton, 1983.

Dennis, David B. *Beethoven in German Politics, 1870-1989*. New Haven, Conn.: Yale University Press, 1996.

DeNora, Tia. *Beethoven and the Construction of Genius: Musical Politics in Vienna, 1792-1803*. Berkeley: University of California Press, 1995.

Deutsch, Otto Erich. *The Schubert Reader: A Life of Franz Schubert in Letters and Documents*, translated by Eric Blom. New York: W.W. Norton, 1947.

Dickinson, A. E. F. *Bach's Fugal Works*. New York: Pitman Publishing, 1956.

Dies, Albert Christoph. "Biographical Accounts of Joseph Haydn," 69-209 in *Haydn: Two Contemporary Portraits*, translated and edited by Vernon Gotwals. Madison: University of Wisconsin Press, 1968.

Dittersdorf, Karl. *The Autobiography of Karl Von Dittersdorf*, translated by A. D. Coleridge. New York: Da Capo Press, 1970.

Dorian, Frederick. *The History of Music in Performance: The Art of Musical Interpretation from the Renaissance to Our Day*. New York: W.W. Norton, 1942.

Duncan, Edmondstoune. *The Story of Minstrelsy*. New York: Charles Scribner's Sons, 1907.

Edler, Arnfried. "The Social Status of Organists in Lutheran Germany from the 16th through the 19th Century," 61-93 in *The Social Status of the Professional Musician from the Middle Ages to the 19th Century*, edited by Walter Salmen, translated by Herbert Kaufman and Barbara Reisman. Hillsdale, N.Y.: Pendragon Press, 1983.

Eidam, Klaus. *The True Life of J. S. Bach*, translated by Hoyt Rogers. New York: Basic Books, 2001.

Einstein, Alfred. *Mozart: His Character, His Work*, translated by Arthur Mendel and Nathan Broder. New York: Oxford University Press, 1945.

Eisen, Cliff, and Stanley Sadie. *The New Grove Mozart*. New York: Grove-Macmillan, 2002.

Elias, Norbert. *Mozart: Portrait of a Genius*, translated by Edmund Jephcott. Berkeley: University of California Press, 1993.

Fauchier-Magnan, Adrien. *The Small German Courts in the 18th Century*. London: Methuen & Co., 1958.

Fassett, Agatha. *The Naked Face of Genius: Béla Bartók's American Years*. New York: Riverside Press, 1958.

Frankl, Victor. *Man's Search for Meaning*. New York: Pocket Books, 1984.

Geiringer, Karl. *Brahms: His Life and Work*. New York: Da Capo Press, 1982.

Goodwin, Frederick K., and Kay Redfield Jamison. *Manic-Depressive Illness*. Oxford: Oxford University Press, 1990.

Gotwals, Vernon, ed. and trans. *Haydn: Two Contemporary Portraits*. Madison: University of Wisconsin Press, 1968.

Grew, Sidney. "Beethoven's 'Grosse Fuge.'" *Music and Letters* Vol. XII, No. 4 (1931): 497-508.

———. "The 'Grosse Fuge': The Hundred Years of Its History," *Music and Letters* Vol. XII, No. 2 (1931): 140-147.

Griesinger, Georg August. "Biographical Notes Concerning Joseph Haydn." 7-66 in *Haydn: Two Contemporary Portraits*, translated and edited by Vernon Gotwals. Madison: University of Wisconsin Press, 1968.

Griffiths, Paul. *The String Quartet: A History*. New York: Thames & Hudson, 1983.

Grout, Donald Jay, with Claude V. Palisca. *A History of Western Music*. New York: Norton, 1980.

Hamburger, Michael, ed. and trans. *Beethoven: Letters, Journals and Conversations*. New York: Anchor Books, 1960.

Hanson, Alice Marie. "Incomes and Outgoings in the Vienna of Beethoven and Schubert." *Music and Letters* Vol. 64 (1983): 173-182.

Heriot, Angus. *The Castrati in Opera*. New York: Da Capo Press, 1974.

Hildesheimer, Wolfgang. *Mozart*, translated by Marion Faber. New York: Vintage, 1983.

Hogwood, Christopher. *Handel*. London: Thames & Hudson, 1984.

Hortschansky, Klaus. "The Musician as Music Dealer in the Second Half of the 18th Century," 189-218 in *The Social Status of the Professional Musician from the Middle Ages to the 19th Century*, edited by Walter Salmen, translated by Herbert Kaufman and Barbara Reisman. Hillsdale, N.Y.: Pendragon Press, 1983.

Isacoff, Stuart. *Temperament: The Idea That Solved Music's Greatest Riddle*. New York: Alfred A. Knopf, 2001.

Jamison, Kay Redfield. *Touched with Fire: Manic-Depressive Illness and the Artistic Temperament*. New York: Free Press, 1994.

———. *An Unquiet Mind*. New York: Vintage, 1995.

Kagan, Susan. *Archduke Rudolph: Beethoven's Patron, Pupil, and Friend*. Stuyvesant, N.Y.: Pendragon Press, 1988.

Katz, Adele T. *Challenge to Musical Tradition: A New Concept of Tonality*. No publisher information, no date. Apparently issued by Katz Press, 2007, a reprint of the original edition published by Alfred A. Knopf, New York, 1946.

Keller, Hans. *The Great Haydn Quartets*. New York: George Braziller, 1986.

Kerman, Joseph. "Beethoven: The Single Journey." *Hudson Review* Vol. V, No. 1 (Spring 1952): 32-55.

———. *The Beethoven Quartets*. New York: W.W. Norton, 1966.

Kerman, Joseph, and Alan Tyson. *The New Grove Beethoven*. New York: W.W. Norton, 1983.

Kerst, Friedrich, and Henry Edward Krehbiel, edited and translated by Krehbiel. *Beethoven: The Man and the Artist, as Revealed in His Own Words*. New York: Dover, 1964.

Kinderman, William. *Beethoven*. Oxford: Oxford University Press, 1997.

Kinderman, William, ed. *Beethoven's Compositional Process*. Lincoln: University of Nebraska Press, 1991.

King, A. Hyatt. *Four Hundred Years of Music Printing*. London: The British Museum, 1968.

Kirkendale, Warren. "The 'Great Fugue' Op. 133: Beethoven's 'Art of Fugue.'" *Acta Musicologica* Vol. 35, No. 1 (January-March 1963): 14-24.

Knight, Frida. *Beethoven and the Age of Revolution*. New York: International Publishers, 1974.

Kramer, Peter D. *Listening to Prozac*. New York: Penguin, 1997.

Kramer, Richard. "Between Cavatina and *Ouverture*: Opus 130 and the Voice of Narrative," 165-189 in *Beethoven Forum, Vol. 1*, edited by Lewis Lockwood and William Webster.

Krehbiel, Henry Edward. *Music and Manners in the Classical Period*. New York: Charles Scribner's Sons, 1899.

Kretschmer, Martin. "Intellectual Property in Music: A Historical Analysis of Rhetoric and Institutional Practices." *Culture and Organization* Vol. 6, No. 2 (December 2000): 197-223.

Kretschmer, Martin, and Friedemann Kawhol. "The History and Philosophy of Copyright," 21-53 in *Music and Copyright*, edited by Simon Frith and Lee Marshall. Edinburgh: Edinburgh University Press, 2004.

Krickeburg, Dieter. "On the Social Status of the *Spielmann* (Folk Musician) in 17th and 18th Century Germany, Particularly in the Northwest," 95-122 in *The Social Status of the Professional Musician from the Middle Ages to the 19th Century*, edited by Walter Salmen, translated by Herbert Kaufman and Barbara Reisman. Hillsdale, N.Y.: Pendragon Press, 1983.

Lang, Paul Henry. *Music in Western Civilization*. New York: W.W. Norton, 1941.

Lang, Paul Henry, ed. *Problems of Modern Music*. New York: W.W. Norton, 1960.

Langer, Susanne K. *Philosophy in a New Key: A Study in the Symbolism of Reason, Rite, and Art*. New York: New American Library, 1951.

Levitin, Daniel J. *This Is Your Brain on Music: The Science of a Human Obsession*. New York: Dutton, 2006.

Lockwood, Lewis. *Beethoven: The Music and the Life*. New York: W.W. Norton, 2003.

Lockwood, Lewis, and Phyllis Benjamin, eds. *Beethoven Essays: Studies in Honor of Elliott Forbes*. Cambridge, Mass.: Harvard University Press, 1984.

Lockwood, Lewis, and James Webster, eds. *Beethoven Forum, Vol. 1*. Lincoln: University of Nebraska Press, 1992.

———. *Beethoven Forum, Vol. 2*. Lincoln: University of Nebraska Press, 1993.

———. *Beethoven Forum, Vol. 3*. Lincoln: University of Nebraska Press, 1994.

———. *Beethoven Forum, Vol. 4*. Lincoln: University of Nebraska Press, 1995.

———. *Beethoven Forum, Vol. 5*. Lincoln: University of Nebraska Press, 1996.

Loesser, Arthur. *Men, Women and Pianos: A Social History*. New York: Simon & Schuster, 1954.

Lonsdale, Roger. *Dr. Charles Burney*. Oxford: Oxford University Press, 1965.

Luria, Alexandr R. *The Mind of a Mnemonist*, translated by Lynn Solotaroff. New York: Avon, 1969.

Mahling, Christoph-Hellmut. "The Origin and Social Status of the Court Orchestral Musician in the 18th and Early 19th Century in Germany," 219-264 in *The Social Status of the Professional Musician from the Middle Ages to the 19th Century*, edited by Walter Salmen, translated by Herbert Kaufman and Barbara Reisman. Hillsdale, N.Y.: Pendragon Press, 1983.

Mai, Francois Martin. *Diagnosing Genius: The Life and Death of Beethoven*. Montreal: McGill-Queen's University Press, 2007.

Mann, Thomas. *Doctor Faustus*, translated by John E. Woods. New York: Vintage, 1999.

Marek, George R. *Beethoven: Biography of a Genius*. New York: Funk & Wagnall's, 1969.

Marliave, Joseph De. *Beethoven's Quartets*, translated by Hilda Andrews. New York: Dover, 1961.

Martin, Russell. *Beethoven's Hair: An Extraordinary Historical Odyssey and a Musical Mystery Solved*. New York: Broadway Books, 2000.

Mason, Daniel Gregory. *The Quartets of Beethoven*. New York: Oxford University Press, 1947.

McArdle, Donald W. "Anton Felix Schindler: Friend of Beethoven." *Music Review* 24 (1963): 50-74.

———. *Beethoven Abstracts*. Detroit: Information Coordinators, 1973.

McKay, Elizabeth Norman. *Franz Schubert: A Biography*. Oxford: Oxford University Press, 2001.

Mendelssohn, Felix. *Felix Mendelssohn Letters*, edited by G. Selden-Goth. New York: Vienna House, 1973.

Meyer, Leonard B. *Emotion and Meaning in Music*. Chicago: University of Chicago Press, 1968.

———. *Music, the Arts, and Ideas*. Chicago: University of Chicago Press, 1969.

Mithen, Steven. *The Singing Neanderthals: The Origins of Music, Language, Mind, and Body*. Cambridge, Mass.: Harvard University Press, 2006.

Moore, Julia V. "Beethoven and Inflation," 191-222 in *Beethoven Forum, Vol. 1*, edited by Lewis Lockwood and William Webster. Lincoln: University of Nebraska Press, 1992.

———. *Beethoven and Musical Economics*. Unpublished Ph.D. dissertation, University of Illinois at Urbana-Champaign, 1987. Available through UMI Dissertation Services, Ann Arbor, Mich.

———. "Mozart in the Market Place." *Journal of the Royal Musical Association* Vol. 114 (1989): 18-42.

Morgenstern, Sam, ed. *Composers on Music, from Palestrina to Copland*. New York: Pantheon, 1956.

Morris, James M., ed. *On Mozart*. New York: Woodrow Wilson Center Press, 1994.

Morrow, Mary Sue. *Concert Life in Haydn's Vienna: Aspects of a Developing Musical and Social Institution*. Stuyvesant, N.Y.: Pendragon Press, 1989.

Nabokov, Vladimir. *Speak, Memory*. New York: Vintage, 1989.

Nettl, Paul. *Beethoven Encyclopedia*. New York: Philosophical Library, 1956.

Newman, Ernest. *The Unconscious Beethoven*. New York: Alfred A. Knopf, 1970.

Norman, Gertrude, and Miriam Lubell Shrifte, eds. *Letters of Composers: An Anthology 1603-1945*. New York: Alfred A. Knopf, 1946.

O'Shea, John. *Was Mozart Poisoned? Medical Investigations into the Lives of the Great Composers*. New York: St. Martin's Press, 1991.

Page, Tim, ed. *The Glenn Gould Reader*. New York: Alfred A. Knopf, 1984.

Patel, Aniruddh D. *Music, Language and the Brain*. Oxford: Oxford University Press, 2008.

Petzoldt, Richard. "The Economic Conditions of the 18th Century Musician," 159-188 in *The Social Status of the Professional Musician from the Middle Ages to the 19th Century*, edited by Walter Salmen, translated by Herbert Kaufman and Barbara Reisman. Hillsdale, N.Y.: Pendragon Press, 1983.

Pinker, Steven. *The Language Instinct: How the Mind Creates Language*. New York: HarperCollins, 2000.

Pinker, Steven, and Paul Bloom. "Natural Language and Natural Selection." *Behavior and Brain Sciences* Vol. 13, No. 4 (1990): 707-784.

Radcliffe, Philip. *Beethoven's String Quartets*. London: Hutchinson & Co., 1965.

Raynor, Henry. *Music and Society Since 1815*. New York: Taplinger, 1978.

———. *A Social History of Music from the Middle Ages to Beethoven*. New York: Taplinger, 1978.

Robbins-Landon, H. C. *Beethoven: A Documentary Study*. New York: Macmillan, 1970.

———. *Haydn: Chronicle and Works. Vol. 1: The Early Years 1732-1765*. Bloomington: Indiana University Press, 1980.

———. *Vol. 2: Haydn at Esterháza 1766-1790*. 1978.

———. *Vol. 3: Haydn in England 1791-1795*. 1976.

———. *Vol. 4: Haydn: The Years of "The Creation" 1796-1800*. 1977.

———. *Vol. 5: Haydn: The Late Years 1801-1809*. 1977.

———. *Mozart: The Golden Years 1781-1791*. New York: Schirmer, 1989.

———. *Mozart and Vienna*. New York: Schirmer, 1991.

———. *1791: Mozart's Last Year*. New York: Schirmer, 1988.

Robertson, Lynn C., and Noam Sagiv, eds. *Synesthesia: Perspectives from Cognitive Neuroscience*. New York: Oxford University Press, 2005.

Rolland, Romain. *Beethoven*, translated by B. Constance Hull. Freeport, N.Y.: Books For Libraries Press, 1969.

———. *Goethe and Beethoven*, translated by G. A. Pfister and E. S. Kemp. New York: Harper & Brothers, 1931.

Rosen, Charles. *Arnold Schoenberg*. New York: Viking Press, 1975.

———. *The Classical Style: Haydn, Mozart, Beethoven* [1971], *Expanded Edition*. New York: W.W. Norton, 1998.

Sachs, Curt. *The Rise of Music in the Ancient World, East and West*. New York: W.W. Norton, 1943.

———. *The Wellsprings of Music*. New York: McGraw-Hill, 1965.

Sacks, Oliver. *Musicophilia: Tales of Music and the Brain*. New York: Alfred A. Knopf, 2007.

Salmen, Walter, ed. *The Social Status of the Professional Musician from the Middle Ages to the 19th Century*, translated by Herbert Kaufman and Barbara Reisman. Hillsdale, N.Y.: Pendragon Press, 1983.

Scherer, F. M. *Quarter Notes and Bank Notes: The Economics of Music Composition in the Eighteenth and Nineteenth Centuries*. Princeton, N.J.: Princeton University Press, 2004.

Scherman, Thomas K., and Louis Biancolli, eds. *The Beethoven Companion*. New York: Doubleday, 1972.

Schindler, Anton Felix. *Beethoven As I Knew Him*, edited by Donald W. McArdle, translated by Constance S. Jolly. New York: W.W. Norton, 1972.

Schoenberg, Arnold. *Structural Functions of Harmony*. New York: W.W. Norton, 1969.

Schonberg, Harold C. *The Lives of the Great Composers*. New York: W.W. Norton, 1970.

———. *The Virtuosi*. New York: Vintage Books, 1988.

Schrade, Leo. *Beethoven in France*. New Haven, Conn.: Yale University Press, 1942.

Schroeder, David. *Mozart in Revolt: Strategies of Resistance, Mischief and Deception*. New Haven: Yale University Press, 1999.

Schullian, Dorothy M., and Max Schoen, eds. *Music and Medicine*. New York: Henry Schuman, 1948.

Schwab, Heinrich W. "The Social Status of the Town Musician," 31-59 in *The Social Status of the Professional Musician from the Middle Ages to the 19th Century*, edited by Walter Salmen, translated by Herbert Kaufman and Barbara Reisman. Hillsdale, N.Y.: Pendragon Press, 1983.

Senner, Wayne M., Robin Wallace, and William Meredith, eds. *The Critical Reception of Beethoven's Compositions by His German Contemporaries, Vol 2*. Lincoln: University of Nebraska Press, 2001.

Sessions, Roger. *Roger Sessions on Music: Collected Essays*. Princeton, N.J.: Princeton University Press, 1979.

Shenk, Joshua Wolf. *Lincoln's Melancholy: How Depression Challenged a President and Fueled His Greatness*. New York: Houghton Mifflin, 2005.

Shepherd, Arthur. *The String Quartets of Ludwig von Beethoven*. Cleveland: The Printing Press, 1935.

Slonimsky, Nicolas. *Lexicon of Musical Invective: Critical Assaults on Composers Since Beethoven's Time*. New York: W.W. Norton, 2000.

Solomon, Andrew. *The Noonday Demon: An Atlas of Depression*. New York: Scribner's, 2002.

Solomon, Maynard. *Beethoven*. New York: Schirmer, 1998.

———. "Beethoven and His Nephew: A Reappraisal," 138-171 in *Beethoven Studies 2*, edited by Alan Tyson. New York: Oxford University Press, 1977

———. *Beethoven Essays*. Cambridge, Mass.: Harvard University Press, 1988.

———. "Beethoven's *Tagebuch* of 1812-1818," 193-288 in *Beethoven Studies 3*, edited by Alan Tyson. New York: W.W. Norton, 1973.

———. *Late Beethoven: Music, Thought, Imagination*. Berkeley: University of California Press, 2003.

———. *Mozart*. New York: Harper Perennial, 1995.

Sonneck, Oscar, ed. *Beethoven: Impressions by His Contemporaries*. New York: Dover, 1967.

Stafford, William. *The Mozart Myths, A Critical Reassessment*. Stanford, Calif.: Stanford University Press, 1991.

Sterba, Editha, and Richard Sterba. *Beethoven and His Nephew: A Psychoanalytical Study of Their Relationship*, translated by Willard B. Trask. New York: Schocken Books, 1971.

Storr, Anthony. *Music and the Mind*. New York: Ballantine, 1992.

Stravinsky, Igor. *Poetics of Music*. Cambridge, Mass.: Harvard University Press, 1975.

Styron, William. *Darkness Visible*. New York: Vintage, 1990.

Sullivan, J. W. N. *Beethoven: His Spiritual Development*. New York: Vintage, 1960.

Thayer, Alexander W. *Thayer's Life Of Beethoven*, revised and edited by Elliot Forbes. Princeton, N.J.: Princeton University Press, 1973.

Thomas, Lewis. *Late Night Thoughts on Listening to Mahler's Ninth Symphony*. New York: Bantam, 1983.

———. *The Medusa and the Snail: More Notes of a Biology Watcher*. New York: Viking Press, 1979.

Tovey, Donald Francis. *Beethoven*. New York: Oxford University Press, 1945.

———. *The Main Stream of Music and Other Essays*. New York: Meridian, 1961.

Truscott, Harold. *Beethoven's Late String Quartets*. London: Dobson Books, 1968.

Tyson, Alan, ed. *Beethoven Studies*. New York: W.W. Norton, 1973.

———. *Beethoven Studies 3*. Cambridge: Cambridge University Press, 1982.

Ulrich, Homer. *Chamber Music*. New York: Columbia University Press, 1966.

Volek, Tomislav, and Jaroslac Macek. "Beethoven's Rehearsals at the Lobkowitz's." *Musical Times* Vol. 127 (1986): 75-80.

Wallace, Robin. *Beethoven's Critics: Aesthetic Dilemmas and Resolutions During the Composer's Lifetime*. Cambridge: Cambridge University Press, 1989.

Watson, James, and Francis Crick. "A Structure for Deoxyribose Nucleic Acid." *Nature*, April 25, 1953.

Weber, William. *Music and the Middle Class*. New York: Holmes and Meier, 1975.

Weber, William, ed. *The Musician as Entrepreneur, 1700-1914. Managers, Charlatans, and Idealists*. Bloomington: Indiana University Press, 2004.

Wegeler, Franz, and Ferdinand Ries. *Beethoven Remembered: The Biographical Notes of Franz Wegeler and Ferdinand Ries*, translated by Frederick Noonan. Arlington, Va.: Great Ocean Publishers, 1987.

Winter, Robert, and Bruce Carr. *Beethoven: Performer and Critic*. Detroit: Wayne State University Press, 1980.

Winter, Robert and Robert Martin, eds. *The Beethoven Quartet Companion*. Berkeley: University of California Press, 1994.

Index

About the Author

Robert S. Kahn received a bachelor's degree in music from Reed College and a master's degree in performance from the Manhattan School of Music, where he studied woodwinds with Joe Allard and the string quartets of Beethoven and Bartók with Phillip Evans.

He has worked as a musician, teacher, freelance journalist, newspaper reporter, correspondent, and editor, as a legal worker in immigration prisons, and as a track coach. His previous books include the novels *An Honest Thief* and *The Violinist*, and the nonfiction book, *Other People's Blood: U.S. Immigration Prisons in the Reagan Decade.*

Kahn lives in Vermont, where he is news editor for Courthouse News Service, a national legal news service.